Penguin Books
The Ladies of Llangollen

Elizabeth Mavor has written three novels and
a biography of the Duchess of Kingston. She
is married to Haro Hodson, the cartoonist,
has two sons and lives in Oxfordshire.

Penguin Books Ltd, Harmondsworth,
Middlesex, England
Penguin Books Australia Ltd, Ringwood,
Victoria, Australia

First published by Michael Joseph 1971
Published in Penguin Books 1973

Copyright © Elizabeth Mavor, 1971

Made and printed in Great Britain by
C. Nicholls & Company Ltd
Set in Linotype Granjon

The Ladies of Llangollen

A Study in Romantic Friendship

Elizabeth Mavor

Penguin Books

For E.M.P. best of Godmothers

Nothing is so hard to bear as a train of happy days.

Goethe

There is indeed no other refuge from the horrors of history but in the mild majesty of private life.

Mrs Elizabeth Carter

Contents

List of Illustrations

I must thank the following who were kind enough to allow me to reproduce as illustrations photographs of works in which they control the copyright: Llangollen Town Council, Tom Hoyne Esq., the Marquis of Ormonde, the National Library of Ireland, Major Charles Hamilton, Miss Sarah Pugh Jones, the British Museum, the Bodleian Library, T. R. Bruen Esq., Sir Michael Leighton Bt., and the Houghton Library, University of Harvard, Cambridge, Mass.

Introduction

There occurred in the summer of 1774 a minor literary tragedy. On the 5th of July Dr Johnson in company with Mrs Thrale and her daughter set out on a tour of North Wales. On his return home two months later he passed by Llangollen just four years too early to meet the celebrated Ladies.

Had he done so he might have retained a stronger impression than that Wales 'offered nothing to the speculation of the traveller'. Eleanor Butler and Sarah Ponsonby, two aristocratic spinsters of thirty-nine and twenty-three respectively, were to provide future Welsh travellers with food for speculation over the next fifty years.

Mrs Piozzi, coming to know them herself, would call them 'enchantresses', Lady Louisa Stuart, never meeting them but by hearsay, would unkindly dub them of the 'genus mountebankum', Prince Puckler Muskau would write of them as 'the two most celebrated virgins in Europe'! In 1782 only two years after taking up house together people were confessing themselves captivated by their romantic mode of life, and three years later their fame had travelled so widely that the Queen was asking for plans of the cottage and garden. This was only the prelude to an adulation accorded to few celebrities in any era, and it was to last until their deaths and after. Their visitors and admirers, though the terms were not always synonymous, were to number nearly everyone of note throughout the period, and while a detailed list would be tedious, it should be recorded that it comprised not only royalty but soldiers, inventors, philanthropists, actors, artists, men of letters and poets. The Duke of Wellington was a cherished friend, Wordsworth and Southey composed beneath their roof, Josiah Wedgwood lectured them upon rock formations, Dr. Darwin and Charles visited them, as did Sir Walter Scott, the Miss Berrys, Sheridan, Lady Caroline Lamb and Sir Humphrey Davy to mention but a few.

What was the cause of such celebrity? For the two women were neither artists nor writers as has often been supposed, though many admired Sarah Ponsonby's beautiful calligraphy and exquisitely careful illuminations and all enjoyed Eleanor Butler's animated conversation, that 'unaccountable knowledge . . . of all living books and people and things', which to Mrs Piozzi had been 'like magic'. For some fascination lay in the strangely picturesque charms of their garden, for others in the gothick witticisms of the cottage, to all the life of the two women represented a perfect picture of that 'retirement' which had become the ideal of an age too long given over to the stridency of the world. Although Dr Johnson had mocked 're-tirement' in *Rasselas* and in 1783 had criticized it as 'Civil sui-cide' he was by then running counter to the thought of the age, for the notion of a dignified withdrawal from the press and vulgarity of the world to a life of virtue and rustic simplicity had already become fashionable.

Inspired anew by Rousseau, but finding its source far back in the Roman poets, the delights of 'retirement' had already been hymned in the works of Pope, Thomson and Gray. Practitioners of this way of life numbered such celebrities as Lady Mary Wortley Montagu, Shenstone and Cowper, not to mention poor foolish Marie Antoinette; and it would not be long before even Hannah More, that pillar of common sense, would remove to her own 'sweet retirement at Cowslip Green', and a whole gen-eration of not so sensible poets would forsake the metropolis for the rigours of life in lakeland cottages.

But it was not only as exemplifiers of a perfect 'retirement' that the Ladies were celebrated, but as perfect friends.

For friendship, as a contemporary had it, could then be ' . . . a divine and spiritual relation of minds, an union of souls, a mar-riage of hearts, a harmony of designs and affections, which being entered into by mutual consent, groweth up into the purest kindness and most endearing love, maintaining itself by the openest freedom, the warmest sympathy, and the closest secrecy'.

In a word, the two women's relationship was what we in

modern terms would consider a marriage. It was to give rise to
their own unique and much envied way of life, for did it not
combine rural innocence and simplicity without lack of comfort
and culture; freedom from unbridled passion with no loss of
pleasure, a balanced reconciliation between the tiresome polarities of existence?

Yet, for the purposes of studying and portraying a friendship
so subtle and so rare, the obvious Freudian interpretation
seemed a bluntish instrument, one at once oversimplified and
too prone in its operation to give rise to that false Duessa of
categorization which now obscures too much of individuality
and interest. Consequently, although an enterprising contributor
to *The Times Literary Supplement* has usefully distinguished
between the homo-erotic and the homo-sexual, I have nevertheless chosen to portray the relationship between the two women
in other terms than Freud's. I have preferred the terms of romantic friendship (a once flourishing but now lost relationship)
as more liberal and inclusive and better suited to the diffuse
feminine nature. Edenic it seems such friendships could be before they were biologically and thus prejudicially defined. De-
pending as they did upon time and leisure, they were aristocratic,
they were idealistic, blissfully free, allowing for a dimension
of sympathy between women that would not now be possible
outside an avowedly lesbian connection. Indeed, much that
we would now associate solely with a sexual attachment was
contained in romantic friendship: tenderness, loyalty, sensibility, shared beds, shared tastes, coquetry, even passion.

Eleanor Butler's and Sarah Ponsonby's friendship was of this
kind, and it was to be celebrated for over half a century in their
journals, day-books and letters; it was celebrated above all in the
journals of Eleanor Butler, though it was those of her more
retiring friend that Colette had been so eager to get a glimpse of.
They, alas, are lost, with the exception of her day-book for 1785
and her account of their first tour of North Wales in 1778 which
she dedicated to 'Her most tenderly Beloved Companion'. Of
other journals that she may have written only one is mentioned
in her letters, one written for the information and, one suspects,

the edification of her methodistical cousin, Mrs Tighe. A loss, in view of that lady's restricted view of life, perhaps not so very great after all.

Of Eleanor Butler's journals, uninhibited, amusing, written for themselves (though occasionally the privileged were permitted to hear extracts), but nine remain. They consist of a Lady's Pocket Book for 1784; a complete journal for January to December 1785; a journal from January 1788 to January 1791 in ten bound parts; an incomplete journal for 1791 and another for only May and June of 1799; one for 1 January to 28 March 1802, and another for 4 August to 31 December 1807. There is a complete journal for 1819 and part of a journal for January to July 1821. There is a day-book for 1806. Extracts from all these, with the exception of the pocket book for 1784, the day-book for 1806 and the journal for 1819, were published in *The Hamwood Papers of the Ladies of Llangollen and Caroline Hamilton* in 1930.

The journal for 1785 is in the possession of Lady Eleanor Butler's kinsman, the Marquis of Ormonde, and I must thank him for his true kindness in entrusting me with that precious possession, and also for his and the late Lady Ormonde's kind hospitality.

The day-book for 1806 and the journal for 1819 are in the keeping of the National Library of Ireland, and to its staff, and in particular to Mr Desmond Kennedy, I should like to express my grateful thanks for much help and kindness.

All the other journals, including Sarah Ponsonby's Welsh Tour and her day-book for 1785, are in the possession of Major Charles Hamilton of Hamwood, Co. Meath, the descendant of Sarah Ponsonby's cousin and correspondent, Mrs Sarah Tighe. To him I owe an immense debt of gratitude both for allowing me to read and work from these documents and for his and Mrs Hamilton's generous hospitality while I did so.

Of a correspondence which was, to say the least of it, voluminous, six main and hitherto unpublished collections survive. First an exceptionally fine sequence of letters from Sarah Ponsonby to her cousin, Mrs Tighe, dating from 1784 to 1813 and comprising 145 items in all. These are in the possession of an-

other of Mrs Tighe's descendants, Mr Evelyn Webber, and for
his kind and protracted loan of them I am immeasurably grateful
as I am to my generous friend, Miss Katharine Kenyon, for her
kind offices in making this possible.

Secondly, there is a sequence of letters from Harriet Bowdler
to Sarah Ponsonby comprising thirty-nine items and dating from
1790 to 1815. These are in the keeping of the Marquis of
Ormonde to whom I am once again indebted for his kindness in
allowing me to work and quote from them.

Thirdly, there is the sequence of letters from Sarah Ponsonby
to her friend Mrs Parker of Sweeney Hall. This collection numbering 131 items and dating from 1809 to 1831 is in the possession of Mrs Parker's descendant, Sir Michael Leighton, Bt., and
I should like to thank him for his kindness in allowing me to
work and quote from this correspondence as well as for permission to reproduce his great-great-grandmother's watercolour
sketches of the Plas Newydd garden.

Of the remaining three collections, one, consisting of a series
of eighteen letters from Eleanor Butler to Harriet Pigott over
the years 1809 to 1822, is in the Bodleian Library; another, consisting of twenty-four letters from the Ladies to Mrs Hester
Piozzi over the years 1796 to 1814 is in the John Rylands Library
at Manchester; while a third miscellaneous collection of both
private and business correspondence numbering eighteen items
and covering the years 1792 to 1827 together with Sarah Ponsonby's Account Book for the years January 1788 to December
1790 are in the keeping of the National Library of Wales. Sarah's
Account Book for 1 January 1791 to 31 December 1800 is at Plas
Newydd and thus in the care of the Llangollen Town Council.
Her plan and description of the Plas Newydd cottage and garden is in the Houghton Library at Harvard. I should like to
express gratitude to all these bodies for permission to work from
these papers and to quote from them.

I should also like to thank all those other people who have
been kind enough to furnish me with letters, pictures and information about these vastly prolific Ladies. All those who so
kindly responded to my letter in *Country Life*, also Mr H. V.
Best, Miss Mary Cosh, Miss Katharine Kenyon, Miss Florence

MacClellan, Mr Francis Needham and Miss M. Wright for so generously lending or making transcriptions of original letters; Dr William Bond of Harvard for help with papers in the Houghton Library; Mr. T. R. Bruen for kind permission to reproduce the watercolour of Plas Newydd in his possession; Mr Fergusson Wood for his kind loan of the excellent collection of family photographs taken at Plas Newydd; Mr Wilfrid Little for photographs of and information about 'Ladies of Llangollen' ware; Mr H. D. Lyon for guiding me to papers of Sarah Ponsonby at Harvard; and Mrs Joan Cliff and Mr John Sparrow for kind loans of books belonging to the two friends. I am also grateful to Lord Dunboyne, Mr John Gore, Mrs Ponsonby of Kilkooly, Sir Charles Ponsonby Bt., and Rear-Admiral W. G. S. Tighe for information about the Butler and Ponsonby families.

I should especially like to thank Mr and Mrs Adrian Blighe, Mr James Delahanty, Mr Tom Hoyne, and Mr Peter O'Brien, those kind Irish friends who helped so much with my research in Ireland and made staying there such a very great pleasure. Similarly in Wales, where I should like to thank Mr Davies the Plas Newydd caretaker, Miss Lloyd Jones, Miss Sarah Pugh Jones, Mr Rowlands and Mr Trevor for much helpful information and kindness, also the Llangollen Town Council and the Librarian of the Llangollen County Library for kind advice and help.

I am indebted to Mr P. B. Carter, the Hon. David Erskine and Mr Andy Hodson for advice on certain legal aspects of the Ladies' story, and I should like to thank most warmly Mr Ronald Blythe and Dr E. M. S. Tompkins for reading this manuscript and for offering such inspiring suggestions and advice.

Nearer home I must thank very especially Felix Pearson and Faith Tolkien, who at separate times not only journeyed to Wales and to Ireland with me but were unfailingly patient and industrious in the matter of making transcriptions from the papers we found there, as they were unfailingly cheerful about the adventures we encountered.

To Haro Hodson I owe most. Not only has he made the Welsh and Irish journeys, numerous transcriptions, and put in much careful work at Somerset House, but he has lived patiently, politely and appreciatively with these two charming but exacting friends for upwards of six years.

Garsington
September 1970

Chapter One

'. . .your being Totally Ignorant who we are.'
Eleanor Butler to Mrs Paulet

Their homes in Ireland are still there. Eleanor Butler's, a grey Norman castle at Kilkenny in the Nore valley; Sarah Ponsonby's, a Georgian mansion high on a hill overlooking the picturesque village of Inistiogue twelve miles off. But the castle is uninhabited; and it is only when the visitor draws near the house that he realizes that the solid-seeming front with its elegant flight of steps is a façade concealing a ruin. Woodstock was burned down in the Troubles. So now pied goats go scrambling incontinently through the reception rooms, where fragments of eighteenth-century plaster-work still cling like cracked icing to the bricks, and in the bedroom where two women long ago took a momentous decision the sapling plane trees have thrust upwards to the light and made a fluttering ceiling of their leaves against the sky.

In July spotted orchids of a freakish inverted variety spring from the crumbling walls of the outside offices and pierce through the neglected lawns like pale candles, and near by, an old beech tree, dropping its mast unheeded year after year, has made a forest. In what was once a water garden the stream has long ago broken out of its stone conduit and gone oozing off to make a morass at the back of the kitchen door; and between picturesquely placed rocks, thickets of esparto grass and frantic-looking ornamental palms have grown together to make, what is in high summer, a tinkling, buzzing jungle.

Two hundred years ago Woodstock and its owners were representative of the extensive power and enlightened tastes of the Irish Protestant Ascendancy; an Ascendancy which, by the third quarter of the eighteenth century, had converted the less remote portions of the country into a replica of Georgian England.

Just as Dublin had been squared and quartered off into the classical pattern of wide streets and comely terraced houses which rivalled those of the English capital, so had the countryside been parcelled out into gentlemen's estates. The aggressive-looking keeps of the previous period had fallen before mild-looking Georgian manor houses, and the scars of early deforestation were rapidly being made good by planting in the English manner.

As early as 1749 Lord Orrery* was writing with satisfaction that 'every gentleman in Ireland is become a planter',[1] and the fashionable enthusiasm was extended to gardening. Lord Orrery himself had already embellished his grounds with statues and a root house, and Bishop Pococke,† travelling through Ireland three years later, would rhapsodize over the profusion of Romantic prospects, wildernesses, obelisks, Chinese bridges, serpentine rivers, hermitages and grottoes, that he had met with on his progress.

A later generation of travellers, while justly admiring such improvements, would yet be able to point out certain disturbing anomalies; the ruinous condition of the Establishment churches, the scantiness of their congregations, besides other and graver symptoms of a society at odds with itself. A society in which the native Irish, for all that their conditions had improved so much since the beginning of the century, were still worse off than any Spanish, Portuguese or even Scots peasants; a society which, after all, seemed less like its English paradigm and rather more like the colonial force of occupation, which in truth it was.

'An aristocracy of five hundred thousand protestants crushing the industry of two millions of poor Catholics . . .'[2] wrote Arthur Young the agriculturist with some frankness. Had not his commonsense English heart revolted at seeing the servants of wealthy gentlemen whipping the carts of the Irish peasants into the ditch in order to make way for their masters' carriages? Had

* John Boyle 5th Earl of Cork and Orrery (1707–62), author and friend of Swift, Pope and Johnson, 'would have been a man of genius', Berkeley said of him, 'had he known how to set about it'.

† Richard Pococke (1704–65), Bishop of Ossory and indefatigable traveller in Europe and the Middle East.

he not learned with indignation that they endured such treatment so patiently for fear of being horse whipped? and had he not been assured by landlords of consequence 'that many of their cottagers would think themselves honoured by having their wives and daughters sent for to the bed of their master . . .?'³

Such abuses would in time bear their own fruit, meanwhile at Woodstock, where all for the time being was gaiety, order and judicious improvement, Arthur Young approvingly noted a five-hundred-acre beech wood 'hanging in a noble shade to the river which flows at the bottom of a winding glen'.⁴

The squire of Woodstock was Sir William Fownes, connected, a shade resentfully it would seem, both by interest and marriage, with the foremost Irish family of the day, the Ponsonbys.

The Ponsonbys, like most of the Ascendancy, were comparative newcomers to Ireland. Originally Cumberland squires they had fought for Cromwell and had been rewarded for their services out of confiscated lands in the beautiful Suir valley. A generation later loyalty and a genuine administrative ability had resulted in a viscountcy, and a generation after that in the earldom of Bessborough. It was to this illustrious and powerful house that Lady Betty, Sir William's wife, belonged, and it would be owing to her kind heart that Sarah, her dead cousin's daughter, would be invited to make a home with her and Sir William at Woodstock.

Sarah Ponsonby's early life is reminscent of some forgotten eighteenth-century novel. Her family was a cadet branch of that powerful Bessborough connection. Her grandfather, Henry Ponsonby, had been an able general commanding troops both in Flanders and in 1743 at Dettingen. But his promising career was to be cut short two years later when, at the head of his troops, he paused to take snuff on the crest of the ridge between Fontenoy and the wood of Barry, in the act of which his head was removed by an untimely round shot. But a few seconds before he had prophetically handed his watch and ring for safe keeping to his son and aide-de-camp, Sarah's father.

Chambre Brabazon Ponsonby's portrait reveals an elegant

languid-looking man with a quizzical expression. He was described to Sarah by an aunt, however, as 'always unhappy amongst strangers as were most of his nearest connections to him'.⁵ This appears to have been the result of his mother educating him in 'too great retirement'. His shyness did not prevent him from making three attempts at marriage none the less, all, as it turned out, conspicuously unsuccessful.

In the course of his first union, which lasted six years, he lost not only his wife but his only son and two out of three daughters. In 1752 he consoled himself with Miss Louisa Lyons, the gay and pretty daughter of the clerk of the Irish Council. The couple waited three years for the birth of a son and heir, and when in 1755 a child arrived at last, it proved to be another disappointment, a daughter, to be christened Sarah. Three years later the second Mrs Ponsonby died, worn out, it was rumoured, by the jealousy of her husband and the languors of 'the great solitude to which he had condemned her'.⁶

Mr Ponsonby tried one more. This time his choice fell on an heiress, Miss Mary Barker. They were married, and then, as if exhausted by this final attempt, poor Mr Ponsonby, unaware that he had begotten a posthumous son and heir, expired himself. The new widow rallied not long after to become the lady of Sir Robert Staples of Dunmore, and Sarah Ponsonby's complement of relations was complete.

The sum effect of these rapid events was to deprive the small girl of her mother at three, her father at seven, and to furnish her with two half-sisters and half a brother who had, by his unexpected appearance, effectively dispossessed her of any fortune she had been entitled to expect from her father.

She was to endure a comfortless, narrow upbringing. 'I do not think', she was to write later, 'that absolute silence and solitude are likely to be the most effectual means of escaping those snares which the enemy of our Souls is perpetually laying for them. To Very Young Minds (I speak from my own recollections of when I was young) I should apprehend them to be particularly dangerous – for surely a propensity to Gloom if not to Despair – May be attended with as fatal effects – from self indulgence – as a Contrary Disposition.'⁷

There was to be yet one more bereavement. Six years later her stepmother, Lady Staples, died, leaving Sarah at the age of thirteen not only orphaned, but destitute.

It was at this point, her stepfather Sir Robert showing no further interest in her, that Sarah Ponsonby was placed under the care of her father's cousin, Lady Betty Fownes, and sent to Miss Parke's boarding school at Kilkenny.

She was 'nice, slight looking'[8] we are told, and, as a miniature shows, fair, with wide-spaced eyes and a small, firm mouth. But her unsettled and lonely childhood dominated by a morose father and a stepmother, who in true Cinderella fashion had too often called her a slattern, had done nothing to soothe a disposition already retiring and over-sensitive, and it had no doubt served to accentuate an inherited vein of melancholy.

Judging by her enthusiastic support in later life of a boarding school education for girls, Miss Parke's must have been a pleasant establishment. We are told that this earnest, shy little girl now set herself to 'learn all she could at school';[9] the elegant handwriting, the neat maps, the fine embroidery which were later to be so characteristic of her.

It was but a short time after beginning at Miss Parke's, that Sarah Ponsonby, still little more than a child, first met her destiny in the sardonic person of Miss Butler from the Castle.

Eleanor Butler was twenty-nine. Sarah's niece, who had no great partiality for her, conceded that although her round features were in no way remarkable she had a good complexion and good teeth, but added that 'she could not be called feminine and she was very satirical'.[10]

Sarah, not unnaturally, was to see her differently: 'uncommonly handsome and like my B[eloved]'[11] she would write years later describing the strong resemblance between Lady Eleanor and one of her Butler nephews.

Her background was very different from Sarah's, contrasting as sharply as the spacious modern house on the hill with the gloomy over-muscular castle by the river, the interior of which, as one visitor disgustedly expressed it, had not 'experienced any important alterations since the latter part of the seventeenth century'.[12] In fact it was a warren, crammed with old-fashioned

Stuart portraits, its huge state-rooms hung with enormous tapestries depicting the vigorous operations of the Emperor Decius against the Goths, its spent magnificence a constant and painful reminder to the Butlers of disgrace and a lost dukedom.

The family was exceedingly ancient, anticipating the advent of the Ponsonbys by nearly five hundred years; the first Butler in Ireland performing for Henry I the very office which his name suggested. Through time the family had rooted wide and deep in their adopted country and, intermarrying with the great Irish chieftains, had at last themselves become part of Irish legend.

In Eleanor Butler's own time Kilkenny mothers still threatened obstreperous children with her great ancestress who had lived two hundred years before: Maighread M'Gearoid, the terrible Margaret of Ormonde, tall and manlike it was said, full of a man's courage, 'a lady of such parts that all the estates of the kingdom crouched under her ...', one who had been 'a secure friend, a bitter enemy'.[13]

The honour of this great family had been snuffed out in the ambiguous person of James, second Duke of Ormonde; an expensive man according to Jonathan Swift, and one either so deceitful or so able that not long after acting Lord of the Bedchamber to James II and quelling Monmouth's rebellion he had found it not dishonourable to change sides and captain the usurping William's horse guards at the Battle of the Boyne, entertaining his new master afterwards to a sumptuous banquet at Kilkenny Castle.

Deceit or ability had carried him suavely through the reign of Anne, but had cut little ice with the first George, who had him impeached for his Jacobite sympathies, his estates forfeited and his honours extinguished.

By 1768 Eleanor Butler's own family had but newly succeeded to the castle, and this by way of a somewhat tortuous pattern of inheritance, for although her father was the only surviving lineal representative of the second Duke, his was a minor branch of the great family, and they had long laboured beneath the added disadvantage of being not only financially impoverished but Roman Catholic.

The Garryricken Butlers had inherited a long tradition of

fervent Catholicism. Eleanor Butler's great-great-grandfather had been a member of the Catholic Confederation, a Lieutenant-General with the Irish army against the English; her great-grandfather had made Garryricken a haven for all persecuted Catholic clergy; her grand-uncle, the famous Archbishop of Cashel, had courageously carried on his episcopate throughout the savage persecution following the Penal Code of 1703; her grand-father had been, and her grandmother, who lived with the family, still was an ardent Jacobite; her father, Walter Butler, as was customary, had been educated overseas at the seminary of Douai.

But the Butlers had paid for their Catholicism. The Penal Code had deprived all those professing the Faith of any civil life whatsoever; had, among many petty and humiliating restrictions, forbidden Catholics to educate their children in the Faith, buy land or inherit an undivided estate. As a consequence the Garryricken Butlers, one-time magnates of Tipperary, had been superseded in political and administrative influence by the new Protestant squirearchy. Bishop Pococke travelling by Garryricken in 1752 was to make no mention of this once influential family, and the name of Butler does not occur in any public capacity until the end of the century by which time the anti-Catholic laws had been relaxed. The name only occurs surreptitiously and in whispers when members of the family attend a Jacobite gathering at the *Wheatsheaf* Inn at Kilkenny in 1715, or are asked, humiliatingly, to stand bail for agrarian disturbances that they are supposed to have fomented during the sixties.

Like most of the Catholic gentry they had evaded the Penal Laws by spending periods abroad; at Avignon, at Douai, at Cambrai; and it was at Cambrai, where a fervently Jacobite grand-aunt was a pensioner at the Convent of the English Benedictines, that Eleanor Butler, youngest of three sisters, was born in 1739.

By 1740 matters must have improved, for that year the family moved back to Garryricken for an event of far greater importance, the birth of a son and heir that December.

The old keep-like house was set deep in the Tipperary countryside, country that from the wine-coloured heights of its mountain, Slievenamon, looks like a seamed green stone fished up

from the sea. It was romantic country for a Butler child to be
reared in, permeated by the proud but tragic family memories
which were also Ireland's. All through Eleanor's childhood her
grand-uncle, the great and much persecuted Archbishop, was
living out his last years with Butler cousins at near-by Callan;
while not far off, at the castle of Kilkash, lived her relation,
Lady Iveagh. Known as Lady 'Vagh, this woman was adored
for her goodness, revered for her devotion to the persecuted
Faith for which she had sacrificed her fortune. By the time
Eleanor was five Lady 'Vagh was dead, and Kilkash, which had
once been so splendid, was but a ghost of itself:

'My deep grief! My sorrow the sorest!' lamented the young
priest whose patron and protector she had once been:

> 'Thy beautiful gates overthrown;
> Thy walks (like rude paths in the forest)
> Neglected, leaf strewn, and grass grown . . .'[14]

Garryricken, like Kilkenny Castle that they were later to inherit, was also dark and old fashioned, the walls of its great hall
most likely decked, as Sir Jonah Barrington* tells us was then
customary, with a profusion of 'fishing rods, fire-arms, stags'
horns, foxes' brushes, powder flasks, shot-pouches, nets and dog
collars'.[15] The walls of the parlour were probably hung with old
portraits and sporting prints, red tape nailed round them by way
of frames. The library, as in most country houses, was very
likely scanty, stocked with farriery, sporting and gardening
books and not much else bar the Bible and a few romances.

The family estate does not appear to have been strikingly well
run. Frequent advertisements in the local paper for the canting
or auctioning of its leases disclose a form of management which,
by giving tenants no security of tenure, resulted in the exploita-
tion and running down of the land, while numerous complaining letters from Mr Harrison, the Butler rent collector, give
evidence of small and scattered rents hardly worth the gathering. It was even said that Garryricken itself was not freehold.[16]

---

*Sir Jonah Barrington (1760–1834), member of the Irish parliament,
trenchant observer of the Golden Age of Dublin and author of *Personal
Sketches*, 1827.

Indeed a perpetual mismanagement of correspondence suggests a state of affairs not unlike that described by Swift: '. . . but one lock and a half in the whole house. The key of the garden door lost . . . The door of the Dean's bedchamber full of large chinks . . . The Dean's bed threatening every night to fall under him . . . Bottles stopped with bits of wood and tow, instead of corks . . . The spit blunted with poking into bogs for timber . . . A great hole in the floor of the ladies' chamber . . .'[17]

Unsurprisingly the family appear to have endured perennial financial disappointment. Some idea of how matters stood is indicated by Eleanor's grandmother who spent much time in making numerous and revealing wills:

First to you my dear Son I leave my pictures and wish they were of more value . . .[18]

. . . What little plate I have which consists only of a dozen spoons.[19]

. . . as for mony I dont expect to have by me at my death what will be sufficient to bury me . . .[20]

She herself was a good old lady, devoted to her family, kind to her servants, and if melancholy, pious with it.

Sarah Ponsonby's niece was to paint Eleanor Butler's father in harsh colours, '. . . an ignorant ill-bred man', who spent one day entertaining his neighbours with lavish hospitality, a servant in gaudy livery standing behind every chair, the next drinking in an ale house and 'completely powered by his wife Madam Butler'.[21] While the account is substantially correct, allowances must be made for the opinions of one who was ignorant of the ways of the old Catholic gentry. Walter Butler's portrait shows an amiable, defeated-looking man in a plain coat.

The Penal Laws, without actually losing him his estate (as an only son the Gavel law which divided a Catholic's estate between brothers had taken no effect), appear to have driven him to the somewhat limited outlets open to a man of his religion and class, '. . . you may be diverted with cock shooting and Hunting in the morning, and whist playing and whoreing in the Evening'[22] his cousin at Kilkash writes by way of invitation.

For all that, his business letters show him to have been as indulgent towards his debtors as he hoped his creditors would be towards him, and his youngest daughter, who in times of stress was apt to reproduce his less startling oaths, appears to have had both affection and respect for him.* In short, he might have been contented enough but for his able and ambitious wife.

'. . . a bigotted Roman Catholic ashamed of her family', wrote Sarah Ponsonby's niece angrily. 'Proud, overbearing, surrounded by Priests.'[23] 'Eleanor De Montmorency Morres', declared a certain Mr Brewer of her, 'had a very masculine turn of mind.'[24] Passionately set on restoring the lost family titles as she was, she appears in her portrait as a comely, intelligent woman nursing a King Charles spaniel on her oyster-satin lap.

Her business correspondence makes it plain that she coped energetically with the financial affairs which appear to have confused her weak husband. He lost letters, she dashed them off with angry vivacity to solicitors, rent collectors, moneylenders and received abject or sullen replies :

'. . . an expression in one of my letters which seemed to give you offence, which I am sorry for and had not the least meaning that it would bear the construction you seemed to put upon it . . .'[25]

'. . . it is not really convenient for me to advance you Two hundred pound now.'[26]

'. . . the making out of your whole Acct which is running on Since you was at Moors house, wou'd take me more time and attention than the little hurry of my affairs will for some time permit . . .'[27]

She was nevertheless able to find the money to send her two eldest daughters, Suzy and Fanny, to the fashionable Convent of the Blue Nuns in Paris to educate them in keeping with their exalted birth, for Madam Butler's own family was as ancient as her husband's, threading back through a labyrinthine pedigree to the Lady Basilia, sister of the famous Strongbow. She numbered centenarians among her immediate ancestors, and this enduring gene was to be transmitted to her youngest and most disappointing daughter.

---

* Thus she writes of one of her Butler nephews : 'James, the image of his grandfather. I trust he will resemble him in his mind as he does in his person and then indeed his family may be proud of him' (Eleanor Butler's Journal, *Hamwood Papers,* ed. Bell, p. 126).

Eleanor's position in such a family was hardly of the first importance, was in a sense almost as solitary as Sarah Ponsonby's own. Any expectations that might have been aroused by the prospect of her birth had been dashed by the arrival of yet another daughter, forgotten altogether at the arrival of a son and heir a year later. Displaced too early, she was to dislike her brother with varying intensity for the remainder of her life, and it was a dislike that was vigorously reciprocated. Her sisters, themselves close in age, were both somewhat older than she was; her father was kind but ineffectual; her mother, dedicated to the revival of the family fortunes, was unsympathetic, seeing her daughters as little more than pawns in the marriage stakes, and Eleanor, alas, was neither rich nor beautiful.

Jottings of elderly Butler relations tend to reinforce such impressions, for early in 1745, when Eleanor would have been six, a grand-aunt living at Cambrai made mention in her will of 'her dear little niece Miss Francis Butler and her sister Susan Butler'[28] but none whatsoever of Eleanor. Seven years later when Eleanor was thirteen the Butler grandmother at Garryricken willed her watch and chain 'to my Dr Grandaughter Suzy', left Fanny all her house linen, bequeathed her 'Dr Grandson John Butler' her silver cup and salvers, and only named '. . . a little ring to Nelly of ye hair that I constantly wear and a writing box . . .'[29]

Ten years later, old Mrs Butler, still disappointingly in the land of the living, had rewilled the little ring to Eleanor's eldest sister, 'I once named it for Nelly but her finger is now too big . . .'[30] Since Suzy Butler was by this time safely married, the old lady rewilled her watch to Eleanor who had become, at twenty-three, the spinster of the family.

Perhaps it was her disappointing thickness of finger which determined Madam Butler not to send Eleanor to the fashionable Convent of the Blue Nuns in Paris but to Cambrai and the aptly named English Benedictine Convent of Our Blessed Lady of Consolation. More likely it was because there were already connections with Cambrai. Eleanor, after all, had been born there, the family appear to have travelled frequently between Cambrai and Ireland, and there were elderly Butler relatives living in the town who could be depended upon to keep a watchful eye on a girl perhaps already becoming strong-willed and difficult.

It is not known at what date Eleanor began boarding at the convent because the papers of the Cambrai house were destroyed during the French Revolution. Such convents were accustomed to boarding little girls of four as well as old gentlewomen of ninety, but the general age of admission was around fourteen, and the length of stay about two years, though both could vary enormously. Given that Continental wars would have limited travel, the likeliest years seem either to be between 1748 and 1756, or between 1763 and 1768. A letter from one of Eleanor's young relations to her father's cousin, John Butler of Kilkash, might possibly point to the first period. 'I should be very much obliged to you Dear Uncle', she was writing in 1753 when Eleanor would have been fourteen, 'if you would let me know in Your next what is become of my Nelly, For it has been so long Since I have heard anything of her which gives me great Uneasyness . . .'[31]

If Nelly were indeed at Cambrai Margaret Stanley had no call to be uneasy. Nelly was happy; would ever after pepper her conversation with French phrases, burst into French songs, swear unswerving devotion to all the Bourbons and to Louis-Quatorze in particular, and confess every time 'dear dear France' was mentioned to 'a sort of Maladie du Pays'.[32] Convent life unquestionably suited her.

The English orders consisted of small companies of liberal, well-educated, and often aristocratic women. The Prioress of the Austins, for instance, was a member of the Fermor family and a niece of Pope's Belinda. In the Convent of the Blue Nuns in Paris, where Eleanor's two sisters had been educated, Lady Anastasia Stafford was Abbess. Conditions were, for the most part, extremely comfortable; a visitor considering that the Abbess of St Louis at Rouen had a private apartment as good as any person of fashion. It had also been noted that most houses had excellent libraries, while some even ran to billiard rooms.

The number of boarders, or pensioners, as they were called, were eight to ten to each convent. They wore habits, and were under the direct control of the Abbess without whose consent they were not so much as allowed to stir outside the walls.

The average payment for boarding was in the region of twenty-five pounds a year. At the English Canonesses of the Holy Sepulchre at Liège, three Miss Meades paid twenty-two guineas a year each, and the convent found them 'washing, dancing, books, paper, quills, pencils, powder, pomatum, combs, dressing hair and postage of letters'.[33] The pupils themselves were mostly drawn from the Catholic nobility and gentry although towards the end of the century Protestants were also attending.

Eleanor's convent at Cambrai, founded by a descendant of Sir Thomas More, was not so fashionable as the Parisian house, but it had nevertheless a high reputation for its education, and particularly for such niceties as the manufacture of artificial flowers and the cutting of exquisite ornaments and devices upon vellum.

The rule for the Religious was fairly strict as such places went, and all were sternly conjured to 'employ the time of work faithfully, profitably, and for the good of the Community, and not lose time in frivolous Trifling . . .'[34] There were, in addition, severe punishments for entering the nuns' cells or the pensioners' rooms without permission, and for raiding the convent larder.

In the world, opinions on convent education varied widely. The Irish peeress, Lady Lucan, thought convents wretched places for education; and Mrs Carter, the bluestocking, writing to Mrs Vesey in 1769 observed 'that a cloyster is by no means such a school of devotion as it is represented'. But Mrs Thrale,* making a tour of France with Dr Johnson in 1775, was of a very different opinion, finding herself enraptured by the convents she had visited. While her daughter, Queeney, ran races on the grass with the pensioners at the Convent of the Austins, Mrs Thrale self-confessedly found her head rapidly becoming '. . . filled with nuns', and as she looked over their cells and walked in

---

*Hester Lynch Thrale (1741–1821). Only child of John Salusbury of Bachycraig, Flintshire, the friend of Dr Johnson, married against her will to Henry Thrale, son of a wealthy brewer. In 1786 published *Anecdotes of the late Samuel Johnson,* and in 1788 her correspondence with him.

their gardens, had mused that she should surely lose her heart among them, 'there is something so caressive in their manner, so Singular in their Profession, which at once inspires Compassion and Respect, that one must love them, and with a Tenderness that would be painful to oneself, but for the Consideration that they feel nothing for us'.[35] And although the Doctor was to lower her romantic flights by making faces at her through the grill, she could not help feeling 'much penetrated' by the sight of an earl's sister serving at table, finding 'all distinction thus thrown down by Religion so lovely'. She was highly intrigued by one nun in particular, '. . . a Beauty about London since my Time', still '. . . uncommonly handsome' who had 'seen a great deal of the world, has travelled and has read. She has many Books in her Room on various Subjects and talks of studying Latin in good earnest.'[36] Indeed so moved was Mrs Thrale by her experiences that, Dr Johnson notwithstanding, she was in half a mind to take refuge in a convent herself, if only for the pleasure of reading Virgil with her friend Miss Canning who had recently taken the veil.

In short such places provided an environment well calculated to engage a mind that was already thirsting for knowledge; to charm a temperament that craved passionately for affection.

The intellectual climate of most convents was extremely liberal for it was a period when all that was brilliant and fashionable, as well as all that was learned and profound, was intensely anti-clerical. Montesquieu, Voltaire, Rousseau, Diderot, D'Alembert, were the undisputed kings of literature, Condillac, Helvétius and Holbach dictated the philosophy of the day. Small wonder that Sarah Ponsonby's niece would write that Eleanor's education in the convent had not only given her 'a certain degree of refinement in literature' but 'a distaste for Irish priests and Irish Popery . . .'[37]

There was, however, another aspect of convent life which could have profoundly affected a nature at once sensitive and passionate. Emotional currents ran strongly in such places. Even Mrs Thrale's enthusiasm for the conventual life had not blinded her to flaws about which she found herself unable to be very specific. To more worldly observers the flaws had long been notorious. Casanova, who knew several nuns intimately, records in his memoirs that homosexuality was considered such a childish sin, and was so common in convents, that confessors imposed no penance for it.[38]

It is worth noting that even Madame de Genlis,* placed for safety in a convent during the absence of her young husband, remembered her visit ever after with acute nostalgia; calling up not only that vision of herself flying through the cloisters in the early hours dressed up as the Devil to frighten the nuns, but also the remembrance of the dances which were given twice a week when the nuns partnered the pensioners. They were dances, as Madame de Genlis later confessed with a certain astonishment, that were for some reason so very much more memorable than all the elegant balls she was later to attend in the world.

It was perhaps unsurprising that with such an educational background, with such a family, Miss Butler of the Castle should have an aura about her that if it was somewhat dark was also interesting.

Culturally, psychologically, the convent education was to leave a lasting impression on her. Even her time-table for the day would resemble a Convent Rule, for the pages of her journal would be divided up in advance thus:

> Rose at eight
> Nine Breakfast
> Half past nine Till Three
> Three Dinner
> Half past three Till Nine
> Nine Till One

the spaces to be filled up hour by hour throughout the day. But in 1768 when she was back in Kilkenny once again for her brother's wedding, a stretch of ten years would lie before her to be endured with growing impatience until the journal could be filled in according to her heart's desire.

* Stephanie-Felicité du Crest de Saint-Aubin, Comtesse de Genlis (1746–1830). French writer and educator. She was governess to the children of the Duke of Chartres, and lived to see her former pupil Louis-Philippe seated on the throne of France. Her 'adopted' daughter Pamela was married to Lord Edward Fitzgerald.

'One of the pleasantest and most antient cities in the kingdom', John Wesley had said of Kilkenny, another considered it 'one of the most considerable and populous inland towns in Ireland'. It was frequently likened to Oxford. But in 1776, Mark Elstob the traveller, jogging through its environs in the Kilkenny stage in company with a lady who could well have been Eleanor Butler from his description, '. . . somewhat to the masculine . . . yet of an obliging disposition, and not unentertaining', had looked through the window and been depressed by the long, narrow, dirty street edged with houses made of mud sods and straw. He found the beautiful cathedral of cloud-coloured stone 'destitute of grandeur' and he had been put out by the paltry congregation and the bare feet of the choir boys, just as he had been put out by having to push through a crowd of peasants waiting to be hired for the potato digging before he could catch a glimpse of the elegant town hall or Tholsel.

But he admired the handsome pavings of local Kilkenny marble, and had been impressed by the remarkable politeness of the townspeople. He had enjoyed discussing Irish customs with the lady traveller: the universal habit of serving potatoes in their jackets at every meal, the cloth afterwards being strewn with peelings; the hard-boiled eggs that everyone took with their morning tea; the slowness with which the peasants worked in the fields. He had asked the lady why some of the peasants' cabins had white flags flying outside them and had received the obliging reply that it meant milk was for sale. She had pointed out other cabins with notices reading, 'good dry lodging and snuff'.

All in all Mr Elstob had been a good deal more generous with his encomiums than that other traveller, Mr Twiss, who had preceded him the year before, and who had insulted everyone by his fault-finding: with the ungenteel manners of the Irish noblemen, with the common voices and fat legs of the ladies. However even he had found Kilkenny 'a pleasant little town', and had enjoyed a delightful walk along the river Nore.

In fact, Kilkenny was a remarkably civilized town by any standards. The excellence of its inns had earned it the proud title of 'The little city of all Ireland the part most reclaimed from sluttishness and slavery, to civility and clean bedding.' Indeed, there was no necessity for the traveller to take his bedding to the *Sheaf* in Rose Inn Street, for it was scrupulously clean, and the cook so refined that he wore ruffles like a gentleman.

The Protestant Ascendancy were apt to call such places 'Ale houses' out of ignorance, but in Kilkenny no man spent the early part of the night at home, preferring to seek out his friends at places like the *Wheatsheaf* or at the *Hole in the Wall* in the High Street. The latter rendezvous was much frequented by Eleanor's brother, John Butler, who was nicknamed 'Jack of the Castle'. The inn was run, and excellently well run, by one of the old Butler family valets :

'No, no, no dissipation, no dissipation', curious inquirers were told of the *Hole in the Wall*. And although this was flatly contradicted by a certain jingle :

> 'If you ever go to Kilkenny
> Remember the *Hole in the Wall*
> You may there get blind drunk for a penny
> Or tipsey for nothing at all '[39]

there was truth in it too, for the Kilkenny inns were not mere drinking clubs, but catered for breakfasts, dinners, suppers and balls, and all manner of other elegant entertainments.

There was no dearth of elegant entertainment in the town, for, housing the garrison, Kilkenny was in close touch with Dublin, and was much frequented by the country gentry. During the Season there were weekly assemblies at the Tholsel ; Tenducci* held concerts, and a variety of plays could be seen at the County Court house, *Maid of the Mill, Comus, Hamlet, The Beggar's Opera,* and *The Clandestine Marriage* among others. There were in addition two public cockpits, while the band of the garrison played regularly on the Parade outside the Castle.

In the local paper, the merchant, Dominick Farrell, with whom Madam Butler was everlastingly locked in financial business of extraordinary complexity, advertised tantalizing cargoes

---

* Described by Horace Walpole as 'a moderate tenor'.

that had just come in, 'lemons and oranges, brandy, sherry, iron, beech logs, french paper', and if the *Leinster Journal* carried accounts of a woman being whipped along the Kilkenny streets for stealing, and of a runaway apprentice being thrown into prison and heavily ironed it also recorded that an infirmary had been opened in 1767, and that there was already a society for bettering the condition and increasing the comforts of the poor.

Yet for all its indisputable pleasantness Kilkenny constituted a life sentence for Eleanor Butler. Life at the Castle, where in winter fumes from the Kilkenny coal hung heavy in the rooms giving everyone but the *de jure* Earl violent wheezing fits, was oppressive in more than one sense. For one educated in the heyday of French liberalism Castle routine must have seemed unendurably rigid, Castle attitudes affrontingly priest-ridden. Nor did there seem to be much relief in the feminine society of Kilkenny for one who, having been too well educated for her sex, found most of its pursuits twaddling.

Frustration, resentment, may have caused those migraines which were to dog her until late in life, for it was now becoming very clear that she was going to play little part in the reviving family fortunes. Four years before, in 1764, her brother John Butler had renounced his Catholicism and conformed to the Established Church as a preliminary to reversing the attainder on the Ormonde titles. In 1769 he followed this up with a brilliant marriage to the heiress of Lord Wandesford. Both of Eleanor's sisters had already been married for some time to prominent Catholics; one to 'Monarch' Kavanagh of Borris, the other to Morgan Kavanagh of Ballyhail. Eleanor, nearly thirty now, apparently of too satirical and too masculine a style to attract men, had every appearance of becoming an old maid and something of a stumbling-block to her family.

It was at this point that deliverance came. We are told that Lady Betty Fownes twelve miles off at Inistiogue had asked Madam Butler of the Castle to keep a watchful eye on Sally Ponsonby at Miss Parke's.[40] It was not long before Madam Butler was to have the strange experience of seeing her bored, cultivated, critical daughter committing herself unreservedly to a friendship with a schoolgirl of thirteen.

Mrs Delany* tells us how rare and how precious congenial feminine friendships were then. Sarah Ponsonby was sensitive and retiring, but also sympathetic and eager to learn. Eleanor, who had long taken refuge in books, was fluent in French, had read extensively in French literature. Given a responsive companion she had much to offer. There was sixteen years' difference between them, but such associations of a romantic pupil-teacher sort were common throughout the period.

Their friendship most likely began, as so many before and since, with books. Richardson was a mutual favourite; they greatly admired *Clarissa*, doted on the noble character of *Sir Charles Grandison*. Perhaps they read and discussed that dulcet ladies' Utopia, *Millenium Hall,* which was then so much in vogue.

From books they no doubt passed on to discuss the world as it was, as it might be, and, leaving that, would have pondered their own futures; slowly discovering over five years of growing intimacy that they both, the one so shy, gentle and over-sensitive, the other bitter, sharp-tongued, yet scarcely less sensitive, had a longing for the simple life, for the *douceurs* of retirement. Then, if at first only as an ideal, they planned such a life which, suppose the opportunity should ever offer, they might lead together.

On the first of May 1773, five years after their first meeting, Sarah Ponsonby, now eighteen, left Miss Parke's school and went to live with Sir William and Lady Betty Fownes at Woodstock.

How much or how little the two friends now saw of each other is uncertain. The Butlers and the Fownes were by no means intimate, although conformity to an established social pattern would ensure their meeting, if only publicly, at the theatres, assemblies and the balls at Dublin Castle and the Rotunda.

---

*Mary Granville Delany (1700–88), wife (after the death of her first husband) of Dr Patrick Delany, friend of Swift. She had known everyone worth knowing in her day, had corresponded with Swift and Young, and left an interesting picture of polite English society in her six volumes of *Autobiography and Letters.*

Sir William's great connection and his own membership of the Irish parliament and Privy Council gave him an entry into the first society of the day. A society which Horace Walpole with unaccustomed generosity had spoke of as 'the staple of wit, and I find coins bons mots for our greatest men'.

The Fownes had an elegant house in the most fashionable part of Dublin. The houses in Dominick Street are now slum property: the beautiful fanlights have lost their glass, and in what is reputedly 37 Dominick Street, where the Fownes lived, the drawing-room is divided across by grimy screens to make two rooms for the lodger who now lives there. It is hard, therefore, to imagine it as it was on nights when the family were expecting great company, or when they themselves were setting out for an evening at the Opera or a reception at the Castle.

But it was not the bustle of the Dublin season that Sarah remembered afterwards, nor yet the elegancies of Bath, where it seems she was briefly mistaken for Mr Speaker Ponsonby's daughter and almost received a proposal of marriage, but the calm happiness of Woodstock. For to begin with she was happy. Content to feel secure at last, to become a second daughter to Lady Betty who was missing her own girl, also named Sarah, who had not long married. Years later she would dream of Woodstock, would remember the favourite flowers Lady Betty grew in the garden, would recall the names of the old servants, and laugh again remembering the pompous sermons of the Inistiogue parson. She would remember galloping round the 'improved' garden with Lady Betty's grandson, Harry Tighe, on her shoulders. Harry, who called her 'Aaa Pouhh' and 'Sally Puppy' and promised to marry her when he grew up.

Kind Lady Betty who was killing herself, so it was said, working enormous cross-stitch carpets and innumerable embroidered chair seats, and when not doing that, indulging her voracious passion for cards. It was a passion shared by her greatest crony and one of Woodstock's most constant visitors, Lucy Goddard, a sprightly and ambitious widow with an eye to the main chance. Great confidante, greater rattle, she was ever recording, while staying with Lady Betty, what she was pleased to call 'boosey' whist parties beneath the Woodstock oaks; or water excursions with the Woodstock ladies; or drives through the woods to Altamount, on the limpid autumn days when the beech trees showered leaves like gold and crimson butterflies. In wintertime she sat with them before the huge Woodstock fires, drinking black cherry whiskey as the rain flailed at the windows and tattling about her chances with that unforthcoming, that deceitful, that mean bachelor, Mr Izod.

It was not until the winter of 1776 that Lucy Goddard recorded in dashing hand her unaccustomed confusion at a clandestine correspondence that had just been brought to her notice. She had, however, for some time been acquainted with the cause of it.

Chapter Two

'How charmingly might you and I
live together and despise them all!'
Miss Howe to Miss Clarissa Harlowe

'At first I believed it almost impossible for so professed a man of honour to throw off the mask so shamefully, and that my prudence would secure me from appearing to understand him'[1] Sarah had written to Mrs Goddard in that neat elegant hand which not so long ago had written very different letters. Letters sending Mrs Goddard compliments from Crab, the Woodstock dog; 10,000,000 good wishes from Lady Betty, 175,468,976 from Sir William.[2]

Sir William! She enclosed a copy of the letter she had written him: 'I desire to be informed in writing and only in writing, whether your motive for behaving to me as you do is a desire that I should quit your house. If so, I promise in the most solemn manner that I will take the first opportunity of doing it, and that my real motive shall ever remain concealed.'[3]

Sir William's own granddaughter would reveal the real motive with commendably un-Victorian candour:

Sir William Fownes was not a kind husband to his excellent wife. The gout made him very ill-tempered and though his daughter was married and had children he still lamented that he had not a male heir, and believing that Lady Betty was in a declining state of health, he fancied that the time was approaching which would leave him at liberty to marry a young wife. He had a pretty face, he thought, and was not much above fifty. In this disposition of mind he cast his eye on Miss Ponsonby after she had lived in his house for a year or two.

Sir William's daughter, anxious no doubt to excuse her father, was of the opinion 'that more was imagined than was intended'.[4]

Sarah Ponsonby however was in no doubt; '... be satisfied' her flying pen informed Mrs Goddard, 'that neither my pride, resentment, nor any other passion shall ever be sufficiently powerful to make me give Lady Betty any uneasiness in my power to spare her, and I sometimes laugh to think of the earnestness with which she presses me to be obliging to him, for I have adopted the most reserved mode of behaviour ever since.' Her quill opened a sardonic bracket: 'Taking no pains when she does not perceive it, to show my disgust and detestation of him.' She closed the bracket contemptuously and added, meaning it, 'I would rather die than wound Lady Betty's heart.'[5]

The last sentiment was undoubtedly hers, but there was something alien in the bitter force of the rest of the letter which suggested that she had been seeking, and receiving, advice from another quarter.

'I found letters from her to Mrs Goddard complaining of her unhappiness,' wrote Sarah's niece long after, 'and alluding to a secret correspondence with Miss Butler, who was equally unhappy.'[6]

Novels of the period confirm that such secret correspondence was not uncommon. Even the impeccable Mrs Delany had, as a girl, conducted one with her friend, Miss Kirkham, whom her father had forbidden her to meet, considering Miss Kirkham 'too free and masculine', although he revised his opinion later, when the over-free Miss Kirkham married and turned into excellent Mrs Chapone.

Such deceptions were made possible by corruptible servants, were necessary at all because parents, having absolute authority over their children in general and their daughters in particular, were frequently tyrannical. For, as Dr Johnson had been at pains to explain to Boswell, the chastity of women was of the utmost importance since all property was dependent upon it.

The civilized editors of the *Spectator* had had much to say upon the subject of parental harshness. Samuel Richardson had written admonishingly on the same theme, for theirs was a society so material that it disregarded everything but the worldly settlement in life. Mrs Delany's aunt, writing to compliment her niece upon a marriage which the niece herself looked upon as one with a tyrant, a jailer, 'one that I was determined to obey and oblige, but found it impossible to love', stoutly defined what constituted happiness as 'riches, honours, and length of years'.[7]

There were exceptions, like one of Sarah Ponsonby's own relations, who deferred accepting a materially advantageous offer of marriage for his young daughter, 'as he has always left his children intirely to their own choice upon this subject'.[8]

Eleanor Butler's parents were not, alas, of this sort. Something now drove her to open her heart secretly to the only friend she could trust. It was a correspondence of mutual complaint, which, by the early spring of 1778, had been going on for at least eighteen months. It transpired that while at Woodstock Sir William's unwanted attentions were causing Sarah both misery and embarrassment, so at the Castle Eleanor was being made wretched by Madam Butler pressing her to enter a convent.

Madam Butler's plan was very likely well intended. Her daughter was thirty-nine, unlikely to marry now, and in the past she had been happy at Cambrai. Needled possibly by the priests who surrounded her, Madam Butler may have suffered twinges of guilt at the bland conversion of her son to the Established Church. She may have imagined that the balance could be restored by her youngest daughter devoting herself to the Faith. The scheme had another merit: it was cheap. At the convent of the Holy Sepulchre at Liège where both men and women could be pensioners, a peer and two servants had stayed in comfort for five months for as little as twenty-six pounds, sixteen shillings and eightpence. Should Eleanor conveniently find a call within herself to take the veil, a down payment of three hundred pounds would take care of her for life and still allow five pounds per annum for extras. Meanwhile her portion of the family fortune guaranteed her by her brother's marriage settlement might be advantageously redeployed.

It was unfortunate for Madam Butler's peace of mind that such excellent arrangements should be strenuously opposed by Eleanor herself. Much as she had enjoyed it then, the life at Cambrai was past. She now had other and more ambitious plans.

They had discussed their idea of the perfect life together long ago. Now the events of the last eighteen months were dramatically to transpose it from the heights of fantasy to the plains of possibility. Their ideal of retiring from society had been inspired not only by natural inclination but by the prevailing fashion for the French nature philosophers. If it were to be realistically interpreted it would mean leading a quiet life together in a country cottage. It was all they could dare because for the time being it was all they could afford.

This must have been the burden of the letters, which, braving interception, discovery and ruin, had gone posting back and forth between the Castle and Woodstock.

By March 1778, while Mrs Goddard gallivanted in Dublin, 'wickedly splenetic' among the company she was entertaining that St Patrick's day, dressing up as Juggy Lannon for a masquerade at Lady Dungannon's,* final arrangements were being made in the privacy of a certain bedroom in the Castle and in another twelve miles off at Woodstock. Tension was mounting. The explosion when it came was brief and shocking. On Friday 3 April Mrs Goddard was abruptly halted in her giddy social round by a letter from Lady Betty Fownes.

Lady Betty's handwriting, never of the most elegant, was now quite wild with anxiety. Headed 'Tuesday Nigh' it spelt out the following extraordinary news:

My dear Mrs Goddard I cant Paint our distress. My Dr Sally lept out of a Window last Night and is gon off. We learn Miss Butler of the Castle is wt her. I can say no more. Help me if you can. We are in the utmost distress and I am sure you pitty us. God Bless you.

> ever Yours E.F.

There was a postscript, 'Mr Butler of ye Castle has sent here in search of his daughter.'[9]

Mrs Goddard was sufficiently disturbed by this news to spend the whole of the following day indoors ruminating about her friends, for as yet there was no word of them. By Saturday

---

*Daughter of Edmund Stafford, Esq., Co. Meath, and widow of Arthur Hill, created Viscount Dungannon. She was the maternal grandmother of the Duke of Wellington.

however a picture was beginning to build up from the letters which were arriving for her from lady correspondents in all quarters.

On the evening of Monday 30 March Lady Betty's married daughter, Sarah Tighe, who was staying at Woodstock with her three children, had been sitting up late with the youngest child who was ill. Sarah Ponsonby had come into the room, knelt down at Mrs Tighe's knee and burst out weeping, a display of emotion which, at the time, Mrs Tighe had naturally attributed to anxiety about the baby. In fact Sarah was taking leave of Mrs Tighe of whom she was very fond. Late that night, when the family was in bed, Sarah, dressed in men's clothes, armed with a pistol and carrying her small dog, Frisk, made her way silently downstairs, as silently pushed up the sash of the parlour window, and, climbing over the sill, dropped to the ground. Outside she was met by the trusted labourer who straightway guided her to the barn where Eleanor Butler was waiting for her.[10]

Earlier that night at about ten, and just as the family were going into supper, Eleanor had crept out of the Castle. Once outside she too had changed into men's clothes, and, on a horse either begged or borrowed, had ridden off to their prearranged rendezvous.[11] Their goal was Waterford twenty-three miles off and the boat for England.

By Tuesday morning Eleanor Butler's father, having at first thought that his daughter had run off with some man, but, significantly, being quite unable to think who, had traced her to Woodstock. He arrived to find that Sir William's men were already out scouring the countryside for the two women. The weather was wet with cold winds, the St George's Channel rumoured to be alive with pirates. The fugitives were within reach of Waterford when the narrative blurs. They either missed the English packet or, being traditionally unreliable, it did not sail at all. Whatever happened they were forced by some such circumstance to postpone their sailing and to hide the whole of that day and night in a barn.

Ironically enough the day following, Wednesday, was April Fools' day. Some time towards evening Sir William's men caught up with them. They were within a mile of Waterford, 'in a Carr in Mens Clouths',[12] betrayed, so it was said, by one of Eleanor's fine ruffles that she had dropped, and by the hysterical barking of Frisk.

As soon as the news got back to Woodstock Lady Betty took a coach for Waterford, and at five in the morning of the same day Eleanor's brother-in-law, Morgan Kavanagh, grimly set out for the same destination with Mrs Hamerton, a close friend of the Butler family.

They arrived on the quay just as the Woodstock coach containing Lady Betty and the two fugitives was starting off for the homeward journey. Sarah had caught an appalling cold from sleeping in the barn and was sneezing her head off. Eleanor, according to Lady Betty, was well enough, and 'very happy' to be going home with her.

If only the Butler contingent had arrived a few minutes later much misery might have been prevented. As it was they stopped Lady Betty's coach and insisted on Eleanor getting out and accompanying them. The unfortunate woman 'begged and intreated'[13] that she might be allowed to go with Sarah and Lady Betty, but Morgan Kavanagh was obdurate. Her father's orders were that she should be taken to 'Monarch' Kavanagh's house at Borris for safekeeping until her outraged family had made up their minds what to do with her.

By now on the verge of hysteria Eleanor begged half an hour longer with Sarah, which was grudgingly permitted. But on her crying for a moment and yet another moment longer the Butler entourage lost patience. Half-fainting she had to be helped into the Butler coach, which now drove off to spend the night at Morgan Kavanagh's house at Ballyhail, leaving Sarah Ponsonby and Lady Betty to travel back to Woodstock alone.

'In the Coach I could not help asking her the Cause of this sudden flight,' wrote Lady Betty to Mrs Goddard, 'she said it was not suddain. Their plan was to go to England, take a house and live together. By all accounts there was no man concerned with either of them.'[14]

This small measure of comfort was echoed by Mrs Tighe, Lady Betty's daughter, '. . . conduct, though it has an appearance of imprudence is I am sure void of serious impropriety', she wrote in her turn to Mrs Goddard. 'There were no gentlemen concerned, nor does it appear to be anything more than a scheme of Romantic Friendship.'[15] 'Romantic',* at the time, inferring no more than what was fanciful or eccentric.

They reached Woodstock, and Sarah was put to bed with a sore throat and high fever. The next day she was worse, reviving only briefly when a letter arrived from Eleanor Butler for Lady Betty. Lady Betty indulgently re-read it to the patient, but it was only a letter of thanks, containing no definite news of what was in store for the writer.

Anxiety on this account now so exacerbated Sarah's fever that by nightfall she was delirious. '. . . very ill all night' Lady Betty reported agitatedly to Mrs Goddard, 'this morning fainted twice, looks quite wild at us.'[16] But at eight o'clock that morning a messenger from Ballyhail brought news from her friend at last. It could scarcely have been worse. Eleanor, forbidden her parents' house, was to be taken that very morning to 'Monarch' Kavanagh at Borris where, virtually a prisoner, she was to wait until being sent abroad to France.

'She is now at Borris' Lady Betty confirmed in her letter to Mrs Goddard that Sunday, 'and by all we can learn very well. Dines with the Family and seems hearty but I can scarcely believe it ... We hear the Butlers are never to forgive their Daughter', she continued, 'and that she is to be sent to France to a convent. I wish she had been safe in one long ago, and she would have made us all happy. Many an unhappy hour she has cost me and I am convinced years to Sally.'[17] This letter ended as all its predecessors with Lady Betty urgently beseeching Mrs Goddard to come to Woodstock and give them the benefit of her comfort and advice.

In Dublin, however, Mrs Goddard had recovered from the initial shock caused by the elopement and was in no mind to forgo her social round. She had been playing whist; had been at

---

*It was, according to Mary Hays, the authoress, 'a vague term, applied to everything we do not understand, or are unwilling to imitate' (J.M.S. Tompkins, *The Popular Novel in England, 1770–1800*, Methuen University Paperback, p. 212).

the Italian opera, and was even now looking forward to a performance of *The School for Scandal*.[18]

Sarah was still extremely ill. Although the fever had abated her distress of mind now so terrified Lady Betty that she wrote in the strongest terms to Eleanor Butler's sister at Borris 'to beg Miss B might not write volumes to her till she was better'. For the letters were arriving daily, each one reducing the unhappy recipient to even further extremes of misery. 'I am astonished she will do it',[19] commented the gentle and unselfish mistress of Woodstock.

But Eleanor Butler was desperate. She stood to lose all: the love and companionship of her friend; the passionate hope of a life together; her very freedom, for every day the dreaded journey to France seemed more likely to take place. To make matters worse it now began to look as though Sally Ponsonby might be succumbing to Lady Betty's kind ministrations, for by the end of the week Lady Betty had been able to write a little more hopefully to her frivolous friend:

My dear G, Sally is much better, but weak, low and dejected. She made me watch the windows all day yesterday, she was so sure you would lose no time. She was most anxious to see your letter to me. I did not read it all, as anything against Miss B. is death to her. Be very cautious till we meet. Storys to be sure there must be in plenty. I cant help giving credit to Sarah Ponsonby's which is that they were to live together. A convent, I used to think – but she said that is what she [Eleanor Butler] flew from and that we are all much mistaken and that if we knew Miss B. we would love her as well as she did. All together it is a most extraordinary affair. I sometimes can hardly think the cause is known by any one but themselves. God knows how it is, or how it will end. I know she is very ill. I am sure nothing could be of so much use to her as seeing you and having you talk to her. I think you will come now, my dear. She has taken my little senses away. I sometimes sitt for hours and cant speak to her. Sally Tighe has been of infinite use to her. If she had not been here I must have died I really think. She is so clever at preaching to her. I fear they [the Tighes] must soon leave me and then indeed if you don't come I shall give myself up at once. God bless you.[20]

Sarah was by now sufficiently recovered to add her own plea in an attempt to influence the careless G.

Not from my Green table but from my Bed.

The 9th of April 1778

My Dear dear friend, I must be indeed fallen, and fallen very low, in your opinion, if you are not convinced that among the many which agitate my heart at this moment the most earnest wishes to behold you once more are not very predominant. Come then for Lady Betty's sake. You know the effect your presence has here at all times. And I know your heart well enough to be convinced that it will soon bring you. As there did not come a letter from you Wednesday I persuaded myself you would have been here that night as much as if you had promised it. I would say more to persuade you, but I am sick and weak. But your good nature requires not incentives, nor does your knowledge of my feelings require any assurance of the gratitude and tender affection of your

Poor S.

There was a footnote: 'Miss B. endures a sufficient portion of anguish already. Spare and vindicate her from the unmerited reproach of being the Principal Cause of Our Common Misfortune, which her Generosity makes her take pains to load herself with. Believe my Solemn Assurance that it is not just – as I will convince you when I am able. Come and assist me to thank Lady Betty.'[21]

Deaf even to this moving appeal the reprehensible G remained fixed in Dublin, and it was to Grafton Street that Lady Betty had again to address her next letter.

For a change it was tolerably optimistic. Sally was recovering, Eleanor reported well at Borris, the only cause for anxiety was that the two friends were longing to meet one another, a circumstance which Lady Betty naturally dreaded. 'Tho' Sally has assured me that I may make myself easy as she never will leave me again.' She drew an optimistic dash and passed on to tentative self-congratulation, '... she is very grateful and between you and me I fancy glad to have returned here where I may say, with great truth, she ought to have been the happiest girl in the world, everything considered and I trust will be so again.'[22]

This suggests that for the time being Sarah Ponsonby, if only for Lady Betty's sake, was unwilling to commit herself to further impulsive behaviour. If only the Butlers would relent in the matter of the convent then surely some other solution could be found. Perhaps in the calm of Woodstock, and removed from Eleanor Butler's immediate influence, it was possible to survey the situation in perspective.

Matters however had gone too far. The Butlers were adamant in the matter of the convent, and the anguish caused by such cruelty to her friend was to provoke not only horrified pity but rebellion in Sarah Ponsonby's tender heart. 'I would do anything' she now wrote mutinously to her friend, Mrs Goddard, 'to save Miss Butler from Popery and a Convent.'[23]

By Monday the thirteenth of April Lady Betty's optimism had begun to evaporate once more. Exactly a fortnight after the attempted elopement she was again reporting to her heedless friend:

How she longed for the Goddards' company. Her patience was worn out, and her heart quailed at the thought of losing the support of her daughter, Sarah Tighe, who was leaving the following day with her children. A certain ambiguity about the true reason for the two friends' elopement was continuing to worry her; something that eluded her, something she could put no name to, but which had to do with the character of Miss Butler herself. 'I hear they say these two friends must not live together', she wrote, 'I cant help thinking as they do',[24] though why she thought thus she was unable to say.

Not unnaturally Kilkenny was seething with rumours, 'sad talk and idle reports which I think is all Falce'[25] commented Lady Betty. Sally herself had after all not really settled, yet on her side at least Lady Betty was certain things would return to normal provided that she did not meet Miss Butler. Once again her mind was drawn to the mysterious cause of the elopement. 'Some times I think we dont know the true cause', she wrote sadly, her heart full of misgivings for the gentle girl of whom she had grown so fond. 'Poor Soul if she had not been so fond of her pen so much would not have happened.' She concluded the letter by thanking Mrs Goddard for the pretty lace 'patrone' that she had sent, no doubt with the object of taking Lady Betty's mind off her troubles, and craved 'a pinch of good snuff'. At the bottom of the sheet she added, 'I dont think I ever told you that Sir Wm and Mr Tighe went to the Castle to plead

for Miss B. Sir Wm said everything for her, but all to no purpose. I pity her tho I fear she has been much to bleam.'[26]

Throughout these uneasy days Sir William, as Lady Betty had
gratefully acknowledged to Mrs Goddard, had 'behaved like an
angell'. He was now clearly most anxious to retrieve, if he
could, the embarrassingly extravagant situation that he had
helped to precipitate. But already the obstinacy of the Butlers,
the selfishness of Mrs Goddard in for too long withholding her
help, the hardening resolution of Sarah Ponsonby, and the wild
desperation of Eleanor Butler were combining to produce a situation which would soon be out of anyone's control.

Yet even at this late stage it appears that there was a faint
hope that the Butlers might be persuaded to relent. The fact that
in later life Eleanor Butler corresponded with her Borris sister,
and remained amicably disposed towards her brother-in-law,
while exchanging no correspondence with her parents, suggests
that the family may have been divided; that the party at Borris
might have been advocating a more humane course of action.

By the sixteenth of April there was still no definite news.
'Proud I was of your letter to day to Sally P.' wrote Lady Betty
to Mrs Goddard in a letter which, in her anxiety, she had dated
three days too early.

She is much better but very nervous and low at not hearing of
Miss B's fate. We sent this morning* but no body yet come. I do
hear from others she is to be sent to France. S.P. says she must and
will go with her. I do nothing but Preach. God knows she will be
undone if she goes, and how to keep her I cannot tell. Oh for your
head! but that we cannot have.[27]

They were waiting on tenterhooks for the news to come back
from Borris. It came late that night and confirmed their worst
fears. Eleanor Butler was to be sent to the convent, worse still
she was not even to be allowed to see Sarah again. They had not
entirely succeeded in breaking her spirit however, 'Miss B sais
she will consent to everything but that, but go without seeing
her she will not.'[28]

There had been a note for Lady Betty from Eleanor, begging

* To Borris.

her to write to Borris and to use her influence to persuade the family there to allow her and Sarah one last interview, if only of half an hour. Much moved, further swayed by Sarah's wretchedness, Lady Betty wrote next morning to this effect, but with little hope.

To everyone's surprise permission for a meeting came by return, and, full of foreboding, Sarah was driven over to Borris that day.

She arrived to find that the Butlers had shifted their position somewhat. It appeared that they were now less outraged by their daughter's refusal to go into a convent than disturbed by the nature of her friendship with Sarah Ponsonby. As with Lady Betty, the friendship seems to have assumed a dubious character in their minds. 'They propose great terms to Miss B if she will reside in a convent some years and give me Up For Ever' wrote Sarah unhappily to Mrs Goddard of the interview. 'I am not Heroick enough to wish she could accept them' she went on 'nor is she I believe to listen to them. Worn out by Misfortunes, I still have the comfort of Self Approbation. Were it to do Again I Would Act as I have Done. If it is any satisfaction to you to know that you possess third place at least in an almost broken heart be assured of it – God bless you.'[29]

Shocked and weak as she was, she was guarding a dangerous secret. In the short half-hour meeting she and Eleanor Butler had agreed on one last desperate move.

The following Wednesday Mrs Goddard, relaxing in the gay comfort of Grafton Street, was to be electrified anew. Eleanor had run away from Borris some time on the Sunday night.

High country separates Borris from the small riverside village of Inistiogue twelve miles away. It was country at that time still dangerous on account of the Whiteboys: agrarian agitators, who with no great particularity were given to attacking priests and tithe collectors. In the twilight of the late spring night she would have looked across the Barrow valley and seen the lodge at the Woodstock gates, the dark hang of the famous beech wood which was newly coming into leaf. She would have set her back at last to those high black mountains behind Borris, descended the short steep hill to Inistiogue, gone over the twelve-arched bridge which spanned the river and up through the sleeping village to Woodstock and her Sally.

On Thursday 22 April Mrs Goddard dashed an entry into her journal, 'Got another letter* to tell Miss Butler was and had been at Woodstock concealed by Miss Ponsonby from Sunday till Monday night without their privity.'[30]

'What had happened since Miss Butler's flight will surprise you', poor Lady Betty had written. 'Last night a man came and said that he could discover where she was. Sir William asked "Where?" "In your Honour's house", he said, "She was let in through the Hall window on Sunday night." I could not believe it till I went up and found the two ladies crying together.'[31] It transpired that Mary Carryll, Lady Betty's own housemaid, had been in the plot, and had been smuggling food in to Miss Butler, who, at the least sign of danger, had concealed herself in the cupboard in Sarah's room.

This news galvanized Mrs Goddard into activity at last. On Friday 24 April she set out from Dublin with Jane, her maid, recorded some excellent mutton chops she dined off on the way, and after a 'most terrible long jaunt'[32] arrived at Woodstock on Saturday.

She found the family 'in distraction', and her arrival was to herald a ten day psychological war of attrition, between Miss Ponsonby and Miss Butler on the one hand and everyone else on the other.

Sir William was already writing desperate letters to Mr Butler of the Castle asking him to come and remove his unwelcome daughter; to Sarah's uncle; to the brother of her stepmother. In all three attempts he drew blank. Mrs Goddard in the meantime nagged.

Sunday 26th April. Saw Miss Pons. again who came down to dinner, but Miss Butler not till evening when she came in to tea but did not speak to me.

Monday 27th April. Spoke to them both. Gave them my best advice which they seemed to take well, and I hop'd from their manner would have followed. They both dined with us.[33]

* From Lady Betty.

Next day Mrs Goddard attempted to push home this advantage that she had gained. It turned out however to have been imaginary; all she encountered was a hardening of their resolution to go away together. Whatever her proposals had been the two women had not seriously considered them, for, as they were probably very well aware, their defiance was about to be rewarded. That same day Mr Butler's solicitor, Mr Park; called, and his news was all they could have wished for. Eleanor's father had relented at last. The two ladies might go away together. Mr Park was to remain at Woodstock for a short period during which he was to arrange some sort of financial provision for Miss Butler and to seek, lost cause, to dissuade them from their purpose.

The defection of the Butlers spelt defeat for the Woodstock opposition. Mrs Goddard took it upon herself none the less to deliver one last broadside.

On 2 May she spoke privately to Sarah,

not to dissuade her from her purpose but to discharge my conscience of the duty I owed her as a friend by letting her know my opinion of Miss Butler and the certainty I had they never would agree living together. I spoke of her with harshness and freedom, said she had a debauched mind, no ingredients for friendship, that ought to be founded on virtue, whereas hers every day more and more showed me was acting in direct opposition to it, as well as to the interest, happiness and reputation of the one she professed to love.[34]

'Debauched' was a strong word with its inference of corruption. Yet she was probably voicing no more than general opinion which, not unnaturally, saw something grotesque in such a violent flouting of parental authority; in such 'imprudence', and in the prospect of a woman of nearly forty running away with a girl of twenty-three. A woman, moreover who, even before this episode, had been considered odd, being in the common view over-educated, masculine and satirical.

Sir William who was present at this interview now made himself ridiculous, '. . . kneel'd, implored, swore twice on the Bible' how much he loved Sarah, 'would never more offend, was sorry for his past folly, that was not meant as she understood it, offer'd to double her allowance of £30 a year, or add what more she pleased to it even tho' she did go'.[35]

Reinforced by Eleanor Butler's strong presence, already secretly packed, every day wearing her travelling habit in expectation of their final flight, Sarah Ponsonby roundly anounced that even if the whole world like Sir William were kneeling at her feet she would not alter her intention which was to 'live and die with Miss Butler'.[36]

She added darkly, furthermore, that if she were opposed in any way '. . . it would provoke her to an act that wd give her friends more trouble than anything she had yet done'.[37]

After all they had been through her friends very understandably blenched at this portentous remark. That evening Mrs Goddard was to record disgustedly that both Miss Ponsonby and Miss Butler had dined with the family, 'and I never saw anything so confident as their behaviour'.[38]

The following day, a Sunday, both ladies in striking contrast to the rest of the household, were in excellent spirits. Sir William gloomily read prayers, which only Sarah attended. That evening, but with little enthusiasm, the company played the popular board game, *Game of the Goose*, '. . . all dull' wrote Mrs Goddard of the occasion, 'but the girls'.[39] Everyone with the exception of poor Lady Betty knew now that the Butler coach had come for them. That evening Sarah intercepted Mrs Goddard on her way to bed and kissed her affectionately; but next morning when she went early to Mrs G's door to say good-bye, her erstwhile friend huffily refused to open it. She could not resist looking out of the window however, and there, at six o'clock on the fine May morning, saw the two friends, in company with the housemaid Mary Carryll, getting into the coach. They were laughing happily.

They were gone at last. Everyone had lived through an experience as traumatic as any occurring in Richardson's fiction, and they were mentally exhausted. An uneasy sort of peace must have settled momentarily upon the unfortunate Woodstock household. Mrs Goddard made kind attempts to distract her afflicted friends: took Lady Betty to Thomastown for a surprise dinner; drove over to have a look at the barn where the two ladies had sheltered; daringly paid a visit to the Castle where, in a thunderous atmosphere, no one had the courage even so much as to mention Miss Butler.

But peace was to be of short duration. Stories were already circulating in Kilkenny of Sir William's gallantry to Miss Ponsonby; while Lady Betty, always a nervous and delicate woman, was prostrated by the anxieties she had endured. Perhaps it was now that she wrote to her husband, or perhaps, long anticipating death, she had had the letter by her some time:

My dear Sir Wm, the greatest Grife I have in leaving this World is parting with you and the thoughts of your sorrow for me. Don't grive my dear Sir Wm, I am, I trust in God going to be happy. You have my sincear Prayers and thanks for your tenderness to me and good behaviour to my dear Child. May God grant you happiness in her. If you Marry again I wish you much happiness. If I ever offended you forgive me. I have never meant any offence, I have always ment to be a good Wife and Mother and hope you think Me so. As to my Funeral I hope youl allow me to be Buried as I like, which is this: When the Women about me are sure I am dead, I would be Carried to the Church and kept out of Ground two days and nights, four Women to sitt up with me. To each Woman give five pound. I would have twenty Pound laid out in Close for the poor People, in all forty. No body to be at My Funeral but my own poor, who I think will be sorry for me. If Nelly be wt me at the time of my death give her fifty Pound, she deserves it much. Take care of yourself (live and do all the good you can) and may God almighty give you as peacefull and happy an End as I think I shall have ...[40]

But she was not, after all, to go first, and Sir William was not to have the kind end she would have wished him.

On the last day of May, six weeks after the dark genius of Miss Butler had clandestinely entered his house to plague him, Sir William woke in the early hours of the summer morning yelling out that he was dying of strangulation of the stomach. He was swiftly bled and bathed in warm water, Mrs Goddard ungenerously informing him that his illness was the result of guilt.

The attack was only the prelude to ten days of torment for the unfortunate man; a torment of repeated enemas, continuous

blood-letting and thorough and scorching applications of can-
tharides with the object of raising restorative blisters on his
exterior parts; '. . . blistered and glistered and physick'd . . . in
the space of half an hour',[41] Mrs Goddard recorded gloatingly in
her journal. Exhaustion as a result of this barbarous treatment
soon rendered him so low in body and mind that in front of
both Mrs Goddard and his daughter, Mrs Tighe, he broke down
and freely confessed that 'his illness . . . was his own fault that
he was punished for'.[42]

At three o'clock in the morning of the next day he was seized
with a paralytic stroke, lost the use of his right side and became
speechless. He was at once 'cupp'd blistered and glistered', and
two days later again blistered on his head, making, as Mrs Goddard meticulously noted, 'the 14th he had on him'.[43]

That lady's notions of divine punishment were to be most
amply confirmed. Poor Sir William was to endure another two
days of anguish before the final death agony of twelve hours. He
was released at last and was buried in the small church at Inistiogue. Three weeks later, his devoted Lady Betty was laid beside him.

Meanwhile, comfortably unaware of the havoc they had
caused, Miss Butler and Miss Ponsonby, attended by a devoted
Mary Carryll, were touring Wales.

Chapter Three

A lady traveller in Wales. 'This awfull scenery makes me feel as if I were only a worm or a grain of dust on the face of the earth.'
Mrs Siddons. 'I feel very differently.'

It was not strange for them to have chosen Wales, since it lay, interposing its 'Beautifully horrid mountains', between London and those western ports where the Irish travellers landed.

While some travellers had begun to use the new passage direct from Dublin to Parkgate near Chester and others, en route for Bath, disembarked at Bristol, most still paid half a guinea for a cabin and caught the Government packets which sailed from Dublin to Holyhead. This was a trip of some twelve hours after which the travellers jolted queasily along the turnpike through Caernarvon, Denbigh, Flint and on to Chester.

The Waterford crossing favoured by Eleanor Butler and Sarah Ponsonby was a more leisurely affair altogether, it was also more expensive. The fare was fifteen guineas, the service, as Arthur Young had discovered to his chagrin, was also eccentric.

They themselves had already suffered from the vagary of the service, and they were to suffer again; for although they had arrived in Waterford on the fourth of May, they were still provokingly landbound four days later. This may have been due to the activities of the American privateer, Paul Jones, who had been terrorizing the St George's Channel in the sloop *Ranger* as late as 20 April, or it may simply have been a consequence of the peculiarity of the Waterford captains, who obstinately refused to sail unless they were carrying sufficient passengers to make the venture worth while.

Thus for four days they had been forced to make anxious daily inquiries in all the press and smell of what Bishop Pococke had called the finest quay in Europe. It was extraordinarily hot, tempers probably rose. Eleanor was notoriously impatient; Sarah, though always conciliatory, might have had second thoughts about the step they were taking. There was the ever present fear that their families might, after all, change their minds and pursue them. They must have made an intriguing trio, the tall gaunt maid and the two ladies, one tall, slender and mild looking, the other shorter, vigorous, and dynamically handsome.

But at last the captain was satisfied, and, low tide being around three in the afternoon, they weighed anchor that night, and in the summer twilight moved slowly down the fifteen miles of the Suir, and out at last into the open, privateer-haunted sea. It was Friday 9 May. They were not to know it, but they had left Ireland for ever.

Some time next day they dropped anchor at Haking on the north shore of Milford Haven, and the day after, full of enthusiasm, the Welsh tour began.

A venture of this sort had become exceedingly fashionable; the dramatic Welsh mountains which had excited awed repulsion in Defoe's breast only a generation before, were arousing quite different sensations in travellers who had drunk the heady if inauthentic wine of Ossian.*

The poet Gray had already visited Wales seeking inspiration, and it would not be long before Coleridge and Southey did likewise. Throughout the long summer days of 1773 the Reverend William Gilpin† had gone sketching his way through the northern part of the principality, criticizing Nature's compositions which, in his opinion, fell sadly short of the hand of art; disguising in his mind's eye, with judicious plantings, all those lumpish hills which offended his over-refined sensibility. And in that same summer, the topographer, Thomas Pennant, albeit in less critical frame, was admiring the turbulence of the Welsh

---

*Purportedly an ancient Gaelic poet whose works had been discovered by James Macpherson (1736–96), a Kingussie farmer's son. Mainly due to Dr Johnson they were proved inauthentic.

†William Gilpin (1724–1804), Vicar of Boldre, remembered for his series of picturesque tours, parodied by William Coombe in *Dr Syntax*.

rivers and the picturesque nature of the scenery; while Mrs Vesey, one of the most charming of the *Bas Bleus*, had even gone so far as to complain that the new turnpike road had already ruined the charms of the thrilling journey between Dublin and London. Could she not recall with the utmost nostalgia that journey with her friend Mrs Hancock in 1767 when, while travelling through these wild regions, they had been overtaken by a highly satisfactory storm, a 'tempest' no less, which had 'greatly heightened the sublime and terrible of the scene'?

In intensity of sensibility Eleanor Butler and Sarah Ponsonby were as highly endowed as any. They had no sooner set foot in Wales than Sarah, in her elegant hand, began recording their impressions. It was the first journal they had kept together, and was bound in marbled boards with a blue leather back and corners.

'An Account of a Journey in Wales,' announced the illuminated title-page, 'Perform'd in May 1778', and then, with a self-consciousness all the more startling considering the trouble everyone had been put to on their account, she had added, 'By Two Fugitive Ladies'. The whole was dedicated to 'Her most tenderly Beloved Companion', and on the opposite page she drew a rather lifeless sketch of Benton Castle, Milford Haven.

In point of fact it was a wonder that there was time to keep a journal at all, however brief, for every day they were out walking or driving to see new sights. Perhaps it was written in the evening with her friend smiling indulgently at her eagerness to record these first precious days together.

'Pembrokeshire', she wrote. They walked and drove round it in five days. Monday walked to Hublonston and Gallowswick, Tuesday sailed over on the ferry from Milford Haven to Pembroke, Wednesday walked to Bushe, Thursday drove out in the evening to look at St David's 'church'. 'Ancient' was all Sarah could think of to write about it, or perhaps time had been short.

They now began to wend their way northwards, sometimes driving as many as twenty-five miles a day. 'Caermarthenshire', wrote Sarah, 'Lay at St Clears a small village.' Carmarthen, reputedly the principal city in Wales, disappointed them, so they passed into Cardiganshire and spent the night at Aberystwyth where the following day Sarah noted that they had 'walked along the strand' together. No doubt they were planning their future. The original scheme had been to take a cottage in England, and certainly succeeding entries are marked by the distance of their stopping places from London.

They were now in North Wales. 'Lay at Machyinileth 198 miles from London.' Three days later on Monday 25 May they were just in England, in Shropshire, where they called in at Oswestry, '172 miles from London'.

Did something cause them to change their minds and give up the idea of a cottage in England after all? For they now turned away from the border, and that Monday night slept for the first time at Llangollen.

Mr Gilpin, who had been there five years before, had found little charm in the town, although the Vale of Llangollen had pleased even his exacting temper, and this in spite of the river Dee being reduced by drought to an unpicturesque trickle. He had found in the vale 'a constitutional strength which no mood or atmosphere could injure'; he found 'amusement' in the view from Llangollen churchyard, although he declared patronisingly that it was 'a *study* rather than a *composition*'.[1]

Mr Pennant* had thought Llangollen a small and poor town although situated in a very romantic spot; indeed he claimed that he knew of no other place in North Wales 'where the refined lover of picturesque scenes, the sentimental or the romantic could give further indulgence to his inclinations'.[2]

Sarah Ponsonby, as refined a lover of the picturesque as any, merely recorded 'a pretty village on the river *Dee*'.[3] She underlined Dee, perhaps so that she should remember it, and then went on to note the bridge built in 1395 and the unremarkable church dedicated, as Mr Pennant had with some pedantry discovered, to 'St Collen ap Gwynnawg, ap Clydawg, ap Cowrda, ap Caradog Freichfras, Llyr ap Merim, ap Einion Yrth, ap Cunedda Wledig . . .'[4] Next morning they climbed Dinas Bran, the odd conical-shaped hill to the north of Llangollen, where they examined the remains of Crow Castle scattered about its top, after which they climbed the nearby Trevor rocks from where,

* Thomas Pennant (1726–98), naturalist, antiquarian and traveller.

enraptured, they gazed over 'an extensive Prospect . . . of the Beautifullest Country in the World'.[5]

It was to be a full day. That afternoon they walked to explore the remains of 'an Abbey called Valede Crucis' where Mr Gilpin's sensitive eye had already been repelled by the lumpishness of the surrounding hills, and his sense of history outraged by a large square pond adorned with a Chinese railing of 'lively' green and a summerhouse tipped with a gilded ball. Sarah Ponsonby, however, recorded ecstatically that 'there could scarcely be imagined a more beautiful situation than this . . .'[6] In the evening, apparently tireless, they walked to Chirk Castle, which produced further encomiums in the journal.

They now left Llangollen and continued their progress back into Wales. On 29 May, while across the channel their friend Mrs Goddard was musingly examining the barn they had slept in during that first unsuccessful flight, Eleanor Butler and Sarah Ponsonby were dining in Aberconway.

They were to spend upwards of a month in Caernarvonshire, happily ignorant of the rumpus over Sir William's seizure, at the end of which they circled back through Flintshire and Denbighshire to Llangollen once again. On Thursday 25 June they were back in Shropshire. 'Went to Oswestry and in search of Lodgings to Llanwryneck a small Village disagreably situated on each side of the road and in the neighbourhood of . . .'[7] The remainder of the page though neatly ruled is empty. In all likelihood Mrs Goddard's letter, written from Woodstock ten days before and announcing Sir William's death, had caught up with them at last.

Sarah's first thoughts must have been for her dear Lady Betty. She would have had overwhelming emotions of remorse, compassion; would have experienced anguished heart-searchings as to whether or no she should return to Ireland. There had been ample time to reflect on their situation during these last weeks. They had not yet found a suitable place in which to live, travelling was expensive, and their resources were dwindling. Did the death of Sir William and with it the removal of the danger which had threatened her but add to a gathering conviction that the whole enterprise was an act of folly, was doomed?

A cloud obscures their movements for a moment, and then, years later by way of Harriet Pigott's* raggedly scribbled day-book, clears once more. A place is noted down, 'Erbistock, Overton, Denbigh'. They have been driving about the country-side like lost souls it seems, trying to find somewhere to settle, have reached Erbistock ferry where, bright as uncorked ale, the Dee swirls to a depth of twenty feet. 'Lady EB nearly drowned'[8] jots Miss Pigott. That is all. But there may be more in the episode than meets the eye. Subconsciously or not Eleanor has settled the question, if indeed there had been any doubt. Sarah knows where her heart lies, and there will be no going back to Ireland.

By now the Welsh tour was turning into a frenzied search for somewhere to live before the winter set in. Later, Sarah Pon-sonby would frankly admit that the time they had spent 'chang-ing habitations before we Fixed upon our Final one'[9] had dan-gerously depleted their small stock of money.

In 1818 she would record 'our 39th winter in Llangollen Vale and our fortieth in Wales !'[10] This first winter which had come on them so swiftly seems to have been spent at Blaen Bache, a remote hamlet in the Cufflymen valley in the hills to the south of Llangollen. It appears to have proved too remote however, for by 1779 they were staying in Llangollen itself, in 'little low lodgings in a narrow street in the town' as Harriet Pigott noted in her day-book ; 'they lived on small means having no fortune assured to either in consequence of this elopement . . .'[11] The rooms were in the cottage of Mr Jones, the Llangollen postman, still to be seen not far from the church and across the road from the *Hand* inn.

They had probably been drawn back to Llangollen by nostal-gia. The River Dee as it flows through Llangollen is strongly reminiscent of the Nore at Inistiogue, with all its memories of Woodstock. They may also have wanted to recapture the care-free happiness that they had both enjoyed on first arriving in Wales, and before they had received the sad news from Ireland. But perhaps that first memorable glimpse of the 'Beautifullest

* Harriet Henriette Pigott, authoress and traveller.

Country in the World' had already made choice of any other place impossible.

Nostalgic and aesthetic considerations apart, there were also financial reasons for their decision to give up the idea of a cottage in England and to settle down in Wales instead. Living was cheap, so cheap that 'anybody may live here without money almost' Cecilia Thrale had opined, though being a rich man's daughter she may have exaggerated.

They were not well off. According to Sarah, Eleanor Butler's father had made her only a 'scanty provision'.[12] This may have been even less than the two hundred pounds a year she was receiving after his death. Sarah herself was in receipt of an allowance of eighty pounds a year from Lady Betty's daughter, Mrs Tighe. The thousand pounds left her by her stepmother was 'from a mistaken kindness'[13] as she gently put it, being withheld from her for the time being by her stepmother's brother, Sir William Barker. They could count therefore on two hundred and eighty pounds a year allowed them by the uncertain liberality of close, but not particularly loving relatives, plus a small amount which they had saved, but which had, for the most part, been dissipated by the folly of the Welsh tour.

Twelve years before, an acquaintance of Dr Johnson's had found it possible to support a family of three with four servants on two hundred and eighteen pounds a year. Peregrine Langton had kept a good table as well as a post-chaise and three horses. By 1794 Miss Harriet Bowdler* considered three to four hundred a year 'comparative poverty', and at about the same time Miss Anna Seward† had written to Mrs Piozzi‡ that it would require the utmost frugality to make her 'moderate income not quite amounting to £400 per annum support the inevitable expense' of her rather large house. Yet to illustrate what might be done, Miss Seward in 1791 was also admiring the thrift of a friend

* Harriet Bowdler (1754–1830), authoress and educator, and sister of the purifier of Shakespeare.

† Anna Seward (1742–1809), daughter of the Prebendary of Lichfield. Critic and poetess, 'Queen Muse of Britain'.

‡ After her husband's death in 1781 Mrs Thrale had married the singer Gabriel Mario Piozzi. Dr Johnson never forgave her.

who, on an income of two hundred pounds a year, had not only farmed, improved and cultivated her small property, but 'had twice visited Switzerland, France and Germany'.[14]

Alas, Eleanor Butler and Sarah Ponsonby had not yet learned to be so frugal, though by now it had become their earnest desire and hope to find a suitable cottage as soon as possible and to retrench. It was not long before just such a cottage offered itself, '. . . a mean cottage', Miss Pigott recorded, 'having only four rooms'.[15] In fact a fifth room, which the two friends were to turn into a library, had been added in 1778.* The cottage itself was a plain square building of stone with a stone slated roof, it was situated among stark fields on a hill behind the village and could be rented along with its four acres for a half-yearly sum of eleven pounds, seven shillings and sixpence. Its possibilities, when they explored them, were on the whole pleasing to the romantic minded. Behind the cottage, to the north-east rose the Eglwyseg mountains; the sublime cone of Dinas Bran, the ruined castle on its top outlined like the Capitoline wolf against the moving sky; further east ran the menacing striations of the Trevor rocks; to the south the range of the Berwyn mountains. Behind the cottage the land dropped steeply to a delicious miniature ravine with a mountain stream flowing through it, while the back windows gave a view over the chimney-pots of Llangollen itself, so that by squinnying out of the top windows the church might be glimpsed, also the graveyard and that interesting road along which the coaches rumbled in to the *Hand*. They made up their minds that the cottage would suit their purpose, and early in 1780 became tenants, rechristening it Plas Newydd.

There was much to do, there was a great deal more they would like to have done. Eleanor, for instance, would have to wait eight years before the 'vile tiles' in the hall were replaced by elegant black and white marble slabs, but in the meantime we know they contented themselves with building bookshelves, buying such furniture as they could afford and having the living-rooms carpeted. These last were ordered from Mr Kendal of Gloucester, 'who deals most extensively in carpets, Cyder etc.'

* The date stone carved with the initials of the then owner, Edwards, has been incorporated into a stone arch to the south-west of Plas Newydd.

In addition it may well have been now that they enlarged the library with an elegant bay to the north-east carrying three pointed Gothick windows.

But such items, even in Wales, were not to be had for nothing. They overspent. They overspent disastrously. Sarah most likely in expectation of the thousand pounds left her by her stepmother, Eleanor in anticipation of that far greater amount, secured her, so she then believed, by the terms of her brother's marriage settlement. For the moment however such considerations did not spoil the rapture of entering their first home together.

'Rose at Eight' 1780–83

To all but the most infatuated the immediate prospects for making a fruitful life in Llangollen were not promising. Though doubtless their enthusiasm would not allow them to see it, Llangollen, for all its charming setting, was a depressing little town. It consisted then of one long badly paved street intersected by another. The houses were sombre and mean looking, the people poverty stricken and rough. A certain vivacity was lent it however by the passage of the Irish travellers with whom it was a favourite stopping place, and it had in addition a weekly market and five fairs a year, while the post went through three times a week and could be heard, and seen, by dint of craning out of the dressing-room window.

Of society equal to their own there was none in the valley even had they wanted it. They knew themselves for the time being to be vulnerable both socially and financially and accordingly preferred to lead retired if not hidden lives. Indeed few people knew of their whereabouts at all, only trusted friends like Lucy Goddard and Mrs Tighe; of the Butlers they were still apprehensive – fourteen years later Eleanor's mother had to obtain her daughter's address from her sister. In the vale they were known simply as 'the ladies'.

But from the outset they sought to put down roots, to build up that store of respect and, more important still, credit, on which their very existence was to depend. Soon they were dealing regularly with people like Mrs Parry of Ruabon, who supplied them with groceries; with the little woman at Brynkinalt, who sold them cheese; with the coalman, whom they paid on the nail each March fair. They were also, no doubt due to Mary Carryll, becoming acquainted with their near neighbours: Mathew the Miller; Robert the Weaver; their landlord, Mr Edwards, who was soon dining each Boxing Day in Mary's kitchen as an annual custom; Mr Edwards of the *Hand*, who begged them to use his pew in church, and who, like landlord Edwards, was soon being enticed, as occasion warranted, into Mary Carryll's hospitable kitchen.

The comparative isolation of these early days was precious to them both, casting them delightedly into one another's company. 'When shall we be alone together' Eleanor would write wistfully in the journal when years later they had more visitors than they really wanted.

They were great walkers, like many women of their period and persuasion. Did not Mrs Carter, the learned translator of Epictetus, walk at least ten miles daily, and her friend Miss Talbot ride sixteen, while brilliant and charming Miss Elisabeth Smith thought nothing of climbing up and down Snowdon itself?

During their stay at Blaen Bache they had already contacted the tanner's son, an agreeable and trustworthy boy who had shown them the best walks round about. Now, with him and their bitch Flirt they spent long days exploring the surrounding hills, which with pardonably romantic exaggeration they preferred to call mountains; climbing the high-banked lanes which snaked up Gwernant to the moors; or ventured northwards, where on the Trevor rocks and the precipices above Tan-y-craig on the Eglwyseg mountain the rare Rock Pepperwort could be found in spring and blue pools of *Scilla verna*, and later in June the dark-flowered Helleborine.

No wonder that their shoe bills were quite as substantial as their hefty yearly bill for cheese, and that Eleanor would record that their habits, 'Particularly mine', were 'absolutely worn to rags'.[1]

Such days grew from a régime that had been firmly established from the moment of taking up house together, a régime planned, dreamed of, passionately discussed, during the frustrating Kilkenny days. It was a régime, or, as they preferred to call it, a 'system', at once romantic, more than a touch conventual, yet withal realistic.

Although never actually written down point for point their correspondence and their journal suggests that their system bound them never to leave home; to devote hearts and minds to self-improvement; to eschew the vanity of society; to beautify their surroundings and to better, in so far as they could, the lot of the poor and unfortunate.

Had they, one wonders, been fired by the philosophy of *Millenium Hall*,* which had been written by one of a pair of friends like themselves?

For although Eleanor Butler and Sarah Ponsonby did not extend their compassion as the *Millenium Hall* heroines did to employing a housekeeper with a claw hand, a kitchen maid with one eye, a cook with crutches, a deaf dairy maid and a musician with 'a violent fit of the stone', their aims appear to have been very alike, '. . . to retire into the country, and though both of an age and fortune to enjoy all the pleasures which most people so eagerly pursue, they were desirous of fixing in a way of life where all their satisfactions might be rational, and as conducive to eternal as to temporal happiness'.[2]

It was essential that every aspect of such a life should be recorded. '. . . my B[eloved] has a Book of (I think) very well chosen Extracts from all the Books she has read since we had a home',[3] Sarah would write Mrs Tighe. But it was a question not only of recording elegant extracts, but recipes, nostrums, garden plants, anecdotes, tradesmen (both reliable and unreliable) and, in a special book, future projects. Added to which, Sarah, with a dutiful sigh, for she was indifferent at sums, recorded their expenditure; Eleanor, for the time being, merely jotting down

---

Millenium Hall (1762) purportedly by 'a gentleman' was in fact written by Mrs Scott (younger sister of the 'bluestocking' Mrs Montagu). She and her friend, Lady Barbara Montagu, lived together at Batheaston where they ran a school for poor children.

impressions and meticulously recording her migraines in a small lady's pocket book.

Their day was predictable. Most mornings they rose at eight, though on irresistible summer mornings they might rise at six or even earlier to walk in the garden. On the days when Eleanor woke with a migraine they did not get up at all, but remained in bed with Tatters, the cat, purring on the coverlet until the head was better. At nine they breakfasted, from half-past nine until three, when they dined, they occupied themselves according to the season: gardening, walking, reading, making transcriptions, painting, learning languages. Nine years later this routine would still hold good. 'In the Mornings after breakfast I try to improve myself in drawing' Sarah would write to Mrs Tighe, 'and am also proceeding in a tedious M.S. ... My B. is also improving herself though that is scarce possible in Italian – She also Amuses herself with Compiling and transcribing Notes illustrative of her admired Madame de Sevigné – After dinner She reads aloud to me 'till nine o'clock when we regularly retire to our dressing room (that Our Domesticks also may go to rest) – where we employ ourselves generally 'till twelve.'[4]

There was much to be done, improvements both inside and out, and particularly about the four-acre plot of land where, in accordance with a garden which was to be useful as it was beautiful, they had plans for a fowl yard, a stable, dairy, potager, melon and mushroom beds, vines, while they were already raising roses and holly bushes from seeds they had collected. In short the project book was full, and they would have been in a state of perfect contentment had it not been for the corroding anxiety about money.

Only fifteen months after moving into Plas Newydd their financial situation had become so serious that Sarah, swallowing both shame and resentment had written for help to her father's cousin, Lord Bessborough.*

The troubles that they had been through since leaving Ireland three years before had obviously rendered the expression of her letter unusually shrill, for the old gentleman, nearly eighty, al-

* William 2nd Earl of Bessborough (1704–93). He filled several high political situations including Lord of the Treasury and Postmaster-General.

most blind and tetchy into the bargain, not only complained about the difficulty of reading her exceptionally fine small hand, but went on '. . . you accuse me of what never existed, for I never did treat you with scorn or contempt which you mention to be the case. I did think, and do so still, that you were in the wrong to leave your friends in Ireland and I hope you will return to them. I remember you sent me quotation from Bruyère which I thought harsh, and that I did not deserve.'[5] He concluded by thanking her rather testily for the pretty cap she had sent him but which was too fine to be of any use, complained himself of scarcity of money, but did, none the less, offer to send her fifty pounds. He wrote again shortly afterwards to say that he had paid the money into her bank, but begged her not to send him the purse she was threatening to make him, 'for I have, I believe twenty by me which are not of any use'.[6]

They were sensitive about their poverty, about their anomalous social position. Yet old friends did call to see them: Sarah's half-sister, Mrs Lowther; her brother, Chambre; Dr and Mrs Bathurst from Oxford; while in the Vale itself no one bearing the illustrious names they did could long remain without social recognition. Not far off, in the decaying mansion of Brynkinalt, plagued by impertinent servants, herself fatally extravagant, lived old Lady Dungannon; a friend not only of Mrs Goddard, but of their families in Ireland.

Miss Pigott tells us that it was from beneath Lady Dungannon's protective and respectable wing that the ladies emerged to be introduced to the local gentry; the Myddletons of Chirk Castle, the Myttons of Halston, the Owens of Porkington, Lloyds of Aston, Kynastons of Hardwick, Wynns of Wynnstay. And it was about this time, by some strange social coincidence recorded but not described, that they met the Misses Elizabeth and Letitia Barrett of Cae Glas in Oswestry, who, being of an age with them, were for the next years to be reckoned among their dearest friends until a misunderstanding dramatically parted them.

So it was that when Mrs Goddard arrived to stay for a fortnight in the late summer of 1782 even her exacting social requirements could be met. Miss Elizabeth Barrett and a Mrs

Bond came to dine, another day all three ladies went over to dine with Lady Dungannon at Brynkinalt, and a visit was squeezed in to Chirk Castle where Mrs Goddard was intrigued to see a 'man of £16000 a year who about four years ago married the nursery maid that wont now accept a settlement of £1000 a year because she thinks she will get more'.[7]

All in all the visit was a success, not least because the G had by this time surmounted some of her prejudices concerning Sarah's Beloved. 'Fair friends', she wrote of them in her journal, finding Plas Newydd 'a very pleasant habitation', the only drawback being that it had rained solidly every day but one. Six months later Eleanor wrote to solicit another visit,

... pray Poll davy when will you come and eat with *us*. I'll give you a bill of Fare. for breakfast you shall have a Couple of new laid Eggs from our Jersey Hens Who are in the Most beautiful Second Mourning you ever beheld. With plumes of Feathers on their Head which the D: of D: would not disdain to wear. Your dinner Shall be boil'd chickens from our own Coop. Asparagus out of our garden. Ham of our own Saving and Mutton from our own Village. Your Supper Shall consist of Goosberry Fool. Cranberry Tarts roast Fowl and Sallad. don't this Tempt you.[8]

By now the interest and charm of their small establishment was beginning to be carried back by their visitors to an outside world that had temporarily forgotten them. 'In the year of our Lord 1782' writes Lady Louisa Stuart,* 'When I first heard of them I was disposed to be captivated by anything so romantic.'[9]

But for all that their life appeared to be running so smoothly they were in dangerous financial straits, and on 3 June of the following year there fell a disastrous blow. Eleanor Butler's father died. When the will came to be read she was not mentioned.

*Lady Mary Wortley Montagu's granddaughter.

Chapter Four

She was now dependent upon the brother who had displaced
her in early childhood and with whom there had never been
much love lost. That brother, as she had written to Mrs Goddard earlier in the year, 'whom we neither love nor honour',
'My *Worthy* Brother' as she had noted bitterly in the small
lady's pocket book in which she recorded her migraines.

The migraines, unsurprisingly, were increasing in number
and volume, also fainting fits and vomiting attacks. They were
now able to count on exactly eighty pounds a year from Mrs
Tighe, and their debts by their frugal standards were enormous.

As though this were not enough, an impertinent and disturbing letter, which seemed to aim at the destruction of the 'retirement', had arrived from St Omer that July. A Mrs Paulet was
writing to suggest that a lady of her acquaintance, a lady of
about forty, widowed, childless, amiable and of an entertaining
disposition, a lady '*always* accustomed to genteel life', a lady,
who it later transpired was none other than Mrs Paulet herself,
was more than agreeable to make a third with Miss Butler and
Miss Ponsonby at Plas Newydd, her own special friend having
retired to a convent.

Eleanor replied vigorously on 1 August.

Madam, I was this morning favoured with your letter. I must beg
leave to say that Miss Ponsonby and I can only attribute the proposal
you make us, to your being Totally Ignorant Who We Are. As you
mention that you are soon to come to England, a few enquiries on
that subject will Satisfy you of the Very great Impropriety (to give
it no harsher term) of such an application to us.

I take Liberty to add that We receive no Visitors with whose names character and Consequence We are not perfectly Well Acquainted.

I am, Madam, Your Humble Servant,
Eleanor Butler[1]

The spirit of 'huff and frettability', as Sarah expressed it, was in the air. Towards the begining of 1784 there were other and less easily removed causes of concern. Rumours were now current in Ireland that the 'retirement' had proved a failure, that they were giving up their cottage and returning home; more oddly still that Sarah was driving Eleanor to despair with her savage temper, while she herself was mortally ill with consumption.[2]

Back in Dublin, Mrs Goddard made a note of the gossip in her journal, and in particular of a party at which a 'Mr C. Williams . . . abused Miss Ponsonby and Miss Butler furiously.'[3] Pressed by the curious she loyally refused to answer questions, and even Mrs Hamerton, family friend of the Butlers, was soundly snubbed when she made inquiries about the two women; no doubt because Lucy Goddard was well aware that every particle of news would be relayed instantly to the hostile Castle.

Letters were now flying back and forth between Llangollen and Kilkenny upon the vexed subject of the will, and were angrily noted down in the pocket book. Trusted friends were drawn into agonized discussion as to what course might best be pursued. 'Mrs Talbot has a perfect recollection of the provision which was made for me, in my Brother's Marriage Settlement,' Eleanor was to write, 'They agree in thinking I have been barbarously treated.'[4]

She was to maintain this view for the rest of her life, and with such vehemence that one can only assume that she was either seriously mistaken or that generous provision had indeed been made for her and later withdrawn as a consequence of her elopement with Sarah Ponsonby.

At last, and after much haggling, her relative Lodge Morres*

---

*Lodge-Evans Morres, prominent in Irish politics 1768–1801. Called to the Upper House by the title of Baron Frankfort of Galmoye, and advanced (1816) to a viscountcy as Viscount Frankfort de Montmorency.

succeeded in securing an allowance of two hundred pounds a year for her from her brother together with a lump sum of five hundred pounds with which to pay off her debts. But Eleanor in the light of her expectations from the enormous wealth into which John Butler had married not unaturally found the allowance pitiable, while five hundred pounds in view of the debts they had contracted was barely adequate.

What, one asks oneself, would have happened to them had it not been for the stabilizing effects of the 'system'?

Passionate letters, smarting with injustice, might be written off in the mornings, but in the autumn afternoons, while they determinedly made transcripts and drew maps, loads of hot dung would go rumbling as usual past the library windows to nourish the new mushroom bed, and near by the man was even now completing the coping to the wall of a new vegetable garden; and, as dark fell, they would close the shutters, light the candles and draw their chairs up to the blazing fire, and Eleanor would resume the nightly readings from Spenser, Milton, Cook's *Voyages* or Harriss's *Philogical Enquiries*, and for a time their troubles could be forgotten.

Occasionally however the 'system' was dropped, and Eleanor marked the occasion in red ink in the pocket-book, as on that January Sunday at the beginning of 1786 when they 'set out for Oswestry at the peril of our lives the road an entire Sheet of Ice'[5] to visit their friends the Barrett sisters at whose house they supped and afterwards slept the night. In September of the same year they were to opt out of the 'system' again, this time to stay with the Bridgeman* family at Weston on the borders of Staffordshire. 'You will be surprised to hear that we have infringed our resolution of never passing a night from our cottage', wrote Sarah in her letter to Mrs Tighe, which rhapsodized over everything Bridgeman; from Mrs S. Bridgeman's skill at drawing, singing and harpsicord playing to young Mr Bridgeman's pleasing conduct of family prayers. But the visit, memorable as it was, had, if anything, only 'Added new Charm to our Retirement'.[6]

* The family of Sir Henry Bridgeman, Bt. Created Baron Bradford of Bradford, Salop, 13 August 1794.

The difficult year came to an end, reaching a climax in mid December when Eleanor summoned resolution to discharge the gardener for his 'Sins and Baseness and Ingratitude'[7] and, re-marking that since he was a Methodist none of this was in the least surprising, retired to bed with another migraine. Here, as on all previous occasions, she was lovingly ministered to by Sarah. 'My Sweet Love', she wrote with gratitude in the pocket book, 'My Sweet Love', which if only in the most private man-ner gave the lie to rumours that they were not happy together.

For no one was there but themselves on that night towards Christmas when Eleanor had woken Sarah and, in the light glimmering through their bed curtains from the fire, had excitedly proposed sending the very next day for the Vicar to teach them Latin. They would master the Sixth Book of the *Aeneid* first, and after that they would set out to make them-selves mistresses of Italian.[8] No one would be there but them-selves when, visiting her by moonlight in her field, they would laugh together at Margaret, the cow, being so 'extremely indelicate'.[9] No one would be there when they ran round the garden in the freezing rain and came in afterwards to the blaz-ing library fire, drawing up their chairs to enjoy 'the Tempest that Thundered around us', or when, 'with a satisfaction and delight unknown to vulgar minds', they sat papering their hair by the kitchen fire and reading *L'Esprit des Croisades*.[10]

It was not only rumours of quarrels that were circulating however. Early in 1785 Sarah was writing to Mrs Tighe that 'I have also a foolish vexation of my own – which I am ashamed of being teazed by but cannot help. Somebody I know not who at Kilkenny wrote to Mrs Goddard word that I was going to be married to I know not whom neither. But I am more tormented by Mrs G's having a momentary doubt of its truth than at the report. I have reproached her for her folly, and told her in the words of Mrs Page in the Merry Wives of Windsor – "What – have I 'scaped such reports in the holy day time of beauty and am *now* a fit subject for them."'[11]

They demanded, both now and later, and at times obsessively, to be taken seriously as exponents of an ideal manner of living; that way of life, which they insisted was the true reason for wanting to live together; that retirement, that lay conventualism which did not readily admit of marriage, that insistence on self-improvement, that useful employment of time, which would make Sarah erase one day that winter because she had ruined a map she was drawing, 'A mistake in the Tropics has left me nothing to show for the last six weeks of my life.'[12]

Of the provoking rumour of her Sally's marriage Eleanor made only brief mention in the small book that by now was growing into something far more like a journal, '. . . a day of Retirement of Sentiment and of *Tenderness*' she had underlined, '*which Increases with every Vexation*'.[13]

There were to be vexations enough to test devotion. There was the knowledge, impossible to forget, that their peace and security depended upon the uncertain benevolence of two people, Lady Betty's daughter, Mrs Tighe, methodistical and more than a shade touchy, and John Butler, ruled himself by an ambitious wife, and still bitterly ashamed of his renegade sister.

Might this dangerous state of dependence be removed, they reasoned as they papered their hair and discussed their poverty before the kitchen fire, by the expedient of a pension?

As Sir Lewis Namier has pointed out the notion of pensions was not invented by modern radicals. The theory of 'State Paupers' is as old as the state itself, and holds that those who make up the political nation have, when in need, a claim to public support, which should be given them as their due with no loss of rank or citizen rights. This same principle, hotly condemned by reformers, prevailed in the eighteenth century although for a restricted circle of recipients. 'I look upon such pensions' Hardwicke had written 'as a kind of obligation upon the Crown for the support of ancient noble families, whose peerages happen to continue after their estates are worn out.' A fair number of peers and their relatives were supported according to this principle, their aristocratic dole being paid out of Secret Service funds or, as in the case of the Irish beneficiaries, from the Concordatum fund established by Charles I and later charged to the Irish Civil List.

As a result of these fireside discussions Sarah gathered up her courage and wrote off to her Irish Ponsonby relations to beg them to exert their influence to obtain her a pension as the granddaughter of a general, who had after all been killed in the service of his country. When it came the reply was discouraging. The family had already put forward the name of an elderly Ponsonby aunt. Further demands were out of the question.

They now went walking in the shrubbery before the library windows, tracing and retracing those immaculate raked gravel paths, trying to 'walk away their troubles'. Then the moon would rise so bewitchingly through the white lilacs that they must stop to watch it, and in doing so the troubles were forgotten. How like a description from Rousseau they would ponder, and Eleanor would recite certain favourite passages that were apropos, or else, gazing up at the stars, would be put in mind not of Rousseau this time but of Shakespeare. 'The Floor of Heaven Thick inlayed with Patterns of bright gold', she would quote, and then and there would determine to touch her brother just once more in hope of an increased allowance.

The worthy brother's answer was cruelly decisive. If he received any more such applications even the present allowance would be discontinued.

They were thus back where they had started, faced with the nagging anxiety not only of having too little money, but from sources that could not be depended upon with any confidence.

If there had been much at stake in the past, there was even more to lose now after five years living together; the cottage had been transformed into a *ferme ornée* of such taste and charm that every year greater numbers of people were coming to see it; their life together, governed by the 'system', which gave everything meaning, had for Eleanor especially opened up a happiness that she had never known before. It was a happiness which made her exult in the journal, at the 'Celestial glorious' days, 'Heavenly' evenings and in the simple delights like being wakened early on a fine spring morning by 'Barbara churning'.

The fear of losing everything, the threat that even worse might follow for lack of money with which to pay their debts, compelled them to subdue their pride once again and to approach Lady Frances Douglas to see whether she could secure them an English pension. The reply was encouraging. This time they had made a good choice, for Lady Frances, daughter of the Duke of Buccleuch and wife of the successful Douglas claimant, plain, kind and reliable, was to prove 'indefatigable in her Endeavours' to serve them.

In the meanwhile, and with a kind of desperate tenacity, they continued to live as usual, though not, it must be confessed, quite so poverty stricken as the frontispiece to Eleanor's journal for 1785 suggested. She had tinkered with the lines of Gray's *Elegy* so as to read:

> Let not Ambition mock their *humble* toil
> Their *rural* joys, and destiny observe;
> Nor Grandeur read with a disdainful smile
> The short and simple annals of the poor.

During this trying period their economy, as in the future, was probably tided over by loans or outright presents from friends. As it was they firmly retained their three booksellers (two English and one French), their gardener, footman and two maids, and defiantly continued their improvements in the garden; built a circular stone dairy with circular windows, laid out new asparagus beds and planted peach trees, while in the flower garden they now had '... every shrub and Perennial that was admired at Woodstock'.[14] That summer, the charm of their miniature estate having by now reached royal ears, they sent off, as requested, a plan of the cottage and garden to Queen Charlotte, together with copies of the Italian sentiments which adorned their trees on painted boards.

They were entertaining, if modestly. Miss Margaret Davies and Miss Harriet Bowdler, both friends of the Barretts, that August; charming General Hervey,* that September, who showed Sarah a novel way of drawing in perspective by dint of holding a taut length of string between her teeth. He was succeeded by the Norburys with a lovesick daughter and Mr Wedgwood,† who gave them a lecture upon the surrounding rock formations and issued them with a warm invitation to visit

---

* Brother of Frederick Augustus, 4th Earl of Bristol and Bishop of Derry.

† Josiah Wedgwood (1730–95), master potter and inventor. At Etruria he had built a model village for his workers, and a mansion for himself, Etruria Hall.

his works at Etruria. In October their neighbour, Sir Watkin Williams Wynn, brought the Sheridans over to see them. Mrs Sheridan had pleased them both, though Eleanor to a lesser degree than Sarah; both had united however in finding her spouse 'a very ill looking fellow'.[15]

The evenings were drawing in, evenings which Eleanor loved to record in the journal, when they shut the windows, built up the fire and lit the candles, after which Eleanor took down Rousseau to read to her 'hearts darling' who listened quietly and netted purses.

They were half-way through *La Nouvelle Héloïse*, a novel that might have been written for them, one which they admired so much and were so greatly influenced by that it can fairly be read as a paradigm of their romantic souls. Were there not, in this tale of a young woman of good family falling in love with her young tutor, opportunities both conscious and not so conscious, of the closest self identification. The trials of the young lovers had, to a great extent, been their own; the secret correspondence, the passion for books, the harshness of parents; the strain of meeting formally in society; the plan to elope. Again, though differently, was not Julie, the heroine, fair, gentle and tender like Sarah, while her cousin and greatest friend and confidante was dark, more fiery, like Eleanor? Indeed, had not Julie's lover Saint-Preux, on seeing them both weeping in each other's arms, been almost more moved by their friendship than by his own love? *'J'étais jaloux d'une amitié si tendre; je lui trouvais je ne sais quoi de plus intéressant que l'amour même, et je me voulais une sorte de mal de ne pouvoir t'offrir des consolations aussi chères, sans les troubler par l'agitation de mes transports. Non, rien, rien sur la terre n'est capable d'exciter un si voluptueux attendrissement que vos mutuelles caresses; et le spectacle de deux amants eût offert à mes yeux une sensation moins délicieuse.'[16]*

But not only was *La Nouvelle Héloïse* a repository of the most refined and delicious sentiment, but a *vade mecum* for 'retirement'. Here, in two absorbing chapters were those rules for study and for simple living which they were to make their own. As far as their studies were concerned their aims were to become identical with Rousseau's. '*Pour nous qui voulons profiter de nos connaissances, nous ne les amassons point pour les revendre, mais pour les convertir à notre usage; ni pour nous en charger, mais pour nous en nourrir.*'[17] They were also, as was Rousseau, devoted to the works of Tasso and Metastasio.

From the point of view of conducting their retirement that ideal life, led by Julie married to the excellent Monsieur Wolmar, was to find its echo in life at Plas Newydd. Here they were to experience, like Julie, those rustic friendships which they opined were so much more precious than those of the fashionable world; here they were to enjoy the pleasures of being self-supporting, of delighting in simple food and restrained pleasures. Like Julie they would disregard fashionable clothes, would discourage too many visitors. Here, too, an ideal was being lived.

Towards the end of the year they took a solemn step. That November, a month of belching chimneys, storms, headaches, maps and three-hour-long readings from *La Nouvelle Héloïse*, they made their wills. While thus engaged, new acquaintances, the Whalleys, from across the river paid them an ill-timed visit. 'Wished them at the Deuce for interrupting us' commented Eleanor, who in more douce mood had made Mr Whalley a present of 'a melon for his melancholy'; 'they staid but a few minutes', she added, which was scarcely surprising. She now sealed, signed and delivered 'My last Will and Testement. That I might Secure all I am possessed of or Entitled to to the Beloved of My Heart.'[18] A statement which would have given substance to those dark suspicions of her family that any fortune she could wrest from them would be bestowed elsewhere.

Eighteen months later there was still no news of the pensions from Lady Frances. It had been eighteen months of active retirement, but a retirement shot through with perturbation.

Unpleasant rumours were still circulating. Sarah had by now been married 'at least half a dozen times';[19] they had decamped and gone back to Ireland; Sarah, according to Dr Dealtry who as a physician should have known better, was dead and buried. Rumours apart her persistent cough had been causing intense anxiety to them both, so much so that the kind Barretts had offered to pay for them to visit the wells at Bristol, a kindness which they had appreciated but declined. In addition there had been constant friction with the outside servants, while two of their close friends were to give them cause for worry; Lady Dungannon wilfully persisting in those extravagant courses, which would soon lead her to the sponging-house; and Miss Elizabeth Barrett herself, laid low with such a severe putrid fever that only a timely application of seven blisters and two cataplasms had recalled her from death.

Yet there had been progress, gains for the system. Italian was being mastered; they were engaging in a flattering correspondence with the French King's aunt, Madame Louise, who was a Carmelite and had asked them to transcribe some favourite texts for her. Views and engravings had been copied; more purses netted, satin portfolios worked, an entire MS of Lady Ann Fanshawe's memoirs had been meticulously transcribed as a present for Mrs Tighe, who had visited Llangollen that summer and had been charmed by the cottage and the delights of Mary Carryll's salmon pie. Nor had spiritual matters been allowed to lapse. In her correspondence with Mrs Tighe, Sarah had been dabbling mildly in Methodist theology, while Eleanor on her side had not been idle, having had a strikingly forceful notion on how to eradicate the all too prevalent sin of adultery. 'My B' wrote Sarah approvingly, 'thinks that if all Ladies who are guilty of that Crime were Branded with its Initial a Great A in the Forehead* – it wou'd be the most likely means to deter others from following the example. Don't you think it' she added 'a good idea'?[20] Mrs Tighe's reply is unfortunately not preserved.

But for all the richness of their daily existence, their purses continued distressingly light, and there was still no news of their English pensions. A letter now arrived from Lodge Morres. It contained not only the present of a pretty gold pencil which Sarah instantly passed on as a gift to her Beloved, but the advice to press again for an Irish pension as the chances of getting one

---

* Mrs Piozzi's remedy was equally stringent: '. . . was a Woman to have her Ring Finger cut off; her Lover would hesitate a little in marrying her . . .' *Thraliana*, ed. Balderston, Clarendon Press, 1951, vol. i, p. 379.

were now better. With some reluctance Sarah wrote once again to her kinsman, Lord Bessborough, but the letter was hardly posted when one arrived from Lady Frances Douglas. It contained wonderful news. The King had granted them a pension of one hundred pounds a year.

Sarah now wrote immediately and jubilantly to Mrs Tighe, but met with an icy reply. Her touchy friend had received the tidings as a personal affront, a reflection upon the generosity of her own annual allowance. Weeks of semi-apologetic explanation of their unhappy financial position now followed before Mrs Tighe's ruffled feathers were smoothed at last, by which time, towards the end of 1787, good news of another and less exceptionable kind seemed forthcoming. A *détente* with the Butlers appeared to be about to take place, for in all the flurry of Christmas mince-pie making Sarah broke off to write that no less a person than Eleanor's sister-in-law, Lady Anne Butler, had visited them on her way to Bath. 'The everlasting Harmony which this visit will establish between My B and her Relations will I am certain give you pleasure' she wrote enthusiastically, adding that she could not express 'how flattering and comfortable'[21] Lady Anne's behaviour had been to them.

Thus, with the certainty of a pension, and the promise of perhaps even further financial support from this interesting and unexpected quarter, the old year ended.

1788-90

The New Year opened with soaking rain and low gloomy clouds. After a seasonable dinner of roast beef and plum pudding Eleanor sat down to make their new account book. There had been other account books, but this one was to be preserved, treasured as a relic by an upper maid, so that its pages can be examined and in so doing, the shifts plotted by which the 'retirement' was upheld.

'How dear the blest retreats' the illuminated legend to the 1788 journal opens :

These Mossy banks and rural seats,
These waving groves, these Hamlets mean
Where poverty with brow serene,
Where innocence and Peace reside,
And down Life's current gently guide.

Poverty's serene brow must have clouded nevertheless to peer into the 1788 accounts and see an income of two hundred and eighty-nine pounds, three shillings and one penny and an expenditure of four hundred and forty-four pounds, thirteen shillings and twopence. It is a fact that the rash ladies might never have got through 1788 at all but for an unexpected windfall of seventy-five pounds from Sarah's brother, Chambre, and a further fifty pounds from old Lord Bessborough together with a loan of twenty pounds from Mr Chambre, their solicitor. The anticipated pensions had still not put in an appearance.

The account book reveals that the retirement was supported by four servants at a total of thirty-nine pounds a year. Richard Grosvenor the gardener cost twenty-six pounds, Parry the footman, ten pounds, ten shillings, and Peggin, the kitchen maid, two pounds, five shilling a year. Mary Carryll took no wages, but was entitled to large vails or tips from visitors.

Snug indispensables to the retirement were candles at around nine pounds, five shillings a year, postage fifteen pounds, three shillings and fivepence, coals at eight pounds, nineteen shillings. Cheese, shoes, bacon and charity all stood at about four pounds each, while the meat bill, almost as impressive as Parson Woodford's, was twenty-three pounds, twelve shillings and ninepence, although it was topped by books which cost them an average of thirty-five pounds a year. Rent came to twenty-two pounds, fifteen shillings, and house and servants' tax four pounds, two shillings and sixpence. 'Evaded the stamp' Eleanor noted with triumph in the journal when the tax gatherer came that November.

'Society is all but rude' Sarah had further inscribed the journal for 1788:

To this delicious Solitude
Where all the flowers and Trees do close
To weave the Garland of Repose.

Outside the harsh January wind blew, 'Scowling and Black', inside they were at dinner. 'Roast Goose. Hog's puddings' runs the journal, 'Mem. eat no more of the latter. too savoury too rich for our abstemious Stomachs.'[1]

Readings continued throughout that spring; Sterne for the mornings, and *Mélanges d'Histoire et de Littérature* for the evening lectures, Sarah drawing maps while she listened. The journal makes it clear that the lectures were carefully prepared beforehand by Eleanor, 'Read with the strictest attention until I perfectly comprehended the sense of the 6th, 1, 2, 3, 4th *Sonetto* [*sic*] *de Petraca*.'[2] Next evening while a storm raged up and down the surrounding mountains she was reading her Beloved Metastasio's *La Betulia Libertata*. 'Explained all the difficult passages' she noted, adding, 'how delightful to teach her . . .'[3]

By the end of April they were taking their books into the garden:

Rose at Six Enchanting Morning – My Beloved and I Went the Home Circuit – the Morning so heavenly Could not leave the Shrubbery 'till, Nine, Breakfast.

Half past Nine Till Three – again went the Home Circuit, how splendid, how heavenly. Came in for a few Minutes to Write, Went out again Staid Till one. Reading, drawing then went again to the Shrubbery, brought our Books namely Gil Blas and Madame de Sevigné with us. Such a day!

Three Dinner. roast breast of Mutton boil'd Veal Bacon and Greens Toasted Cheese.

Half past Three Till Nine.

Such a heavenly evening – blue Sky with patches of Cloud Scattered over it. So picturesque, like little Islands studding it – My beloved and I went to the Shrubbery. Spent the Evening there. brought out Books, planted out our hundred Carnations in different parts of the Borders. heavenly evening. Reading. Writing.

Nine till One in the dressing room. Reading. A day of such Exquisite Such enjoyed retirement. So still. So silent.[4]

If still, if silent, it was without question also a vigorous retirement. A list of the reading matter which had been absorbed in three months shows twenty-three works in French and Italian and includes, as single works, nine volumes of Madame de Maintenon's letters, and ten of Madame de Sevigné's.

They were not only reading however but improving the garden. In March, and with the knowledge that a good dinner of 'boil'd fowl and boil'd muttone' was before her Eleanor had sacked the gardener. Moses Jones succeeded to the post. Moses Jones, himself to be sacked and reinstated half a dozen times in the course of the succeeding months, was now set to lay out a new kitchen garden with gravel walks, and to plant a new thicket of 'Lilaks Laburnums, Seringas, White Broom, Weeping Willow, Apple Trees, poplar . . .'⁵ Beside this a new rustic shed was built and thatched by a 'snuffy sauntering, lazy creature' of a thatcher. 'Think the Thatcher horrible' wrote Eleanor who had been down to supervise the work. 'Told him so. Fought him.'⁶

They were, in addition, tinkering with the stream at the bottom of the dell. 'Sat in the rustic seat' Eleanor noted that June, 'disliked the appearance of the Stones over which the Water falls, thought it appeared too formal. Sent our workmen to it with a spade and Mattock.'⁷ By December they were planning another seat, this time in the new vegetable garden, beneath 'a Gothic Arch between two hollies'.

But the picturesque was by now permeating not only garden matters, 'Got a bundle of Moss Rose buds. Threw them in a careless manner over the Library table which had a beautiful effect' wrote Eleanor in the journal.

The journal was, it must be confessed, growing more than a shade self-conscious. Migraines still featured as usual, but now a list, more than a little self-congratulatory, of books read, visits paid and received, began to take up an increasing space at the end of each month.

There was now a fairly constant stream of visitors, since it was the practice for travelling gentry to leave their carriages at the local inns and go on foot to pay their respects to any eminent figures in the neighbourhood.

Thus, besides recording their more regular visitors like Sarah's brother, 'Chum', the Barretts and the usual contingent of local gentry, the journal was also to record more exotic calls.

There were those who like Frizzle* only stayed for a few minutes, [*sic*] : 'Saturday April 4th Frizzle, for a Moment. Monday
April 7th Frizzle again for another Moment'; there were those
who came for an hour or two, for coffee, tea or a meal, but only
close favourites like Harriet Bowdler or Margaret Davies were
invited to stay the night in that spare room so grandly desig-
nated 'the State Bedchamber'. Among those fortunate enough
to have their names inscribed in the journal that spring and
summer were Mr de Luc, the noted geologist; Mrs Crewe† the
society beauty; Lady Dungannon who arrived with her 'Handsome fashioned tall and elegant' grandson Arthur Wellesley;‡
and that 'handsome graceful Conway', Mr Stuart.§ More
encouraging than anything, Eleanor's sister-in-law, Lady Anne
Butler, spent three days with them as arranged on her way back
from Bath. The visit went off promisingly, with all three women
sitting 'most comfortably over the fire talking of old times and
laughing'.[8]

But as the year advanced the hopes that had been raised by
Lady Anne's affability slowly shrivelled. No money came. Debts
were still mounting, and although the warrants for their pensions arrived that September, a letter from their solicitor a
month later warned them that they must not expect payment for
at least several months more. 'The Lord help the poor creatures
who have nothing to subsist on but the Royal bounty'[9] wrote
Eleanor feelingly, while as far back as July, Sarah had written
alongside the weekly accounts, 'in arrears from want of money
from 19th to 20th from 26th to . . .' The quarterly fifty pounds
of Eleanor's had fortunately arrived on the 8th August, just in

* Agent to Eleanor Butler's brother-in-law. 'The Very Essence of
Vulgarity, a perfect comedy worthy of Foote, affection of Taste and
Science but under this fantastic husk I believe there lies a good heart'
(Eleanor Butler, the Journal, *Hamwood Papers*, ed. Bell, p. 194).

† Mrs Piozzi gave her a charm rating of 16 out of 20 for 'Worth of
Heart', 15 for 'Conversation Powers', 19 for 'Person Mien and Manner',
10 for 'Ornamental Knowledge', but zero for 'Useful Knowledge' and
'Good Humour'!

‡ Later the Duke of Wellington.

§ Later Lord Castlereagh.

time to tide them over, but even then they had, with shame, to turn creditors away that October.

In November however a kind letter from Lord Mornington* heartened them once more, for it explained that the delay in the payment of their pensions was due to a deficiency in the Civil List revenue, but he would make every effort to dispatch what was owing to them as soon as he could, and he did not anticipate much difficulty in doing this as Mr Pitt himself was acquainted with their situation and 'with the motive which so justly recommended them to His Majesty's favour'.[10]

'My beloved and I went to the field before our cottage', Eleanor wrote just before Christmas. For a time they stood in silence watching the lights of the village prickling through the rising mist, and then they turned to look back at their cottage where they could see 'the fire and Candles in Our Kitchen gleaming . . .' For the time being at least their home was saved.

'From Home since the First of January 1789', she wrote, 'Not once Thank Heaven.'

The times hardly invited it. The cold was more bitter than they ever remembered, with a 'cutting shaving wind' and a lead-coloured sky, and although they exulted in the snugness of the dressing-room at night, when they closed the shutters, let down the curtain, lit the candles and laid out their pens and ink, they thought anxiously about the poor of the parish, 'who are in great want this piercing season'. When Mr Jones, the vicar, came to collect for these unfortunates they gave him ten and sixpence, which they could ill afford, while the account books would bear witness to the numerous shillings and sixpences bestowed on 'A poor man', a 'poor woman', 'Shanette the witch', 'poor Mary Green' and others.

But not only the weather gave cause for anxiety, the political news was disquieting, and in particular the tidings of the King's illness. From her post at Bath Harriet Bowdler was writing voluminous bulletins upon the subject, bulletins all the more eagerly awaited as the stagecoaches had now stopped going

---

* Richard 2nd Earl of Mornington (1760–1842). Created Marquess Wellesley 1799. Governor-General of India and twice Lord-Lieutenant of Ireland.

through Llangollen, and with them the news from the travellers. 'We are I hope returning to our original State of Retirement' wrote Sarah to Mrs Tighe. Eleanor, however, may have had secret regrets, for the journal was for a time to become intensely political as it followed, with much violent castigation of the Prince of Wales, the painful fluctuations of the King's madness.

In April, prematurely as it turned out, one pound, sixteen shillings went down in the account book for 'Bonfire Sheep and Bell ringing for the King's recovery', and it was gratifyingly reported in *The World* how 'Miss Ponsonby and Miss Butler, the Irish Ladies who have settled in so romantic a manner in Denbighshire' had been 'very conspicuous in their Rejoicings for the King and Queen'.

Miss Bowdler's news service would soon report of other and yet more shocking events, but in the meantime, debts notwithstanding, they had the cottage painted, '. . . the Parlour and Library a beautiful rich white, the Doors varnished Skirting boards chocolate colour. Kitchen window white. Seat and Settle chocolate colour and linen press Door Varnished. Hall and Door going to the cellar and Larder varnished. Stairs and Skirting board and Bannisters painted – the ceilings of the Library, Parlour, Hall, Kitchen, Whitened.'[11] There were pleasant excursions in the *Hand* chaise, among others to the Myttons of Halston, to the Barretts at Oswestry, on the way back from which 'one of the horses got the colic and had many times a great mind to Lye down on the precipice'.[12] They were receiving agreeable visits in return, in particular from Mr Sneyde of Belmont, 'the Botanist in England', who gave them obliging and timely advice on the treatment of die-back in their Dunmore apricot and leaf curl in one of the nectarines.

Among multifarious activities; the unearthing of an alabaster statue of St Cuthline from beneath a pile of rubbish in the churchyard; the setting-up of a large Aeolian harp in the library window, which, when the wind blew, 'had all the sublime effect Thomson so admirably describes in his Ode and Castle of Indolence';[13] walks 'on the Velvet Carpet of the Mountain' – they found time to continue their reading.

At the end of June, together with a list of all the people who had been to see the cottage Eleanor, in what can only be called her own form of Esperanto, wrote down all the books they had read since the first of April. The result is stupefying:

> *Le Rime D'Angelo di Costanzo*
> *Memoires de Madame de Metternique.* 5 tomes.
> *L'idea del Theatro dei M. Giulio Camillo.*
> *Les Oeuvres de Jean Baptiste Poquelin de Moliere* – 4 tomes.
> *Il Cortigano del Conte Baldassare Castiglione.*
> *Theatro du grand Corneille* – 12 tomes.
> *Le Rime di Francesco Petraco* – 2 tomi.
> *Theatro et Oeuvres de Racine* – 9 tomes.
> *Poesies Variés et Chansons Choisies de M. de Coulanges* – 2 tomes.
> *Fables Choisies de la Fontaine* – 4 tomes.
> *Poesies, Maximes et Reflexions Morales de Francis Duc de la Roch-
>   foucault*
> *La Divina Commedia Di Dante Aligheri* – 2 tomes
> *Reflections Critiques Sur la Poesie et la Peinture* – 3 tomes.
> *Les Caracteres ou les Moeurs de le Siecle* – 2 tomes.
> *Opera del Signor Pietro Metastasio* – 16 tomi.
> *Journal d'une Voyage fait en 1775 et 1776 par J. G. Seltzer*
> *Oeuvres de M. Boileau-Depreaux* – 2 tomes.
> *Zayde Mistaire Espagnole* – 2 tomes.
> *La Princesse de Cleves* – 2 tomes.
> *Gilpin's Northern Tour* 2 vols.
> *Warrington's History of Wales*
> *Memoire de St Simon* 3 tomes.
> *Gray's Works* 4 tomes.[14]

Such innocent and improving employment was soon to be disturbed however. On Monday 13 July there was another letter from Miss Bowdler at Bath. It was to be copied out into the journal verbatim, 'The Palais Royal is a scene of riot, murder, and everything that's dreadful. The King has been publicly insulted and has now sent for a great number of Swiss troops, who will be a very weak support against an outraged nation.'[15] The following day, while Eleanor recorded a white sky and millions of rooks on the mountains of Pengwern; wished she could understand their language; turned aside to expatiate on the beauty of her neighbour Mrs Kynaston, the Bastille was stormed.

A minor revolution was about to take place at Plas Newydd.

On the first of August the Ladies' retirement was rudely inter-rupted by Mr Edwards of the *Hand* inn presenting an enormous and unexpected bill for fifty-two pounds, six shillings and seven-pence halfpenny. 'Exorbitant to the last degree' fumed Eleanor, in all probability forgetting the frequent outings in the *Hand* chaise, which had been mounting up over the months.

Retribution was swift. Mr Edwards was sent for and closely interrogated. Two days later Mr Trevor of Aston was asked if the Plas Newydd household might transfer from the *Hand*'s to his pew in church.

'Light airy Clouds' exulted Eleanor shortly after, 'purple mountains, lilac and silver rocks, hum of Bees, rush of waters.'[16] When Mr Edwards of the *Hand* came up that evening to apolo-gize he was brusquely informed that his submission had come too late. The Plas Newydd Ladies had transferred their custom to the rival establishment, the *Lyon*.

It was not until October that there was an embarrassing sequel to the episode.

On the twentieth of the month the dear Barretts drove over to pay a visit, but made the grave error of ordering their carriage not to the now favoured *Lyon*, but, as they always had done, to the recently disgraced *Hand*. 'We had presence of mind suffi-cient to remember we were in our own house' scribbled Eleanor furiously, 'therefore determined that neither by look or word our Resentment at this offence should transpire.'[17] The Barrett sisters, innocently unaware of arousing any such resentment, left at five. Miss Butler and Miss Ponsonby were not to speak to them for a year.

The quarrel with the Barrets was to have its own unhappy consequences, for they had borrowed money from the two sis-ters, which they were now unable to repay. How, they found themselves wondering, were indebtedness and dignity to be maintained?

For 1789 was proving the most financially anxious year yet. Although at the end of 1788 Lord Mornington had encouraged them in a daily expectation of their pensions, they had not re-ceived a farthing by the end of February 1789, and when the first quarter of the pension did at last arrive in mid March, lawyers' fees had reduced it from twenty-five pounds to twenty pounds, thirteen shillings and fourpence.

By the following November shortage of ready money had become so pressing that Sarah wrote in despair for a loan to Mrs Tighe, having already sounded Mrs Lowther, her half-sister, who promised help but did nothing further about it. Mrs Tighe replied kindly, but her letter filled Sarah with remorse. Mrs Tighe, it transpired, was herself in financial difficulties and could do nothing.

On Christmas night Sarah took up her pen, 'My Heart is heavy' she wrote Mrs Tighe, 'And though I begged you would not think of what made it so – I cannot alas Help thinking of it Myself.' She, after all, kept their accounts, which did not balance to the tune of over sixty pounds.

Eleanor for the same day merely recorded a tall thin old man, who had come to the door and sung a Christmas carol in 'Melodious solemn Voice'. She also noted that for dinner there had been Roast Beef and 'minced pies'.

The quarrel with the Barretts was to rankle all through 1790, so that when towards the end of March a letter arrived from their kind friend, Lodge Morres, containing the unexpected gift of one hundred pounds from John Butler, they at once fervently thanked God and set aside fifty pounds of it to repay that 'heavy debt' to Elizabeth and Letitia Barrett, 'which pressed like a dagger to our heart'.[18]

By June they were looking over the journals of the last two years. Two years ago to the day Margaret Davies and Miss Elizabeth Barrett had dined with them. What a change two years had seen Eleanor mused, 'Miss Davies, Mrs Barrett* and we meet no more. The Barretts having manifested themselves ungrateful, unworthy, treacherous and in every respect the reverse of what we so long thought them. Miss Davies' Eleanor added, 'violently their adherent.'[19]

By October, although relations had been re-established with the *Hand* after a further and yet more abject apology from Mr Edwards, Eleanor remained adamant where the Barretts were

* Although unmarried she was allowed, as was then common, the married woman's prefix out of courtesy.

concerned. 'It is precisely a year this day since we received Mrs Barrett here' she noted on the twentieth. 'We have never had reason for a single instants regret' she continued defiantly, 'since we broke off with those false and perfidious Friends. *Au contraire – au contraire.*'[20]

Life had, of course, held compensations for them all this while; a February evening when they had opened the library window, lighted candles and attracted 'millions of birds who sang so sweetly'; delightful expeditions up the winding lane to Blaen Bache to collect holly berries to raise for hedges and primrose and wild strawberry plants for their banks; days spent planting out trees in their shrubbery, and afternoons dining in the shade of the lime tree by their front door; jaunts in the *Lyon* chaise and long favourite walks in the evening along the brook to the Pengwern woods.

But that July something occurred which, for the time being, drove all other vexations out of their heads: perfidious Barretts, drunken gardeners, insufficiently thorough chimney-sweeps, headaches, bills. On 24 July they opened the *General Evening Post* and read something there which made Eleanor note down in the journal that she had instantly written to cancel the paper 'for Essential reasons'.

Beneath the suggestive heading, *Extraordinary Female Affection,* they had read the following:

Miss Butler and Miss Ponsonby have retired from society into a certain Welch Vale.

Both Ladies are daughters of the great Irish families whose names they retain.

Miss Butler, who is of the Ormonde family had several offers of marriage, all of which she rejected. Miss Ponsonby, her particular friend and companion, was supposed to be the bar to all matrimonial union, it was thought proper to separate them, and Miss Butler was confined.

The two Ladies, however found means to elope together. But being soon overtaken, they were each brought back by their respective relations. Many attempts were renewed to draw Miss Butler into marriage. But upon her solemnly and repeatedly declaring that nothing could induce her to wed any one, her parents ceased to persecute her by any more offers.

Not many months after, the ladies concerted and executed a fresh elopement. Each having a small sum with them, and having been allowed a trifling income the place of their retreat was confided to a female servant of the Butler family, who was sworn to secrecy as to the place of their retirement. She was only to say that they were well and safe and hoped that their friends would without further enquiry, continue their annuities, which has not only been done but increased.

The beautiful above-mentioned vale is the spot they fixed on where they have resided for several years unknown to the neighbouring villages by any other appellation than *the Ladies of the Vale*!

About a twelve month since three Ladies and a Gentleman stopping one night at an inn in the village, not being able to procure beds, the inhabitants applied to the Female Hermits for accommodation to some foreign strangers. This was readily granted – when lo! in these foreigners they described some of their own relations! But no entreaties could prevail on the Ladies to quit their sweet retreat.

Miss Butler is tall and masculine, she wears always a riding habit, hangs her hat with the air of a sportsman in the hall, and appears in all respects as a young man, if we except the petticoats which she still retains.

Miss Ponsonby, on the contrary, is polite and effeminate, fair and beautiful. In Mr Secretary Steel's list of Pensions for 1788, there are the names of Elinor [*sic*] Butler and Sarah Ponsonby, for annuities of fifty pounds each. We have many reasons to imagine that these pensioners are the Ladies of the Vale; their female confidante continues to send them their Irish annuities beside.

They live in neatness, elegance and taste. Two females are their only servants.

Miss Ponsonby does the duties and honours of the house, while Miss Butler superintends the gardens and the rest of the grounds.

The piece though garbled yet contained much that was broadly true: about the circumstances of their flight, about the details of their financial arrangements, all of which they would doubtless have preferred to go unbroadcast. What was worse however was its unmistakable innuendo of perversity. What effect might such a piece have upon their reputations, upon their respective families, upon their great benefactor, the King? What of their already precarious allowances, and their pensions?

So far from being tall and masculine and 'in all respects as a young man', Miss Butler, shortish, inclined to be fat and all of fifty-one, indignantly sat down to solicit help from their friend, Edmund Burke. How could their reputations be cleared? Surely the wretch who had written the piece or the villain who had published it could be brought to book? What would this cost?

Burke, rather more man of letters than lawyer, wrote back sympathetically. He had not yet seen the paper himself, but had spoken to a friend who had, and who spoke of the article 'with the indignation felt by every worthy mind', but his friend had doubted whether redress could be had by an appeal to the law. There were offences, Burke explained, like this one, which were deserving of the severest punishment, but on which it was extremely difficult if not impossible to bring the offenders to justice. Nevertheless he and his son would make a thorough perusal of the offending article, and if there was the slightest chance of obtaining a legal sentence on the offenders it would be done, and without expense to the Ladies. He was not sanguine however, 'Your consolation' he asserted bleakly, 'must be that you suffer only by the baseness of the age you live in, that you suffer from the violence of calumny for the virtues that entitle you to the esteem of all who know how to esteem honour, friendship, principle, and dignity of thinking, and that you suffer along with everything that is excellent in the world.' He understood that minds as tenderly sensible of reputation as theirs should for a moment feel shocked at such licence, but he would be sorry and ashamed if such profligacy were to shorten or even embitter such useful lives as theirs. 'I trust' he continued, 'that the piety, good sense, and fortitude that hitherto have distinguished you and make you the mark of envy in your retreat will enable you on recollection perfectly to despise the scandals of those whom if you knew them, you would despise on every other account, and which, I faithfully assure you, make no impressions except those of contempt on any person living.'

He concluded what must for them have been an exceptionally disappointing letter by enclosing Mrs Burke's compliments and making vague promises of browbeating the newspaper proprietors 'to attend to their behaviour in future.'[21]

There was nothing to be done. Burke's inability to help the two women reflected neither negative nor positive assumptions about their relationship. Rather it reflected the failings of the law of libel as it then stood, and by which it was exceedingly difficult to get a successful prosecution in cases of purely personal abuse.

On 3 August Eleanor noted that Edmund Burke's letter had been acknowledged. She made no comment. Indeed the reader of the journal might be forgiven for thinking that she was greatly more concerned with a dramatic occurrence in the shrubbery. For here, amidst the lilacs and laburnums a presumptuous visitor had been discovered: 'Sent to the village for hounds to hunt it. No noses. Nor indeed eyes' she wrote tartly, 'Could neither smell nor see the Rabbit which sat before them by the library windows.'[22]

Nevertheless tension sent them both to bed next day with 'emetical' headaches, yet even then, Eleanor, true to the spirit of the sage Burke's advice, courageously concluded the day's entry with the usual comment: 'a day of delightful retirement'.

But for all Burke's assurance that the profligacy of the *Evening Post* article would excite nothing but contempt in people's minds, people, not unnaturally, did gossip.

While Horace Walpole was writing languidly to Lady Ossory* that 'little acquainted with Miss Ponsonby and Miss Buttershaw' as he was, he had seen something in the papers about them, but could not remember what; Harriet Bowdler was writing to Sarah at the end of August to reassure her that 'the contemptible attack is now forgotten by all, except those who know how much pain it has given to the most aimable of human beings'. She had had some conversation on the subject with an Irish lady, she continued, 'who told me many of your friends were inclined to suspect the *Hand*. The character you gave me of that man, and my dread of vulgar malice, had for a moment given me the same suspicion, but a very little reflection convinced me that the odious writer was as little acquainted with the

---

* Anne, daughter of Henry Liddell, Baron Ravensworth, eloped with John Fitzpatrick, Earl of Upper Ossory, and married him on 26 March 1769 – the day after her divorce was enacted.

situation of your sweet Paradise as with the character of its angelic Inhabitants.'[23]

Indignation on behalf of poor persecuted Miss Butler and Miss Ponsonby lapped and spread. Had Edwards of the *Hand* really read their letters discussing the disgraceful bill and warning their friends against patronizing his establishment? The mystery was mulled over in London, Bath, Shrewsbury, Oswestry, but, as time went on, less and less avidly, so that by the year's end the subject had faded even from Harriet Bowdler's correspondence.

But for all that, the unhappy innuendo made by the *General Evening Post* article stuck and was to stick, that Eleanor Butler and Sarah Ponsonby were Lesbians.

Chapter Five

'Impossibilities . . . whenever two
Ladies live too much together.'
Mrs Piozzi, *Thraliana*

It was no random coincidence that the article in the *General Evening Post* should appear in 1790. Mrs Piozzi, writing in *Thraliana* on the first of April 1789, makes it clear that for people like herself a new and hitherto unsuspected form of female friendship had appeared.

Musing how over-civilized everyone was becoming and how 'Original Feelings' were being strangely refined away, she went on to call upon the talents of Petronius and Juvenal in order to combat the latest unnatural vice. This, like so much that was thoroughly undesirable, had come over from France. 'The queen of France' reported Mrs Piozzi indignantly, 'is at the Head of a Set of Monsters call'd by each other *Sapphists*, who boast her example; and deserve to be thrown with the He Demons that haunt each other likewise, into Mount Vesuvius.'[1]

A year later, and about a month before Eleanor Butler's and Sarah Ponsonby's unhappy publicity, Mrs Piozzi returned to the subject; noted that Horace Walpole's second cousin, Mrs Damer the sculptress, was now much suspected of 'liking her own sex in a Criminal way', and had been seen so much with Miss Farren, the comedienne, that Miss Farren's protector, Lord Derby, had forbidden the two ladies to meet. Mrs Siddons's husband had already made up a verse about them:

> Her little Stock of private Fame
> Will fall a Wreck to public Clamour,
> If Farren leagues with one Whose Name
> Comes near – Aye very near – to Damn her.[2]

It was only necessary for such a category to come into being for a damaging guessing game to ensue, a game to which Mrs Piozzi succumbed instantly: 'Why was Miss Weston so averse to *any Marriage* I am wondering; – and why did Miss Trefusis call Colonel Barry *Hylas** of all names; and why did Miss Weston make such an Ado about little Sally Siddon's Wit and Beauty and Stuff? The Girl is just like every *other* Girl – but Miss Weston did use to like *Every Girl* so.'[3] Poor Miss Weston, friend of Mrs Siddons, Helen Williams,† Anna Seward, leading spirit of a 'knot of ingenious and charming females at Ludlow in Shropshire'; a woman who, by virtue of her elegant letters, Eleanor Butler and Sarah Ponsonby themselves were agog to meet. Misjudged Miss Weston, later to engage in a long and happy marriage with the Master of Ceremonies at Clifton.

In 1795 Mrs Piozzi was drawn to the interesting subject once more, '. . . 'tis now grown common to suspect Impossibilities – (such I think 'em) whenever two Ladies live too much together.'[4]

She expanded in a footnote; pondered how odd it was that the Roman women did not borrow 'this Horrible Vice from Greece'; remarked that Mrs Siddons herself had told her that her own sister had been 'in personal Danger once from a female Fiend of this Sort'; confided to *Thraliana* her opinion that Bath was 'a cage of these unclean Birds'.

English social history had hitherto been reticent upon the intriguing subject‡ which had so newly been brought to Mrs Piozzi's attention. The English, happily less given to close definition than the French, merely recognized the existence of what was a more diffuse relationship altogether, that of 'romantic friendship'.

---

* The favourite of Heracles who was abducted by Dryope and her sister nymphs.

† Helena Maria Williams (1762–1827), writer and revolutionary sympathizer. In Mrs Piozzi's words she sacrificed 'her Reputation to her Spirit of Politics' by living in France with Mr Stone, a married man. In 1794 he divorced his wife and she married him.

‡ Although 'the arbitrary taste for which there is no accounting', the 'secret bias' had been familiar to readers of *Fanny Hill* forty years before, there are few traces of feminine homosexuality in English social history. 'In Charles II's Court', the *Memoires de Grammont* tells us, 'Miss Hobart

The term, 'romantic friendship', had been used by contemporaries to describe Eleanor Butler's and Sarah Ponsonby's attachment at the time of their elopement in 1778. While the very term 'elopement' had not then, as it has now, a specifically sexual connotation, for it could simply mean an escape, a running away; 'romantic' was at that time only just beginning to lose its derisory meaning and to take on one slightly more complimentary. The epithet 'romantic', a notoriously vague one, had hitherto been generally applied to anything that was fanciful, whimsical, impracticable, absurd. John Foster, writing as late as 1806 on its usage, was to distinguish four modes of uncontrolled imagination, the last of which speaks of the romantic who forms schemes or indulges expectations 'Essentially incongruous with the nature of man – such as schemes for retiring from society, and for promoting wisdom and nobility by new schemes of education'.[5] In the light of which it is not difficult to see why Eleanor's and Sarah's retirement, excluding as it did marriage, money and position, should have been seen by contemporaries as 'romantic' and extravagant, and they in consequence judged 'romantic friends'.

Very generally speaking symptoms of romantic friendship were 'retirement', good works, cottages, gardening, impecuniosity, the intellectual pursuits of reading aloud and the study of languages, enthusiasm for the Gothick, journals, migraines, sensibility and often, but not always, the single state.

Such relationships had been produced by the emergence of a cultivated and leisured body of middle and upper-class women

was credited with Lesbian tendencies. ''Soon the rumour, true or false, of this singularity spread through the court. They were gross enough there never to have heard of that refinement of ancient Greece in the tastes of tenderness, and the idea came into their heads that the illustrious Hobart, who seemed so affectionate to pretty women, must be different from what she appeared.'' This passage is interesting because it shows us how rare was the exception. A century later, however, homosexuality among English women seems to have been regarded by the French as common, and Bacchaumont, on January 1st, 1773, recording that Mlle. Heinel of the Opera was settling in England added: 'Her taste for women will there find attractive satisfaction, for though Paris furnishes many tribades it is said that London is herein superior'' (Havelock Ellis, *Studies in the Psychology of Sex*, vol. II, p. 261 n.).

in a society in which, with a few notable exceptions, the sexes were traditionally and culturally divided. In time French influence would help to eradicate this unpleasing feature from English society. In the meantime, however, many ladies already refined into awareness by Addison and Steele's *Spectator*, the poets of solitude and Richardson's novels, found little cultural reciprocity from the more conservative gentlemen, and as a consequence of this sympathetic discrepancy turned to their own sex.

A glance at the more notable correspondence of the period will show that what we would now associate solely with a sexual relationship; tenderness, sensibility, shared tastes, coquetry; were then very largely confined to friendships between women.

'Miss Talbot is absolutely my passion; I think of her all day, dream of her all night, and one way or other introduce her into every subject I talk of.'[6]

What time of day is it? 1741. And who is speaking? Is it perhaps some lover of Miss Talbot's? No, it is Miss Carter, twenty-two, a clergyman's daughter, fated to be the learned translator of Epictetus, and to be revered by Dr Johnson for her intellect. Miss Carter, who reads and writes eight to twelve hours a day, takes snuff, binds a wet towel round her head and another round her stomach, and chews green tea to keep her awake; Miss Carter who has a packthread running from a bell on her bed-head into the garden below, where it is twitched at four each morning by the sexton to awake her and prevent the wastage of precious hours in sleep.

And Miss Talbot. Who is Miss Talbot? She and her widowed mother live with the Bishop of Oxford and his sister at Cuddesdon in Oxfordshire. Miss Talbot is younger than Miss Carter by three years, is perhaps not quite so learned, having no Greek, but is nevertheless well able to discuss the merits of Akenside's *Pleasures of the Imagination* or Voltaire's *Merope,* the latter, if necessary, in French.

Like her friend she will become an authoress, like her she revels in physical exercise. Both agree in the strict planning of their time. As we have seen Miss Carter rises at four or five; Miss Talbot at the more indulgent hour of seven. Both unite in despising the Town and its pleasures, preferring the soothing retirement of the country. Both enjoy melancholy and sublime scenes, romantic gloom; both are deeply mistrustful of marriage and extol, at its expense, friendship. Indeed the tidings that a friend is about to be married will throw Miss Carter into a splenetic fit, for she dreads after the event to be forced to talk to her erstwhile companion in 'the dull, formal indifferent way of common acquaintances'.[7] Miss Talbot will reply sympathetically on the subject, 'We must 'een lower our ideas of friendship to the pitch of common life, and be content with loving and esteeming people constantly and affectionately amid the variety of thwarting and awkward circumstances that forbid all possibility of spending our lives together.'[8]

But unlike romantic love, romantic friendship could be inclusive. Miss Talbot has other friends: 'We two [Miss Talbot and Lady Mary Grey] amuse ourselves by the exercise of walking in a large unfurnished room, where sometimes we have the advantage of moonlight, and always that of conversation in that way that makes this hour the most agreeable of the four and twenty.'[9]

Miss Carter, however, as Miss Talbot will teasingly suggest, in something of a flirt as regards her romantic friendships. There is Mrs Montagu* for instance. 'I longed for you extremely the other night at Reading' Miss Carter will write to her in 1759, 'To ramble by moonlight amongst the ruins of an old Abbey.'[10] There is also Mrs Vesey.† Mrs Carter will read Mrs Vesey's letters sitting on the seashore in the 'soft melancholy light of this fair autumnal moon', her mind in 'that pensive kind of tranquility which has such an inexplicable union with the tenderest feelings of the heart.[11] Mrs Vesey, meanwhile, though far away, is by arrangement also gazing at that same moon.

Sometimes, perhaps understandably, Miss Talbot feels a trifle

*Elizabeth Montagu *née* Robinson (1720–1800) married Edward Montagu, grandson of the 1st Earl of Sandwich. Authoress, beauty and wit, she was one of the leaders of the bluestocking circles. Mrs Piozzi gave her the highest charm rating of any, 101 out of a possible 120.

†Elizabeth Vesey *née* Vesey (?1715–91) married the Rt Hon. Agmondsham Vesey, M.P. Bluestocking and friend of Mrs Montagu. According to Mrs Piozzi she adored Mrs Montagu almost as much as she hated her husband.

neglected. What has become of Miss C and her elegant letters? It is August 1763 and Miss Carter is touring France with Mrs Montagu. When is the next instalment going to arrive telling Miss Talbot more about that fascinating Baronne over whom Miss C was rhapsodizing in her last? Perhaps Miss C is ill? 'No' the Bishop comforts Miss Talbot, who passes on what he says to her friend, 'you are only fallen in love with another woman and the first is forgot. A pretty gentleman you will come home indeed. *Fi volage!*'[12]

Romantic pollinations, now grave, now gay, were taking place between an ever growing number of cultivated women. Letters that were admired were transcribed with, and sometimes without, the permission of their authoress; sent to friends and the friends of friends; likewise Tracts, Tours, Journals, Novels and Poetry. Had not Miss Carter written much admired verses to Miss Talbot beginning, 'Come Musidora'; to Miss D'aeth advocating Retirement; to Miss Lynch 'At Midnight in a Thunderstorm'; as well as numerous verses to the delightful Vesey and Montagu? Reputations could be made without so much as publishing a book; opinions on such grave matters as the Abolition of Slavery could alter overnight; there was soon, spreading over England, and particularly in the cathedral towns, an ever growing web of liberal culture and refinement, which would one day trap even gentlemen in its polite gossamer.

Miss Carter and Miss Talbot, Mrs Vesey and Mrs Montagu were all in the first generation of romantic friends; steeped in the classics, their sensibility was of a more disciplined order than that of the generation which followed them and in which Eleanor Butler and Sarah Ponsonby were to figure. This second generation, glutted on French, and particularly Italian lyric poets and with a sensibility so refined that it more often than not touched on the absurd, were to be portrayed in the charming novel, *Millenium Hall*; the *vade mecum* of romantic friendship which, at the time of Eleanor Butler's and Sarah Ponsonby's elopement, had run into four editions.

The plot was simple. Two gentlemen taking a country airing are caught in a cloudburst. While sheltering beneath a tree they see, embosomed in fields that are prettily hedged with roses and (with a fine disregard for season) underplanted with hyacinths and lily of the valley, a delightful mansion. They seek refuge in the mansion, are most graciously received by two charming ladies, and discover that they have, in fact, happened upon a feminine Utopia.

The grounds are interesting enough, where 'Man never appears as a Merciless Destroyer'; where animals go unmolested 'by gun or trap'; where there are temples dedicated to solitude, and where grottoes of spars and corals put one in mind of devout anchorites; where the very cascades, for some unexplained reason, do not even appear to cause dampness.

Inside the mansion there is an even more interesting state of affairs. For here is an asylum, not only for the indigent gentlewomen who, to the strains of *Judas Maccabeus*, are training to become governesses, but for the other outcasts of society: giants and dwarfs, the physically disabled, the aged and the orphaned. It is not long before Miss Mancel and Mrs Morgan, the two principals of the establishment, are showing the admiring gentlemen over a carpet factory which employs workers from six to eighty, 'all busy singing and whistling'; and they soon learn of free furnished houses for young couples setting up house together; of sick benefits where people are paid during their incapacity what they would have earned had they been working; of alms-houses for the old and schools for the very young. Soon the intrigued gentlemen are questioning the delightful lady principals about their own lives. Not unlike Eleanor Butler and Sarah Ponsonby they had first met at boarding school, where Mrs Morgan (then a Miss Melvyn and a baronet's daughter) had taught the beautiful and orphaned Miss Mancel, Geography, Philosophy and Religion. An unfortunate marriage on Miss Melvyn's part had separated the friends for a space, but the timely death of Mr Morgan had brought them together once more whereupon, backed by his money, they were enabled to achieve their ambition of retiring into the country to lead what appeared to them to be the only rational existence. An existence where all was simplicity, where there were no card parties, assemblies nor masquerades, for, as they explained, 'we do not desire to drown conversation in noise'.[13]

It was not long before they were joined in their retreat by other like-minded and fugitive ladies; Miss Trentham, plain and disfigured with the smallpox, but withal highly cultivated; Lady Mary Jones disgusted, *femme du monde* as she was, with the folly of London high life.

What is the ladies' conception of society? '. . . a state of mutual confidence' replied Lady Mary, 'reciprocal services and correspondent affections.'[14] And marriage? the gentlemen slyly ask. Why does Miss Mancel promote but not practise it? 'We consider matrimony as absolutely essential to the good of society' she responds gravely, '. . . but, as according to all ancient tenures those obliged to perform knights' service might if they chose to enjoy their own fireside, be excused by sending deputies to supply their places; so we, using the same privilege substitute many others, and certainly much more promote wedlock, than we could do by entering into it ourselves.'[15]

Miss Trentham of the pocked face is more outspoken however, declaring with some force that she would rather face the enemy's cannon than put her happiness 'into the hands of a person, who perhaps will not once reflect on the importance of the trust committed to his care'.[16]

Such revelations of the feminine rationale no doubt give the visiting gentlemen much food for thought. After a round of purportedly rustic pleasures, but which nevertheless appear sophisticated enough, since they comprise balls, water parties and concerts, they take leave of their foundress friends, wiser, and it is to be hoped better gentlemen.

In addition to its own grave charm the novel is revealing in the light it casts upon the liberal notions of the authoress. *Millenium Hall* appeared thirty years before the publication of Paine's *Rights of Man*. Two hundred years later we have not yet caught up with the benevolent practices of *Millenium Hall,* with its ban on blood sports, its ready place for the outcasts of society, its free furnished homes for young couples, and its maximum compensation for sick workers. The novel is in fact the blueprint of a woman's panacea for the ills of the society in which she lived. It was not unnaturally the judgement of that society however to find the panacea impracticable, absurd, and 'romantic'.

That *Millenium Hall* represented a true and not merely an imaginary picture of what was taking place at the time is frequently borne out. There were other lay convents than that at Batheaston, where the authoress of *Millenium Hall* and her friend expended their modest income running a school for poor children.

In the September of 1790, Thomas Crabbe,* aged five and resplendent in his first boy's suit of vivid scarlet, climbed into the old family gig, and accompanied his indulgent parents into Suffolk where they made a round of family visits. One such was to his grandmother at Beccles, where he was taken to a

sweet little villa called Normanston ... Here four or five spinsters of independent fortune had formed a sort of Protestant nunnery, the abbess being Miss Blacknell, a lady of distinguished elegance in her tastes and manners, who afterwards deserted it to become the wife of Admiral Sir Thomas Graves. Another of the sisterhood was Miss Waldron, who could sing a jovial song like a fox hunter, and like him I had almost said toss a glass, and yet there was such an air of "ton", and such intellect mingled with these manners, that the perfect lady was not veiled for a moment – no not when, with a face rosy red, and an eye beaming with mirth, she would seize a cup and sing "Toby Fillpot" glorying as it were in her own jollity. When we took our morning rides, she generally drove my father in her phaeton and interested him exceedingly by her strong understanding and conversational powers.[17]

Yet although romantic friendships and their manifestations were to grow increasingly common as the years went by, both society in general and ladies like Miss Talbot and Miss Harriet Bowdler in particular, were, if only vaguely, aware that passions might be involved which could, unrestrained, be dangerous.

Miss Talbot, for all that she wrote in so coquettish a vein to her friend, Miss Carter, could yet stand back from the scene and sound the formal note that religion must be the only unshaken basis of friendship. Dr Johnson would have regarded this as mere cant. 'How many friendships have you known formed

* Son of the poet George Crabbe (1754-1832).

upon principles of virtue?' he asked Boswell. 'Most friendships are formed by caprice or by chance, mere confederacies in vice or leagues in folly.'[18] Miss Talbot's warning against excess of delicacy in friendship is perhaps of more psychological interest. 'In friendships especially', she wrote 'this excess of delicacy is often of fatal ill consequences. From hence spring suspicions and jealousies.'[19]

She was to be most earnestly and fully supported in this observation by one of the second generation of romantic friends, Eleanor Butler's and Sarah Ponsonby's own friend, Harriet Bowdler. This second generation was to be only too prone to the dangers of which Miss Talbot had complained.

In an essay on *The Proper Employment of Time Talents and Fortune*, Harriet Bowdler, while enthusiastically extolling friendship, had some warnings to impart should the relationship become too intense. Friends for instance who weakened the attachment between parents and children, or brothers and sisters, must be flown from 'as from a serpent'. She further cautioned those aspiring to friendship not to allow their minds 'to be so far engrossed by one dear object as to make them neglect anything which duty or affection should require'.[20]

Yet Miss Bowdler, like Miss Talbot, was to prove the perfect example of her own warning to others. For the same pseudo-sexual coquetry already noticed between Miss Talbot and Miss Carter was also to find a place in Harriet Bowdler's correspondence with Sarah Ponsonby, one in which Eleanor Butler is constantly referred to by Harriet Bowdler as 'my *Veillard*' (my old man). Doubtless a joking Valentine had provoked the following which was written on 29 April 1794: 'I have a letter from my *Veillard* wch I shall answer on the first of April 1795, if I can think of anything in the meantime to teaze and provoke him heartily. Till then I have nothing to say except I receive a letter wch is worth answering; I wish I knew where to get another Husband.'[21] And again that September, the eminently respectable sister of the founder of the Society for the Suppression of Vice and Encouragement of Religion was to write, 'I dare say my profligate *Veillard* is gone off with some new favourite, and I must as usual wait patiently till he is pleased to return.'[22] All of which is highly reminiscent of Miss Talbot's affectionate jibe at the promiscuous Miss Carter, 'A pretty gentleman you will come home indeed. *Fi volage!*'

But it was with Miss Anna Seward, of whom Miss Bowdler heartily disapproved on account of her chaste love for the unhappily married choir master of Lichfield, that sentimental adoration of one woman for another was to reach new heights.

Here she is, aged forty-one, indulging her 'Siddonian idolatry', having, in the most lover-like manner, only got into the theatre 'at the hazard of my life, by struggling through the terrible fierce maddening crowd into the pit'. Mrs Siddons is playing Callista, it is possible someone will claim Miss Seward's seat later in the evening. 'Oh, even when the siren spoke with all her graces and melting tones, I wished to have the speech over, so ardently did I long for the moment when possession for the night might become secure.'[23]

The sexual imagery is unconscious, but it is unmistakable. One must now attempt to discover what were the views of Anna Seward and women like her upon men and marriage.

'. . . few *men* know what love is',[24] Harriet Bowdler will whisper to Sarah Ponsonby, while Anna Seward, for all that she has, or thinks she has, fallen in love with several men, will agree. 'Mixed company', by which was meant the company of both men and women, was about as tedious to her as to Miss Carter. Of the love of men she will write to Mrs Hayley,

Men are rarely capable of pure unmixed tenderness to any fellow creature except their children. In general even the best of them give their friendship to their male acquaintances, and their fondness to their offspring. For their mistress, or wife, they feel, during a time, a tenderness more ardent and more secret, a friendship softer and more animated. But this inexplicable, this fascinating sentiment, which we understand by the name of love, often proves an illusion of the imagination; – a meteor that misleads her who trusts it, vanishing when she has followed it into pools and quicksands where peace and liberty are swallowed up and lost.[25]

Yet it will be to a man that Anna Seward will confide a strange friendship that for a time will disturb her exceedingly.

There is no record of what the Reverend Dr Whalley* thought about the episode, for Miss Seward did not include his side of the correspondence in her published letters. One can only judge from the turbulence of Miss Seward's effusions that he was sympathetic; in any case, Dr Whalley, married himself, was a good friend of other romantic ladies including both Eleanor Butler and Sarah Ponsonby.

Here is a very odd state of affairs indeed, and one which seems perfectly to express the strange ambivalence of the pre-Freudian romantic friendships. Miss Seward, now sixty-one, had this August of 1803 just lost her lover of thirty-seven years' standing, that same married, choir-conducting Mr Saville of Lichfield. She has become, in her agony of grief, perfectly ridiculous, dwelling, to poor Dr Whalley, upon '... the perfect shapeliness of his [Mr Saville's] limbs to his last hour, with a form neither slender nor in the slightest degree corpulent'[26] yet now, only four months later, she has renewed a passionate friendship with a young woman of twenty-five whom she had met some years before.

Elizabeth Cornwallis, renamed Clarissa by Miss Seward for obvious reasons, is the only daughter of the Bishop of Lichfield and his wife who unite in having a great dislike of female friendships, deeming them 'romantic, and where there is the least inequality of station, highly improper'. Miss Cornwallis is unfortunate enough to detest the young man her parents want her to marry, and, needless to add, despises the frivols of society, loves retirement and books. Indeed it is through books that she has made the acquaintance of Miss Seward. Books, it has already been seen, can be dangerous in every aspect, in their lending, their borrowing and their perusal; so with poor Miss Cornwallis. 'The fervent disinterested attachment of such a heart' writes Miss Seward of Miss Cornwallis's adoration 'originally and solely inspired by my publications, I have ever considered as the most flattering and precious circumstance of my authorism.'[27]

As with poor Miss Cornwallis's other friendship the Bishop disapproves heartily of this one. Miss Cornwallis, like her

* The Rev. Thomas Sedgwick Whalley (1746–1828), Prebendary of Wells, poet, collector and friend of Mrs Piozzi.

fictional namesake, is confined, forbidden to make any female friends, and is presented with another suitor, one whom, if it were possible, she dislikes even more than the first. She takes refuge in delirium, recovering sufficiently from time to time none the less to enjoy a lively but clandestine correspondence with Miss Seward.

'It is hard that our attachment to each other should be a secret' complains Miss Seward to Dr Whalley, 'the disclosure of which must involve as much distress and misery to both of us as if we were of a different sex, and our intercourse guilty.'[28]

There is an additional difficulty. Miss Seward's house in Lichfield Close is in the gift of the Bishop. Too great an impropriety could even lose her her home. Clarissa notwithstanding contrives to visit her idol. 'Our interview was stolen and dangerous,' writes Miss Seward thrillingly to Dr Whalley, 'and her escape from him fortunate.'[29] Yet in all the excitement of subterfuge, Miss Seward manages with curious consistency to observe the exact hour of beloved Saville's death.

This was the last communiqué. What happened to poor Miss Cornwallis between now and her spinster's death ten years later? What did Dr Whalley advise? Perhaps some rational course was arrived at, for whatever else occurred Miss Seward continued on at the Close.

Clearly Anna Seward was more than ordinarily susceptible, for Elizabeth Cornwallis was by no means her first attachment. There had been a passionate friendship with her foster-sister, Honora Sneyd, ruined, at least in Anna Seward's eyes, by her subsequent marriage to Richard Lovell Edgeworth;* there had been another with Miss Penelope Weston, about whose proclivities Mrs Piozzi had expressed such grave doubts, and another with Mrs Mompesson, '. . . many years my senior, and beginning to love me in the giddy, romantic, hoping happy years of my teens . . . ',[30] and there were doubtless many others.

Compared with Anna Seward, Harriet Bowdler was less flamboyant, more plaintive in her attachments. They seemed, in full accordance with Miss Talbot's warnings, to inspire jealousy.

---

*Richard Lovell Edgeworth (1744–1818), educationist father of the novelist Maria Edgeworth.

There had been Margaret Davies, Elizabeth and Letitia Barret's friend, with whom she had visited Plas Newydd in 1785, a friendship which however had ended unsatisfactorily: '... my Margaret saw a rival in everybody ...',[31] very likely in Sarah Ponsonby, to whom, and as far as the 'retirement' and the *Viellard* permitted, Harriet Bowdler was extremely drawn. The tenderest of Harriet Bowdler's feelings were to be reserved, however, for her charming pupil, Elizabeth Smith, whose fluctuating family fortunes were to take up so great a space in the Bowdler letters to Plas Newydd.

Alas for poor Miss Bowdler. The protégé with whom she had sketched and walked and studied the stars; the young girl whom she had delighted to observe teaching herself French, Italian, Spanish, German, Latin, Greek, Arabic and Persic, caught a tragically romantic chill sitting on a mossy stone reading poetry by a lakeside, contracted tuberculosis and soon died.

It was dear Dr Whalley who had written her requiem:

> ... unobtrusive, serious and meek
> the first to listen, and the last to speak.

Dr Whalley, tender and compassionate, as full of sensibility as any lady, who in 'the wild bosom of one of the vast Mendip mountains' had created his own romantic retirement complete with Gothick cottage, roothouse and rustic seats bearing the names of favourite friends was one of that new order of men, who had been first produced by mixing with learned ladies in the salons of the *Bas Bleus*. There men of the stature of Dr Johnson and Sir Joshua Reynolds had been pleased to converse with women like Miss Carter and Mrs Vesey and Mrs Montagu; men who by the last quarter of the century were beginning to take over the tender, foolish, loverlike coquetry which had once belonged almost exclusively to the romantic friends.

It was to the band of romantic friends, rapidly growing discredited, that Eleanor Butler and Sarah Ponsonby belonged.

Yet their relationship was not only 'romantic', abounding in all those features associated with the word, but, to them, sacred. A quality hard to appreciate now when friendships between members of the same sex tend either to be valued lightly or viewed with suspicion.

In an essay their friend Harriet Bowdler had quoted with approval from an earlier authority: 'True friendship is a divine and spiritual relation of minds, an union of souls, a marriage of hearts, a harmony of designs and affections, which being entered into by mutual consent, groweth up into the purest kindness and most endearing love, maintaining itself by the openest freedom, the warmest sympathy, and the closest secrecy.'[32]

It was this conception of the relationship, one more nearly akin to the modern idea of marriage, that Eleanor Butler and Sarah Ponsonby were to make their own.

'When shall we be quite alone?'
Journal of Eleanor Butler, 25 October 1785

That the relationship between Eleanor Butler and Sarah Ponsonby exhibited most of the features of romantic friendship is self-evident. Everyone thought so. They thought so themselves. As early as 1782 Lady Louisa Stuart, using the epithet with approval, was acknowledging that she had never heard of anything so romantic as their mode of life; while in 1789 the *World* was writing glowingly of their having settled in 'so romantic a manner' in Denbigh.

Numerous bad but admiring poems were to testify to this general impression, the following verses by a Mrs Grant being representative:

In the Vale of Llangollen a Cottage is seen
Well shelter'd from tempests by shades ever green
Where the daisy first opens its eye – to the day
And the hawthorn first flowers on the bosom of May.

There far from the haunts of ambition and pride
Contentment, and virtue, and friendship abide,
And nature, complacent smiles sweet on the pair
Who have splendour forsaken to worship her there.

Bright patterns of wisdom affection and truth
Retired to the shade in the gay bloom of youth
Your sweet rural cottage and pastoral views
Are the charm of the Vale, and the theme of the Muse.

To the Shade for concealment in vain you retire,
We follow to wonder – to gaze – and admire.
Those graces which fancy, and feeling refine,
Like the glow-worm thro' deepest obscurity shine

While ambition exults in her storm-beaten dome,
Like the tower on your Mountain that frowns o'er your home
With tranquil seclusion, and friendship your lot
How blest, how secure, and how envied your cot![1]

The poem obviously gave the Ladies such a pleasing picture of themselves, that they not only kept the original, but made transcripts for their friends.

Of their more literary admirers, Anna Seward, Harriet Bowdler, Mrs Piozzi, Madame de Genlis and the Reverend Mr Chappelow,* not to mention William Wordsworth, were all to describe Plas Newydd and the friends.

To Anna Seward, her head quite turned by the Ladies' Aeolian harps, Gothick lanterns and wavy gravel walks, the friends were Minervas; they were Enchantresses, they were Rosalind and Celia and Plas Newydd was Arcadia, and she wrote a long, impassioned, and disastrous poem upon the subject. Harriet Bowdler's visits to the cottage were to prove 'the most delicious days' of her life, cherished in memory, impossible of repetition, after which she had nothing to look forward to 'except joys behind the tomb'.[2] Mrs Piozzi, with unusual sensibility for her, saw the Ladies as 'fair and noble recluses', 'charming cottagers', 'conquering, and keeping in their enchanted Castle all travellers passing that particular road'.[3] Madame de Genlis would note their intriguing looks, Eleanor's *charmante visage, éclatant de fraîcheur et de santé la plus franche*', Sarah's '*belle figure pâle et melancolique*'.[4] But it was

* The Rev. Leonard Chappelow (d. 1820) of Royden, near Diss, Norfolk, was an amateur botanist and poet.

Mr Chappelow, author of that yet unublished work, *The Sentimental Naturalist*, who was to outdo everyone else in his praise of Plas Newydd and its occupants. With vision almost apocalyptical he described his hesitant approach to the 'Gothick Cottage', how he was tremblingly diffident and afraid '– till I found the Door wide open, a Female beckoned me, so that I entered with Confidence and found myself in a most heavenly Retreat – a Convent in Miniature. We pass'd through the Refectory under a pointed Arch composed of various Coloured Glass illuminated by Lamps and etc. it was Dusk – I looked thro' a Gothic Window and saw the British Chartreuse encircled with Mountains on one of which stood Dynas Castle. The sides of it were bright as burnished Gold with the departing Sun, exhibiting at once the most brilliant and yet temperate Glow –'[5] all of which had so greatly excited Mrs Piozzi that she copied it straight into *Thraliana*.

These, however, were mere external impressions. But a glance into Sarah Ponsonby's day-book, her accounts, or Eleanor Butler's journal, reinforces the impression that the characteristics of romantic friendship were also present in their private life.

As in *Millenium Hall*, not a moment of the day was wasted. The public rooms of the Gothick cottage burbled and scratched and rustled with readings, writings, illuminations and purse nettings. In the domestic offices six species of soft fruit were being expertly converted into wines; bread baked, meat salted, sheets stitched; while outside in the dairy, fowl yard and potager, there were regular milkings and churnings, wringings of turkey necks, generous dungings and vigorous rakings of the gravel paths.

But when work was at last laid aside the romantic was to penetrate yet more private areas of their existence. There were the favourite walks along the banks of the rushing Cufflymen to the picturesque ruins of ancient Pengwern Hall; pensive strolls round their small four-acre estate in the moonlight; long close conversations in the flickering light from the kitchen fire.

While Eleanor described such evenings in the journal Sarah was jotting down *pensées* in her small day-book:

'I am sorry not to give so much but to repay so little.'

'When any Calamity has been suffered, the first thing to be remembered is, how much has been escaped.'

'Those that have loved longest love best.' And, pertinently, one might suppose, 'Esteem of great powers, or amiable qualities newly discovered may embroider a day or a week, but a frendship of twenty years is interwoven with the texture of life.'[6]

There was also Sarah's answer to a friend who had written warning her of the dangers of Poetry and Love:

> Song
>
> By Vulgar Eros long misled
> I call'd thee Tyrant, mighty love!
> With idle fears my fancy fled
> Nor ev'ne thy pleasures wish'd to prove.
>
> Condem'd at length to wear thy chains
> Trembling I felt and ow'd thy might
> But soon I found my fears were vain
> Soon hugg'd my chain, and thought it light.[7]

But to know them, really to know them, if such a thing is indeed possible, one must go behind and beyond sensibility; beyond Sarah's verses and Eleanor's overcharged description of the fiery skies over Dinas Bran; behind and beyond the piquancy of those exquisitely sentimental readings from *La Nouvelle Héloïse*; beyond even the shared conspiracy of their smothered giggles in church or their amusement at Lady Dungannon's bitch, Phillis, being so over-complaisant to the dogs, beyond the snug tutorials by the library fire and the games of backgammon late at night in the dressing-room, when the storm raged outside and rattled the shuttered windows.

There are clues here and there, some dropped unawares. They share everything. Their bound books are gold-lettered, E.B. on the front, S.P. on the back; so with their china and with nearly every possession they have. Their letters are signed jointly, the initials of the Beloved followed by the full name of the writer of the letter. In speech they use always the collective 'We'. They call one another 'Beloved' always, as Dorothy and William

Wordsworth do. 'Beloved', which had about the same weight then as 'Darling', and which even in Sarah's account book was shortened to 'My B'.

Yet none of this compares with the subtlety of the concealed relationship, for to all appearances Eleanor Butler seems to be the stronger character; people notice that it is she who appears to make the decisions; to do most of the talking; who is the active principle. Yet when the library chimney catches fire and their precious cottage is likely to burn down it is not Eleanor but Sarah who has the presence of mind to thrust her arm up the chimney, burning it as she does so, and to pull down Lady Dungannon's dull, voluminous smouldering letter, which has started the trouble. When a drunken man calls at the cottage and puts his foot in the kitchen door it is not Eleanor but Sarah who goes down to send him away. For Eleanor is afraid of men. In the pages of the journal strange men lurk as in nightmares; in the darkening fields or in the shadow of empty side streets, and once, one is seen bound and mad in a nightcap changing horses at the *Hand* en route, who knows, for Bedlam. It is Sarah who is the bridge with reality and Eleanor knows it. 'Sally relates the dismal part of our Story which I hate to think on'[9] she writes to Mrs Goddard, aware of her tendency to suppress disturbing events, merely recording them in the journal without comment as with the unpleasant newspaper article of 1790. She is the child who hides her eyes, it is Sally who faces the accounts.

Here, late at night by the dressing-room fire their voices ring clear; Eleanor's Irish, racy, peppered with expletives; Sarah's, perhaps because she is a good deal younger, less marked with an Irish accent, more English, more how poor James Boswell so yearned to speak; yet for all that vigorous enough, not in the least afraid to use expressions like 'drunken idiot', or to call someone a 'poisonous reptile' or to use words like 'stink' or 'bloody'.

Eleanor, liable on the least provocation to burst into French songs, garnishes her whole conversation with French phrases. She speaks of 'Vile Mrs Vent' in the pages of the journal, of 'Madame Pluie'; she is also inclined to use the pious ejaculations of her nursery days, 'Mother of God!', she will exclaim in the journal, *'Laus Deo!'*, 'God rest his soul!' She does not hesitate to call a malefactor 'a dirty thief!' or to condemn social pests of any kind violently 'to the deuce!' In the journal she regularly uses expressions like 'crazy', 'calm and collected'; and she has, as we already know, 'splitting headaches'. Where Sarah is concerned, however, her epithets become Arabian. She is 'My Sally', 'My Love', 'The Beloved of My Soul', 'The Delight of my Heart', 'The Joy of My Life'.

Even now though, here in the dressing-room with the dice box rattling and Eleanor crying out 'Faith!' as she does over a lucky throw, we can, such is the power of private letters, penetrate even further; to the privacy of their bedroom with its grey carpet, moreen hangings, Gothick stools and large bookcase,[10] to the privacy of their bed itself.

It is an ark of a bed, a capital four-poster with back, roof, tester and posts of 'very rich Carved oak in high relief'.[11] It has an excellent mattress with a palliasse, and on top of the palliasse, a seasoned goose-feathered bed. In winter its moreen curtains are left slightly parted so that its interior is always dimly lit from the glowing coals of their bedroom fire.

It is here they lie tossing on their hot pillows worrying about money, or soaking them with tears, because their little bitch Gypsy has died in whelp; it is here that they close their eyes beneath the enormous warm nightcaps which they find so exceedingly efficacious for the toothache; here, where Sarah will fall asleep to dream of past happy days at Woodstock, picnics with Lady Betty and the Goddard to Altamount or water excursions to the Red House; here, where Eleanor will wake up with terrifying nightmares to be soothed by Sally into sleep once more. It is here, where in accordance with Harriet Bowdler's definition of true friendship, '. . . the purest kindness and most endearing love . . . the warmest sympathy and the closest secrecy . . .' will find expression:

I kept my bed all day with one of My dreadful Headaches. My Sally. My Tender, My Sweet Love lay beside me holding and supporting My Head till one o'clock when I by Much entreaty prevailed with her to rise and get my breakfast. She never left me for half a Moment the entire day Except at Two o'clock when she perceived

Mr Whalley* and little Richard coming down the Field. She ran out to Prevent his rapping at the door and to borrow the 1st Volume of the *Tab. de Suisse*† which she knew I was pining for ... My beloved Sat by My Bed Side reading it to me for near Two Hours – I wou'd not permit her to Continue–lest it shou'd impair her precious Health. Mrs Tatters uneasy that we did not come down Stairs at the usual hour Scratched at our Door for admittance, came on the bed to me and lay there till Ten o'clock at night Purring all the Time – a day of Tenderness and Sensibility'

she concluded, 'My Sally How can I acknowledge the grateful Sense My Heart labours under of Your Tenderness, anxiety and incessant attention to your B.'[12]

Or:

Rose at Eight after a tedious night Spent in coughing and with a most dreadful head ache. My dearest. My Kindest love did not sleep even for one moment the entire night but lay beside me watching and lamenting my illness and soothing by her tenderness the distressing pain of My Head.[13]

Such entries were common, for the migraines occurred with monthly regularity, and at times of stress more frequently. They were always recorded. So, later on, were the 'Emeticks' or vomits, which Sarah administered to cure them:

My beloved ... the darling of My heart came got me some warm water which gave me a momentary relief but it returned with greater violence and continued till 3 during which time My beloved Sally never left me for a single moment.[14]

The journals show nothing more revealing than this, and their pages are innocent of any signs other than the coloured ink in which their days away from home were written. Such meticulous recordings of migraines and vomits could be read as more significant than the robust interest taken by contemporaries in such matters; more significant than the unsophisticated acknowledgement of '... purest kindness and most endearing love'. They could be read as a code; as the only permissible expression of a yet more intimate relationship; or as the unconscious expression of the desire for such a relationship.

* The Rev. Richard Chapple Whalley (1748–1816), Vicar of Horsington, Somerset, and brother of Dr Whalley. 'A great many men are *near* heaven,' wrote Hannah More, 'but Richard Whalley is *in* heaven.'

† A book of Swiss views.

What were the personal relations between Eleanor Butler and Sarah Ponsonby, and what was their nature? After reading the extracts from the journals the reader will know as much as I. Psychologically the character of their relationship seems clear, but technically an inquiry must be inconclusive. Certainly love speaks in these entries.

My beloved with her accustomed kindness and anxiety Made me go to the dressing Room. procured me an Emetick which She administered herself. When I grew Easier She read to me . . .[15]

Four days later on a hot August afternoon Eleanor turned the current journal upside down and wrote, 'A Cottage August 13th. The having but one Heart between my beloved and —',[16] and then she crossed this out as an inadequate expression of the great love she felt.

Chapter Six

'Three o'clock. Dinner.' 1791–4

New Year's day 1791 opened with soaking rain and wind. In the kitchen Mary Carryll was entertaining the kitchen maid Anne Jones and her granddaughter, also 'old Parkes', the landlord of the *Lyon*. The occasion, for reasons which Eleanor forbore to enlarge upon, was not an unqualified success. 'Mem.' she wrote of Old Parkes, 'the latter old brute never again to be invited.'[1] There had been other provocations, 'Owen Mr Myddleton's bailiff came to demand a Christmas Box. Asked him – for what? Sent him about his business'[2] she wrote with what might be deemed unseasonable irritability, but which was probably caused by the anxiety of having literally no money with which to pay their bills.

Bar the recording of disturbances of this sort, her splitting headaches, exceptionally picturesque scenery, and the usual scrupulous details of what they had eaten, the journal was becoming less intimate, consisting in the main of lists of people written to, letters received, visitors who had called. From time to time either dismal weather or the extreme regularity of their lives induced that sort of torpor which caused Eleanor to write the same date two days running. 25 January as it happened was destined for some reason to last three consecutive days!

Imperceptibly a shift of emphasis was taking place in their relationship. They had lived together for thirteen years now, had grown predictable to one another. As the journal shows, the expression 'Better Half' was beginning to oust 'Beloved', and an increasing social life was beginning to make inroads on the 'retirement'.

An important event was to underline this trend. 'Bellringers'

Sarah wrote in the account book for the twelfth of April, 'for my dst. Lady Eleanor. *10.6.*'

The lost Ormonde titles had been restored at last.

'It is otherwise a very Unsubstantial honour,' Sarah wrote to Mrs Tighe in a letter which thanked that lady for her congratulations, 'and though the World seems unanimously of the opinion that it affords her a new claim to that One hundred per Annum in relation to her present *two* which wd. gratify Our Utmost ambition – We have no reason to think Ld. Ormond will be prevailed with to adopt it . . .' They had known for some time, Sarah went on to explain, that Eleanor had the right to the title of 'Ladyship', but she had only just been induced to accept it, 'from a report having been propagated in Kilkenny . . . that she disapproved the restoration of her truly illustrious family to the Hereditary Honours . . . She would otherwise have been much better pleased to have resigned that share in them which seems attended with much more pain than satisfaction, to her truly amiable feelings.'[3]

Eleanor Butler's exalted sentiments upon the subject, their united protestations at seeing no financial benefit in this event were perhaps not quite so sincere as they pretended. The foretune concerned was reputedly enormous; '. . . the income of his estates is indeed monstrous !' an aunt of Sarah's had written of Eleanor's brother; seventy thousand pounds a year she pointed out, more than what many German princes had to maintain armies upon. Should she try and touch the new lord for an income of five hundred pounds a year for his youngest sister? She was most willing to, had indeed formed the idea of approaching Eleanor's mother the Dowager, 'but she I fear is not made, pardon me dear Lady Eleanor ? of "penetrable stuff".'[4]

A few weeks later a letter arrived from the 'impenetrable' Dowager herself. From her ignorance of her youngest daughter's address it would appear to have been the first she had written in thirteen years. It was not of the most encouraging:

Dear Daughter, I received your obliging letter of Congratulations on the Titles being restore'd, it makes me very happy on account of the Family but it comes a little Late for me and besides, it brings some incumberances with it but no addition to my income. I would have answered yours sooner but wait'd to get your address from your sister Kavanagh, who lives at Ballyragget and comes very seldom here;

> I am Dear Daughter
> Your Affect. mother
> E. Ormonde.[5]

Magnificently undeterred they began a new shrubbery that July, followed six months later by an ambitious programme of alterations to the cottage itself.

Mulish tenacity, incredulity that Eleanor would not in the end benefit from the family's accession to the titles, may both have stimulated such impetuous activity, but they also had their own secret. Lady Frances Douglas, the indefatigable, had been again exerting her influence on their behalf, and had, to their great joy, secured them the promise of an addition to their pension. What they had professed their 'Utmost ambition' was in fact about to be realized, namely, an increase in income of one hundred pounds a year.

At the prospect of yet another shrubbery, it is worth pausing to conjure up a picture of that Plas Newydd garden, so greatly admired at the time, itself so characteristic an expression of the taste of the two women.

Unfortunately the plan of the miniature estate, which had been sent to Queen Charlotte in 1785, has been lost, or more likely was destroyed at the time, being fatally impregnated with the scent of musk, which the Ladies perpetually employed but which the Queen detested.*

Most views of the cottage show its south-west facing front demurely nestling behind white palings and overlooking a field of grazing sheep.

The garden proper, consisting of four separate enclosures for

---

* 'We find by experience that the Smell of Musk is Obnoxious to Royal Personages – the Queen of G.B. was on the point of looking at some of my Works, the Inscriptions in our Garden (have you got them?) and a Plan of our House but was obliged to order them out of the Room – lest the Perfume should put us all into Mourning, this happened last Summer But We Did not hear it 'till last Week! We are busy in unsweetening our Drawers.' Sarah Ponsonby – Sarah Tighe, 7 June 1786, Webber MSS.

fruit, vegetables and flowers, lay to the south-eastern side of the
cottage, and was approached through a Gothick arch with a
pendant bell by which the gardener was summoned. Immediately behind the cottage a small lawn sloped away from the
library windows to a shrubbery. It was on this lawn, as Madame
de Genlis recalled, that the two friends loved to sit in summer
reading Ossian; Eleanor pronouncing the heart-stirring lines
while Sarah, lifting her eyes from time to time to the romantic
bulk of Dinas Bran over the valley, netted purses. Here, protected by lilacs, laburnums, syringas and white broom, they were
perfectly and charmingly secluded. For a shrubbery, before the
Victorians converted it into a jungle of ponticums, was a far
more inviting place, something more akin to the wild gardens of
Francis Bacon, Batty Langley or Gertrude Jekyll. A purely English inspiration, it was a retreat from the excessive formality of
the French gardens, and at its best it was a terrestrial Paradise,
beautiful as it was romantic.

Henry Phillips, a botanist whose books were to find a place in
the Plas Newydd library, devoted a complete work to the subject
of shrubberies; painting an inviting picture of a grove of carefully contrasted lilacs, laburnums, yews, filberts and wild white
cherries, and below them banks of yellow and silvery purple
crocus and drifts of wild wood anemones and primroses. Daisies
were to be encouraged in the turf, and even wild white convol-
vulus was to be persuaded to clamber through the powdery blue
foliage of young cedar trees. No wonder Eleanor and Sarah
enjoyed taking their books to such a spot on the hot June afternoons, or loved walking there inbreathing the scent of the white
lilacs on warm spring nights.

'. . . each walk' Mr Phillips continues of the shrubbery,
'should lead to some particular object; to the orchard, kitchen
garden, botanical borders, green-house, dairy, ice house, mushroom hut, aviary, poultry house or stables. The intention of the
plantation should seem to be to conduct the walker in the most
agreeable manner to each outlet and building of utility or pleasure.'[6] All of which corresponds to that 'wavy and shaded' gravel
walk which the Ladies were pleased to call the 'Home Circuit',
and which wound its way now to their model dairy, the fowl

yard and drying green, now to the flower, vegetable and fruit gardens.

Of the flowers, little remains to indicate how they were ordered, but letters from Sarah to her friend, Mrs Tighe, speak of borders of Snowdon pinks and gentianella that were 'above fifty yards long', as to variety, they had not been five years in the cottage before they had 'every Shrub and Perennial that was admired at Woodstock . . .' while Sarah's day-book for 1789 lists forty-four different kinds of roses that they were growing including old favourites like Maiden's Blush, Rosa Mundi, Rose d'Amour and the gorgeous and intensely fragrant 'Cabbage' or Provence roses.

But it was the fruit and vegetable gardens that peculiarly excited the admiration of their friend, Anna Seward, and about which she wrote ecstatically to a clergyman friend in the autumn of 1795; extolling the talents of the two friends who had converted two and a half acres of 'turnip ground' into 'a fairy palace amid the bowers of Calypso' !

'The kitchen garden is neatness itself' she reported.

Neither there, nor in the whole precincts, can a single weed be discovered. The fruit trees are of the rarest and finest sort, and luxuriant in their produce, the garden house and its implements, arranged in the exactest order.

Nor is the dairy house for one cow the least curiously elegant object of this magic domain. A short steep declivity shadowed over with tall shrubs, conducts us to the cool and clean repository. The white and shining utensils that contain the milk, and cream, and butter, are pure 'as snows thrice bolted in the northern blast'. In the midst, a little machine, answering the purpose of a churn enables the ladies to manufacture half a pound of butter for their own breakfast, with an apparatus which finishes the whole process without manual operation.

The wavy and shaded gravel walk which encircles this Elysium, is enriched with curious shrubs and flowers. It is nothing in extent and everything in grace and beauty and in variety of foliage; its gravel smooth as marble. In one part of it we turn upon a small knoll which overhangs a deep hollow glen. In its tangled bottom, a frothing brook leaps and clamours over the rough stones in its channel. A large spreading beech canopies the knoll and a semicircular seat beneath its boughs admits four people. A board, nailed to the elm [*sic*] has this inscription '*O cara Selva! e Fiunicello amato*.'[7]

In all likelihood they had culled the inscription from their favourite gardening book, Christopher Hirschfeld's *De l'Art des Jardins*. Published a year after their flight from Ireland, it still remains a delightful catalogue of everything to do with romantic gardening; its engravings ranging from designs for orangeries to hermit cabins, from funeral urns to rustic bridges. Sarah herself was much given to meticulously copying its beautiful illustrations.

For it must be confessed that the two Ladies were gardeners of the most picturesque sort; their library containing all the works of Gilpin and at least two copies of Price* on *The Picturesque*, besides other gardening manuals of a less exalted character.

They had most probably originally conceived of the 'two and a half acre turnip field' in the style of the *ferme ornée*, which the poet, William Shenstone, had made famous at his farmhouse, the Leasowes. Here, as Dr Johnson tells us: '. . . he began to point his prospects, to diversify his surface, to entangle his walks, and to wind his waters: which he did with such judgement and fancy, as made his little domain the envy of the great and the admiration of the skilful; a place to be visited by travellers and copied by designers.'[8]

The principles of this style, suitable for even the most modest-sized gardens, were laid out by Shenstone himself in an essay, *Unconnected Thoughts on Gardening*. The first consideration for the gardener was to study the character of his ground, to decide 'whether it be the grand, the savage, the sprightly, the melancholy, the horrid or the beautiful',[9] after which he must seek to introduce that all-important quality called Variety.

There was to be Variety within the garden itself in a series of pictures; variety in tone, texture and position of objects. Avenues, for instance, should show the art of distancing by a gradual tonal diminution, starting with yew, say, and grading through fir to almond-willow, to silver osier; an effect which

---

* Sir Uvedale Price (1747–1829), amateur gardener and with Payne Knight passionate advocate of the 'picturesque' as opposed to the Reptonian mode of gardening.

Eleanor Butler and Sarah Ponsonby had achieved by judicious planting in that part of the shrubbery which, for obvious reasons, they called the 'Infini', and beneath whose trees they had planted drifts of snowdrops and dropwort.

Another quality besides 'Variety' in the *ferme ornée* aesthetic was 'Novelty'; woods suddenly opening to disclose a prospect; a corner turned to reveal an obelisk, a cascade, a grot, a root house. In the jargon of the later Picturesque gardeners 'Novelty', which to Alexander Pope had been 'Surprise', was to be redubbed 'Unexpectedness'. It was a quality which, as readers of *Headlong Hall* will remember, could lead, when discussed, to some absurdity:

> 'Allow me,' said Mr Gall. 'I distinguish the picturesque and the beautiful, and I add to them in the laying out of grounds, a third and distinct character, which I call *unexpectedness*.'
> 'Pray sir,' said Mr Milestone 'by what name do you distinguish this character, when a person walks round the ground for the second time?'[10]

Eleanor Butler and Sarah Ponsonby were, to begin with at least, less concerned to startle with cascades and grots than with the miniature charm of their domestic offices; with the evocative sentiments in various romance languages that adorned their trees; with Gothic garden seats and a delightful summerhouse,* which was perched above the rushing stream and furnished with a miniature library of carefully selected books.

As the years went by, the two women were to become progressively more interested in wild gardening; renting land on both sides of the Cufflymen, that energetic brook Anna Seward had admired frothing in the 'tangled bottom', land which in due course was judiciously cleared and planted with 'a long birch avenue', giving thereby a view upstream of 'two mills at the same time'.[11] Rustic bridges, directly inspired by *L'Art des Jardins*, were then constructed across the deliciously picturesque torrent, thus giving opportunities for delightful airings on both banks, while a font, purloined from the ruins of a Valle Crucis abbey, was placed beneath the runnel of a piped spring and

---

* The foundations remain today.

allowed to develop romantic accretions of fern and moss.

By 1799 the Cufflymen itself was being artfully disciplined into cascades and pools, into one of which, that 'Dark deep pool above the cascade', they 'Ingurgitated' one fine Saturday afternoon in June, 'three live trouts'[12] that the miller's boy had given them.

By the end of the old century the garden was complete in its essentials, and although, as time went by, its character would become increasingly, not to say grotesquely Gothick, this may only have been because Eleanor and Sarah themselves were by then directing their attention ever more towards farming.

Back in 1791 however Eleanor Butler's accession to her Ormonde title and the expectancy of Lady Frances Douglas's pension had not only resulted in a new shrubbery but in plans to alter Plas Newydd itself.

The cottage as originally built had been simple enough; a substantial square stone building roofed with stone tiles. There were three upper over two lower windows on either side of a central door that was crowned by a stone pediment. It will be remembered that the room, part of which became the library, had been added to the south-eastern side of the cottage in 1778 before the two friends had taken up residence. By 1788 when Sarah Ponsonby sent a plan and drawings of Plas Newydd to Lady Frances Douglas this room had been converted into a brewing kitchen to the front of the cottage and at the back into a library with a bay and windows of pointed Gothick, though an inaccurate view of the cottage taken in 1792 shows them as being of a sash pattern. Two years later, an engraving in the *European Magazine* confirms that the windows were Gothick. A burst of activity recorded in the account book for 1792 further reveals that a new room and cellar were added to the back of the cottage that February, taking eight days to build and costing seven pounds, while in April 'carriage of Library Doors' costing seven shillings was recorded as an item in the account book. The doors, probably replacing plain square ones, were in the height of fashion, and the intriguing manner in which they were fitted was to send susceptible Miss Seward into transports of delight when she saw them three years later:

The ingenious friends have invented a kind of prismatic lantern which occupies the whole eliptic arch of the Gothick door. This lantern* is of cut glass variously coloured, enclosing the two lamps with their reflectors. The light it imparts resembles that of a volcano – sanguine and solemn. It is assisted by two glow worm lamps, that, in little marble reservoirs, stand on the opposite chimney-piece, and these supply the place of the here always chastised day-light, when the dusk of evening sables, or when night wholly involves the thrice lovely solitude.[13]

It seems that with this impressive contrivance the Ladies had to some degree anticipated the effect achieved later on by William Beckford† at Fonthill. James Storer's description of the famous octagon brings the Plas Newydd library at once to mind:

'... the light emitted through the painted windows of the octagon presents a most enchanting play of colours, and the effect produced by the sombre hue of twilight, contrasted with the vivid appearance at different hours of the day is indescribably pleasing.'[14]

By 1798 the first phase in the evolution of Plas Newydd was over. An unsigned though dated watercolour sketch, most probably taken by Harriet Bowdler, who was staying with them that October, shows the development thus far. As yet the projecting oriel windows which remain to this day have not appeared; instead the square windows on the first floor have been replaced with windows of a trefoil pattern while the pointed Gothick arch of the dressing-room window above the library can clearly be seen. Between 1798 and 1814, the charming confection will regrettably develop oriel windows aloft and richly carved oaken canopies below; later still, worse will happen; but for the time being it is perhaps at its most charming, a white-washed Gothick cottage of the earlier and lighter Strawberry Hill inspiration, gay, wittily literary, nestling amid its floral walks and fan-trained fruit, and facing on to its green field dotted with white sheep. It is a cottage of 'four small apartments' Anna Seward tells us, '... the exquisite cleanliness of the kitchen, its utensils

* Still to be seen at Plas Newydd today.

† William Beckford (1759–1844), collector of curios and works of art, lived in almost complete seclusion at Fonthill. He was the author of *Vathek* and two books of travel.

and its auxiliary offices vieing with the finished elegance of the gay, the lightsome little dining room* as that contrasts the gloomy yet superior grace of the library into which it opens'.[15]

Unsurprisingly Madame de Genlis, visiting the cottage that same year of 1792 with her accomplished 'adopted' daughter and pupil, Pamela, was overwhelmed by their rooms, views, pieces and garden, all of which she found 'ravissantes'. It was only after a night spent listening to the mournful wails of the Aeolian harp which the Ladies had secretly concealed beneath her window that the educatress, perhaps understandably, had second and graver thoughts about the whole ménage.

New room, new cellar, new library doors, new marble chimney-piece, carpets, curtains, upholstery. Nemesis struck almost immediately. By the fourth of June 1792 the account book was recording the 'Miraculous Intervention of Providence through a real Freind of my B's'. This was the sum of two hundred pounds from an unnamed donor. Without it they would have ended the year nearly two hundred and fifty pounds in debt, half their year's income. They were now in desperate straits; nothing had accrued from the accession of the Ormonde titles, nothing had yet been seen of the additional pension that Lady Frances Douglas had secured for them, while their original pension was now months in arrears. In their plight they wrote for help to Lady Frances, who, that November, appears to have succeeded in wresting a promise of two hundred pounds from the Treasury; a sum possibly made up of back instalments of the new pension already owing, together with a small advance. A month later this sum still had not arrived, and Eleanor was writing to the Treasury to inquire of its whereabouts, delicately but firmly stressing '... the particular Circumstances which Make the receipt of this Sum Most peculiarly important to me'.[16] Even then nothing was to arrive until the following June.

'The Times are so alarmingly frightful' Sarah was writing feelingly to Mrs Tighe. 'We believe the end of the World is at no great distance. What is your opinion?'[17]

---

*The dining-room was painted white, the seats of its Sheraton chairs worked in pale blue convolvuli on a white background.

She alluded not only to their own affairs. Back in the July of 1791 while they were peacefully planning the new shrubbery the Birmingham dissenters had by all accounts antagonized the entire town by celebrating the anniversary of the French Revolution, drinking treasonable toasts 'as confusion to the present Government and etc.' The consequent rioting and burning had lasted for the best part of a week until dragoons from Nottingham had restored order.

Sarah Ponsonby had written to Mrs Tighe of the events ten days later,

'... the Coach which passed through Llangollen a few hours since, brought intelligence that the Birmingham riots had begun again – and though that town is ninety-one miles from hence we are assured that the Inhabitants of Shrewsbury which is but thirty entertain serious apprehensions for their own safety on account of the many dissenters it contains and if a very numerous Mob should assemble so near us – have we not some reason, my dear friend, to tremble for the Safety of Our Cottage?'[18]

In a true sense the end of the world was at no great distance, that is to say the world of the old régime. Had not Harriet Bowdler written of a preacher at Bath who had spoken of the *right* of the poor to relief, and that 'the power of bestowing it was the most valuable privilege of the rich'?[19]

By 1792 in the name of this very right France was at war with Austria; now in the February of 1793, having endured the ghastly purge of the September massacres, having executed her King, she declared war simultaneously on Holland and England. 'Here is an odd Idea now' Mrs Piozzi confided to *Thraliana*, 'that the Beast of the Revelations is this French Democracy.'[20]

At home in England a situation perilously akin to civil war appeared to be developing. The inflammatory offers of French aid to the oppressed of all nations had, unsurprisingly, thrown the governing classes into such a state of panic that all judgement was flung to the winds. Against a background of increasing poverty a witch hunt was set afoot to root out all those symptoms of the radicalism which, even before the Republican decree of 'fraternity and assistance', had been seeking by constitutional and other means to reform and democratize English society.

In the February of 1793 John Frost, an attorney and member of the Corresponding Society, which advocated manhood suffrage, annual parliaments and controls over the enclosure movement, was pilloried and sent to prison for 'seditious conversation'; while in the following August another lawyer, Thomas Muir, founder of the Scottish Friends of the People, was sentenced to fourteen years' transportation for the same offence. Such persecutions were only the prelude to many more, though they did not succeed in muffling the Jacobinical voices which were to be heard as far afield as the Ladies' own North Wales, which was 'infested', we are told, 'by itinerant Methodist preachers who descant on the Rights of Man and attack Kingly Government'.[21]

There were to be concurrent troubles, if on a minor scale, at Plas Newydd. In that forward spring, when in February Mrs Piozzi was recording 'Blackbirds already beginning to whistle tho faintly', and Hens all wanting to sit, and Primroses and Polyanthus crowding the hedges, Mary Carryll tripped over her favourite cat on her way upstairs and nearly broke her skull; while that summer Eleanor, ever accident-prone, would fall likewise and fracture her arm. She would soon recover, however, and Harriet Bowdler, staying with them, would conjure Sarah to let the patient '. . . sing French songs as much as she pleases, but lock up her pen and ink'.[22]

Around them the times continued uneasy: not only was Jacobinism threatening but financial disruption, the complexities of paper money contributing to the failure of numerous private banks. Harriet Bowdler was to write to them of a family known to her where the father was actually in hiding, 'a Banker is liable to arrest for every five guinea Bill, and it is impossible to know into what wretched hands they may fall'.[23] Rebellion too was imminent in Ireland, and no one, not even the Austrians, seemed capable of holding the terrible French. The Ladies consoled themselves for the horror of the times by taking refuge in Judgement Day prophesies and in learning Spanish. In April 1793 Sarah was able to report to Mrs Tighe that Eleanor was able to read '. . . whole Cantos of the Araucana without even once or twice looking into the dictionary'[24] while she herself was able to read three or four successive lines after her dearest Better Half had explained them to her.

But in spite of such pleasant diversions money affairs still clamoured for attention, for neither Lady Douglas's new pension, which took effect that June, nor yet their own very considerable retrenchment, could mitigate the effect of steeply rising prices.

A certain amount of what would seem to have been well-justified spleen was now directed at Eleanor's sister-in-law in their correspondence. 'She knows that one hundred pounds would remove any present or future *pecuniary* thorn from our pillows – that one syllable from her, would instantly procure it, for my B. has been besought to utter that syllable in vain . . .' Sarah wrote indignantly to Mrs Tighe that October on behalf of Eleanor, 'the *Sole*' in Sarah's opinion 'Inheritrix of all the Ormonde Virtues'. She ended the letter a day later after having just heard the appalling news from Europe: 'Alas! for the poor Queen of France!' and she concluded with the diurnal refrain, not only common to them now but to Mrs Piozzi and all like ladies, 'don't you think the end of the world approaches?'[25]

On New Year's Eve Harriet Bowdler took up a commiserating pen upon the subject of the 'pecuniary thorn'. 'I should indeed have been *agreeably surprised* if I had heard of anything worthy of the Ormonde name from its present possessors, but I hoped that no circumstances cd now arise to make it necessary that you should deprive yourselves of Attendants wch must be very essential to your comfort . . .'[26]

Shortage of money had by now become so pressing that they were cutting down on their domestic staff; discharging their quasi-footman Edward Parry that September, and following this up by retiring the gardener and engaging Simon, a man of all work, for a reduced wage of nine shillings a week. Edward Parry, for all that he had been given two months' wages in lieu of notice, had protested vehemently. 'That most ungrateful and mean', Sarah wrote of him with peevishness in the account book.

Her ruffled temper was soon soothed however by Harriet Bowdler's wholehearted approbation of her course of action, '. . . from the bottom of my heart I honour you for doing it' wrote that lady of their economies, adding that she personally would rather live on bread and water in the poorest cottage than have to worry about debts.

As Miss Bowdler's pen was scratching the old year away at Hammersmith, the Dowager Lady Ormonde, the proud restorer of the family fortunes, the impenetrable, the unforgiving, was breathing her last in the restored grandeur of Kilkenny Castle.

'. . . nothing could induce us ever to re-visit Ireland' Sarah had written that autumn to Mrs Tighe, 'except the Dowager Lady Ormonde were to make it a point of duty with My Better half to go for her last Blessing, which however, we tremble but to think of – with that we dare not refuse to comply lest our future life should be embittered by self reproach.'[27]

They need not have concerned themselves. When the time came, not only did the Dowager prove totally undesirous of bestowing a blessing upon her youngest daughter, but it seemed that she had not even mentioned her in her will.

It was the most bitter blow yet. With each change in the family fortunes: at her father's death, on her brother's accession to the titles, and now at the death of her mother, Eleanor Butler had counted upon recognition, and with recognition upon the impressive expectation which she believed was due to her under the terms of her brother's marriage settlement. But it was clear now, as it should have been long ago, that the expectancy would never be forthcoming; that, in short, she was not to be forgiven for her rash flight with Sarah Ponsonby fifteen years before.

Appalled at the pass to which she had brought them both, her sleep became plagued with nightmares, while her waking hours were obsessed with fears of what might happen as a result of their increasing poverty; fears that they might have to give up the cottage and return to Ireland, fears even of the debtors' prison itself. Meanwhile Sarah saw with anguish that her friend was fast approaching a nervous breakdown.

In letters to Mrs Tighe Sarah tended to emphasize Eleanor's

humiliation at being forgotten by her mother rather than her despair at their financial predicament; it no doubt struck her as more seemly. In actual fact although the humiliations of her friend's childhood, and in particular the remembrance of the bitter feud between brother and sister, must have been brought to mind with painful force once more, it is hard to credit a wholehearted affection in Eleanor for a mother with whom she never corresponded and news of whom would always provoke a proud 'as if we cared' in the journal. Added to which a very obvious spurt of building in the account book for the beginning of 1794, and at a time when retrenchment was the order of the day, suggests that Madam Butler may have been poorly for some time, and her death not a little slyly anticipated.

Soon slightly more cheering news was to come leaking back from the Castle. Eleanor it now appeared had not been forgotten after all! In her mother's will, of which she had not yet seen a copy, she had been left the sum of one hundred pounds. It was paltry enough but, as Sarah was quick to write Mrs Tighe, '. . . the instant She had reason to know that she was not totally forgot by her last surviving Parent it is impossible for me to describe its effect on her Noble Mind, and She immediately sent to the nearest Roman Catholick Clergyman to have Masses and every other proper respect showed to her Mother's Memory — which having left so few of Her own persuasion amongst her numerous descendants it is possible might have been totally unprofessed, since then' Sarah concluded 'her dear mind has been easy indeed.'[28]

This in fact was something short of the truth, for it was not long before they were bitterly reflecting on the injustice of the legacy in their correspondence with friends. '. . . the Legacy would have been much greater' Sarah explained to Mrs Tighe, 'had she [the Dowager] been suffered to have followed her own inclination – which in fact would have induced her not to make any will and in that case My B would have been intitled to her Legal portion of an immense property. But Lady Ormonde longed for her Diamonds and Pearls and etc etc *all* of which She has now taken *entire* possession of – and to compleat the meaness, (I might be justified in saying the *Treasury* of her Conduct)'

Kilkenny Castle
Woodstock House

Madam Butler

Walter Butler de jure
Earl of Ormonde

John Butler Earl of
Ormonde, from a
painting by
George Stubbs

Lady Betty Fownes

Sir William Fownes

A miniature of Sarah Ponsonby, aged about twenty-one

Lady in a Tall Hat said to be a portrait of Eleanor Butler

Mary Carryll

Mrs Sarah Tighe

As they found it

1788

1794

98, from a sketch
Harriet Bowdler

above left c. 1810
centre c. 1815
below left, c. 1815, from a sketch by Harriet Pigot
above Miss Lolly and Miss Andrew take over
below Finale under Mrs G. H. Robertson, including
General Yorke's alterations

The souvenir portfolio for Lady Frances Douglas, drawn by Sarah Ponsonby

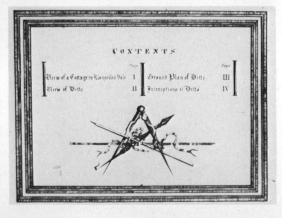

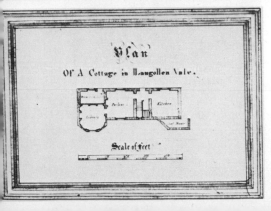

Plan

Of A Cottage in Llangollen Vale.

Scale of feet

Garden Gothick

The new porch, 1814

The entrance to the
grounds, from a
sketch by Lady
Leighton

The bird table, from a sketch by Lady Leighton

The font from Vale Crucis Abbey

The tomb of the Ladies and their maid, from a sketch
by Lady Leighton

she indignantly punned, 'a large collection of Books, known to be Lawfully belonging to Lady Eleanor are amongst these ill acquired treasures – and she wishes to have it thought that My B's name was omitted in her Mother's will . . . the Deceit in respect of this will' she concluded 'is still more shocking than that practised about the late Lord Ormonde's – though that was bad enough, but since then Lady Ormonde has *professed* herself our *friend*'.[29]

When this shocking news reached Harriet Bowdler in one of those numerous letters that habitually winged back and forth between her and Sarah Ponsonby, she was suitably indignant: 'As to diamonds and Pearls if they can adorn the little person or please the little mind of the countess God bless her with them they are only playthings for children, but why is my sweet Viellard to lose the Books? I cannot think they can be of any use to her Sister in Law.'[30]

On 20 February, and after repeated applications, the post brought a copy of the will at last. There it was, exactly as reported, a legacy for one hundred pounds, and although loyal Miss Bowdler expressed a wish that a nought might be added to the sum, even one thousand pounds would have been negligible in view of those great expectations which had now been finally and cruelly disappointed.

It was now, with apparently so little to lose, that Eleanor Butler made one last effort to secure that additional one hundred a year which they both so fondly believed could completely alter their circumstances. It was little enough to ask of Lady Ormonde, a woman whose own private income was sixteen thousand pounds a year, or so it was reported. A woman too, who, for all Eleanor Butler's angry scorn, was well liked in society and much loved by her dependants.* But alas, Eleanor's letter, with its undertones of menace, was hardly likely to arouse much sympathy.

Dear Lady Ormonde, Your silence to the recent application I troubled you with the first of this month (an instance of disregard to

---

* It was said that an aged tenant whose family had been lords of Lady Ormonde's estate in pre-Cromwellian times had 'willed' it to her on his death-bed.

yourself and me for which I was totally unprepared) will influence my abridging (much as is possible) the present intrusion on your attention.

Last Thursday's post brought a Duplicate of the Will accompanied by your promise of letting me know 'when' I may be permitted to draw for the One Hundred Pounds my Mother had the goodness to bequeath me. In Seven Weeks from the Event which added so considerably to your already Princely Resources could nothing be afforded except a promise of future information when I might apply for such a sum?

I shall only lead your Observation to the evident, the unmerited cruelty of this treatment! It may indeed be pronounced so unexampled, that with difficulty will it obtain belief. Equally incredible must it appear that my remonstrance to *Your Friendship* and my *Brother's justice* experienced no other return than a *Silent* Contempt. But now (impelled by many powerful motives, independent of my own particular interests) I once more conjure you to bestow even a momentary consideration on the *Moderate Object* of that remonstrance, and the claims I have upon those to whom it was addressed. Let me also remind you that though for near sixteen Years the constant Inhabitant of 'so remote a dwelling' yet when the Title of Ormande is pronounced at St James this ensuing Birthday the recollections of a Daughter and Sister of that House will consequently be awakened to the minds of some distinguished Characters in the circle, many of whom, as your Ladyship cannot be ignorant, I have the happiness to count in the list of acquaintance and not a few in that of my *real* friends. If the eyes of these persons should unanimously turn towards you on your first introduction to their majesties, let it be I entreat with that degree of approbation which it shall prove my immediate business to convince them you are entitled to from all who feel an interest in my welfare, if by obtaining me the slender addition of One hundred a year you at once fulfill my utmost ambition and Secure to yourself my liveliest Gratitude. I have only one additional favour to solicit, it is the Obligation of not being kept in a state of painful suspense, but that whatever may be your determination, you will without delay communicate it to, dear Lady Ormonde,

Your Most faithful and most Obedient Humble Servant,
Eleanor Butler[31]

As desired she was not kept long in suspense:

Madam, I applyed to your Brother on your first application to me some years ago, for an addition of One Hundred a Year to your allowance, and he refused my request, as he says that the addition he has already made to it, is in his opinion, more than you could expect from your former conduct towards him, and also he thinks it sufficient for you. I *then* and not till then, that I might not do you an injury, showed him your last Letters to me. You can't be surprised that after such unmerited ill treatment as I have experienced from you in your last two letters, that I should decline all future correspondence. Your Brother desires I may inform you that your Legacy is lodged at Mr Le Touches and that you may draw for it when you chuse.

I am, Madam,
Yours,
Anne Ormonde[32]

The matter was closed. The money, when she finally received it, had been reduced by the poor rate of exchange to ninety-two pounds, three shillings and fourpence.

Chapter Seven

'Three-thirty till Nine.' 1794–1809

The times were growing worse. By the end of 1793 the French Royalist rising at Toulon, which had been supported by the English navy under Hood, had been decisively crushed by the Republican artillery commanded by the rising young officer, Napoleon Buonaparte.

'The accounts from Toulon haunt me night and day', Harriet Bowdler was writing to her two friends early in the New Year. 'I fear this affair will kill our generous high-spirited Lord Hood, he has however, and the Nation has, one powerful consolation, in the consciousness that from first to last the English have done all that Men cd do . . .'¹ By March a French invasion was hourly expected, Mrs Piozzi noting in *Thraliana* that '. . . the Carmagnols are even said to be upon the sea'² while Harriet Bowdler, begging Sarah Ponsonby on the one hand not to lose confidence in Mr Pitt, was advising her on the other to '. . . remember what I said last year, and keep a few guineas in the Drawer . . . I am persuaded our people wd fight like Lions but we might feel the want of a guinea to purchase bread before all was settled.'²

It was all very fine for Miss Bowdler to prate about guineas in drawers. Their need for ready money was becoming desperate. There was no longer the remotest hope of relief from the Ormondes, and their pensions were now eight months in arrears. By October they were anticipating fifty pounds of Mrs Goddard's promised legacy to Sarah, while all through the next year, with the exception of a fifty-pound gift from Sarah's brother, Chambre, they were driven to buttress their economy with loans; among others, so grave was their plight, from Letitia Barrett, with whom there must have been some form of reconciliation.

At the beginning of 1796 news reached them which was to increase their anxiety to fever pitch; they were to learn that on Christmas Day Lord Ormonde had died, bringing a feud of fifty five years' standing between brother and sister to an end at last. Would it also bring with it, they anxiously asked each other, the cessation of Eleanor's allowance as well? Asides in the journal suggest that the new head of the family was by no means strikingly sympathetic towards them, and if he were as much under his mother's influence as his father had been, would he devote much thought to that disgraced aunt dwelling in her remote Welsh mountains?

By June the Civil List had stopped payment and their pensions were six quarters in arrears and 'likely to continue increasingly so – while the War endures',[3] and in the same letter Sarah was writing to Mrs Tighe that Eleanor was prostrate as a result of 'the shock Her noble mind has *sustained* in consequence of an application to her nephew (the present Lord Ormonde) being ineffectual'.[4]

The application may either have been for a loan or an increased allowance. As it was, while the account book reveals no loan, it does show that the usual allowance was being continued. By the year's end a gift from Eleanor's relative, the open-handed Lord Thurles, together with some back payments of their pension, had seen them through, though not before they had been driven to consider, albeit not very seriously, the possibility of mortgaging their pensions. 'I think being in debt, very often makes people look thin and feel apt to take cold'[5] Sarah wrote pathetically to Mrs Tighe.

Their private distress was reflected in the country as a whole, where people like themselves on fixed incomes were in desperate straits, where bankruptcies had become a common occurrence, and where the poor, as a result of low wages and astronomical prices, were actually starving. 'Famine and insurrection threatening us *within*' Mrs Piozzi was writing gloomily, 'whilst Invasion is avowedly the Design of our Neighbour the French – *without*.'[6]

How did they maintain their spirits? Anna Seward, meeting them both for the first time in that anxious summer of 1795, had commented on Eleanor's face, 'round and fair with the glow of luxuriant health', and had described her figure as 'somewhat beyond the enbonpoint as to plumpness', which hardly suggests the ravages of excessive worry. Perhaps the description of Sarah was more telling: 'A face rather long than round, a complexion clear, but without bloom, with a countenance which from its soft melancholy has peculiar interest.'[7]

If Sarah both by temperament and as a consequence of keeping the accounts did most of the worrying, she also had her own explanation of how they coped: 'We ... endeavour to amuse our working hours with all the comfortable day dreams of which we are capable praying and endeavouring to hope for better times.'[8]

Their prayers were needed. In the autumn, piqued by British activity in the West Indies, Spain declared war, and it seemed that Britain, having given up Corsica and Elba, must lose all influence in the Mediterranean. But in fact, as the Ladies bravely prepared to settle down for the winter, welcoming the frost and snow, 'which will I hope keep us a good while alone and allow us to amuse ourselves',[9] matters were already growing slightly better.

Early in 1797, Mary Carryll, whose health had been causing them great anxiety throughout the previous autumn, seemed, after a barrage of emetics and nostrums from the 'little doctor', to be improving; and soon Anna Seward was writing, as was customary, to congratulate her friends on the 'dispersion' of the Spanish fleet by Jervis and Nelson at Cape St Vincent. Meanwhile in the account book Sarah was recording a minor triumph: 'February 10th from Evan Williams for Potatoes we sold him, £1 : 10 :0.' Small as the amount was it was a presage of things to come. The two Ladies, in response to the demands of the time, were turning farmers.

They had always kept one cow, but by September 1796 they had acquired another. They were already renting extra land on which they had grown two rood and a quarter of lucerne, and by the end of the year were leasing Aber Adda field from the vicar.

Soon the correspondence with Mrs Tighe would be full, not as once with religious discussion of a methodistical hue, but with vivacious dialogues as to the respective merits of different wheats and cattle feeds.

By the summer of 1797 their financial affairs had been so far improved by a timely gift of a hundred pounds from the new Lord Ormonde and the back payment of several instalments of their pensions, that in July they took what appears to have been their first and only holiday.

On the twenty-fifth of the month they climbed into the *Hand* chaise, and with Dick Morris driving them, set out for the coastal resort of Barmouth.

Their way took them along the well-worn tourist route, now contained in the southern portion of the Snowdonia National Park; past rounded green hills covered with browsing sheep; past the broad lapping Bala lake where the woman leech-gatherer lived and the wise old man who attended the accouchements of their cows; on to Dolgellau with a pause to inspect Cymer Abbey, and on again, past smooth winding rivers until one, the Mawddach, opened out at last into a great estuary, beyond which they could glimpse the cloudy green sea that they had not set eyes on for nineteen years.

According to contemporary accounts Barmouth then was no more seductive than it is now. Although the fishermen's cottages were quoined into the mauve shale cliffs with a picturesque irregularity that put tourists in mind of Edinburgh and Gibraltar, and caused them to marvel how 'one neighbour, as he stands at his door, may look down the chimney of another', the houses at the foot of the cliff were regularly inundated with the flying sand which blew everywhere and rendered the town impassable in rainy weather.

This charmless spot was redeemed however by the presence of a first-rate inn, the *Corsygedol Arms*, run by Mrs Lewis. It was here, where a disillusioned tourist noted with some astonishment that the dining-room contained 'Upwards of thirty persons, most of them of fortune and fashion',[10] that the Ladies stayed.

With reawakened memories of that first tour that they had made together nineteen years ago they determined to see all they could in the short time at their disposal; had no sooner arrived that evening than they set out for a 'water excursion' which cost them two shillings, while the following day Dick drove them over the flatly unpicturesque road to Harlech Castle. The day after they began leisurely wending their way home, probably halted to inspect a waterfall or two, certainly spent the night at Bala, and arrived back at the cottage on the evening of the twenty-eighth. The whole trip had cost them the not inconsiderable sum of eight pounds, ten shillings and ninepence.

Blowing sand notwithstanding, the jaunt to Barmouth must have been a sweetener for all that had gone before, yet the trying period they had just been through had not been without its compensations.

In spite of scarifying financial anxiety their life in fact had continued uninterrupted even to its minutest details. That is to say they could still find a shilling for the 'Poor little dancing dogs' which had wrung their hearts. No doubt this had been a troupe of terriers like the one Bewick drew; pathetically balancing on their hind legs after a man with a fife, each with a sad little gauze skirt around its middle. They could still spare a shilling for 'Little Molly encouragement for going well dressed to Church'; spend sixpence on holly berries or on their gardener's small son rolling the lawn; while they could always spare sums for the crowd of unfortunates which haunted Llangollen: the blind harpers; 'lame handed' women; old soldiers; 'two terrific sailors', as well as 'Poor Mary Green' who was regularly supported at the rate of a shilling a week.

There had been the usual expeditions to Oswestry and Wrexham to look forward to besides visits to their country neighbours. Recorded in the account book are frequent airings with Miss Letitia Barrett, among which was one to see an aqueduct and another to picnic at the Eglwyseg rocks, which suggests that by 1796, there had been a *détente*, possibly as a consequence of the death of Miss Elizabeth Barrett in 1792. They had also made two flattering and delightful new friendships: Anna Seward and Hester Piozzi.

In the August of 1795, Miss Anna Seward, that celebrated authoress, whose verses upon the voyages of Captain Cook even so harsh a critic as Dr Johnson had seen fit to admire, was visiting friends at Dinbren close to Llangollen. Her hosts, the Reverend Mr and Mrs Roberts, were already friends of the Ladies, and it was not long before an introduction was effected. In all the poetess was thrice invited to tea at Plas Newydd; had met and been charmed there by Mrs Tighe's son, Harry, and his wife, Mary,* also a poetess; had, as a climax to her visit, been invited, at the Ladies' instigation, to a 'rural dinner' given by Mrs Ormsby, among the ruins of Valle Crucis Abbey.

Three chaise and two phaetons full of guests arrived to dine in a setting that could scarcely have been more romantic.

'We found the scenery of Valle-Crucis grand, silent, impressive, awful'[11] wrote Miss Seward to a friend of this serene and unalarming spot. While the guests strolled about the grass and the hired harper played his soul-haunting airs; while Miss Seward and the Ladies, no doubt plagued by midges, mutually pondered 'the deep repose, resulting from the high umbrageous mountains'; the friendship ripened. By the time her visit was over Miss Seward left Denbighshire resolved to nurture such an interesting new acquaintanceship.

An agreeable correspondence now sprang up between the three women in which Miss Seward sent her poems and her own long criticisms of other people's, to which Eleanor Butler and Sarah Ponsonby responded with further criticisms (eulogies in the case of Miss Seward's work) and long transcriptions of verbal distinctions culled from *Chambers's Encyclopedia* interspersed with presents of fruit trees.

It was a correspondence of which only Anna Seward's side was to be published, but from which it is possible to infer that all three discovered themselves to be in perfect agreement upon such matters as the power of beautiful scenery to ameliorate sorrow; the 'false Duessa' of Republican freedom; the indelicacy of certain of Madame Roland's memoirs; the superiority of the wild and extravagant as exemplified in *The Mysteries of Udolpho* over the 'mild *Evelina* or the rigid *Cecilia* of Miss Burney'; and they were unanimous in their praise of the admirably 'forestian' quality of the Reverend Mr Munday's long

* Mary Tighe (1773–1810), authoress of *Psyche*.

poem, *Needwood Forest*, deeming it far preferable to William Cowper's on *Windsor*.

Unsurprisingly it was not long before the sentiments aroused by her visit to Plas Newydd drove Anna Seward to composition, and soon *Llangollen Vale** was dispatched to the two friends. They received it with ecstasy. Sarah Ponsonby was now invited by the authoress to design a vignette of the cottage with Dinas Bran in the background by way of a frontispiece to the published work. The vignette, carefully executed, as if by a diligent mouse, but hardly original in its composition, duly arrived, and it was now Anna Seward's turn to express rapture. She had, however, some difficulty in defending the vignette in a long letter to her friend, Mrs Powys, herself a lady of taste and judgement, who had disturbingly expressed discontent with nearly every aspect of the cottage's situation.

'I hope to reconcile you to the vignette by observing that it was my request to the Rosalind and Celia of Llangollen Vale, that my poem on that Vale might be enriched with a view of their habitation on its title page . . .'[12] Miss Seward was at pains to explain to the uncompromising Mrs Powys. She agreed that the view might have presented a more striking part of the Vale, but it would then have been less eligible as having less connection with the poetry. Certainly Lady Eleanor Butler's and Miss Ponsonby's interesting retreat might have been placed where it would have had sublimer scenic accompaniments, but its site was sufficiently lovely, sufficiently romantic. Mrs Powys should realize that when the two females had meant to sit down for life in a sylvan retirement with a small establishment of servants, it had become necessary that the desire of landscape-charms should become subservient to the more material considerations of health, protection and convenience. Their scene, not on those

---

* The final lines run thus :

> ' Through Eleanora and her Zara's mind
> Early though genius, taste, and fancy flowed,
> Through all the graceful arts their powers combined,
> And her last polish brilliant life bestowed ;
> The lavish promises in life's soft morn,
> Pride, pomp, and love, their friends the sweet enthusiasts scorn.'

wild heights which must have exposed them to the mountain storms, was yet on a dry gravelly bank, favourable to health and exercise, and sheltered by a background of rocks and hills. Instead of seeking the picturesque banks of the dashing river foaming through its craggy channel, whose spray and mists would have been confined, and therefore unwholesome, by the vast rocks and mountains towering on either hand, they had contented themselves with the briery dell and its prattling brook, which descended abruptly from a reach of that winding walk, which formed the bounds of their smiling, though small domain. Situated in an opener part of the valley, Anna Seward firmly explained, they breathed a purer air, while their vicinity to the town of Llangollen afforded the comforts of convenience and the confidence of safety.[13]

At about the same time as Mrs Powys was being so minutely enlightened, Mr Chappelow, the botanizing parson, who had long been a friend of the Ladies, and in particular a much treasured correspondent of Eleanor's* was meditating another introduction. It was one that had been 'an important object in the confessed ambition of the Ladies *for many years past*'.[14] So it was that in July 1796, when, to meet the exigencies of the times, it was fashionable to be cutting out pastry and reducing each servant to a quartern loaf a week in order to set a good example, Mr Chappelow contrived a meeting between his two Ladies and Mrs Hester Piozzi. She, in response to the call of her ancient Cambrian blood, had newly come to settle with her Italian husband just over the hills from Llangollen in the valley of the Clywd.

Soon visits and counter-visits were taking place between Plas Newydd and Brynbella, Mrs Piozzi's elegant villa. 'Eel and trouts for Mr and Mrs Piozzi', or 'Preparations for the Piozzis who dined here', were to become familiar entries in the account book as the two friends ensnared the singer and his wife on their

* 'Mr Chappelow has renounced My Correspondence I believe, and 'tis no Small Loss to me: he used to tell me Twenty pretty things that Were going forward . . .' Lady Eleanor Butler to Mrs Piozzi. Undated. Rylands English MS. 892. *Ladies of Llangollen.*

way to and from Bath; and on one occasion they were so obliging as to arrange for the carriage of Mr Piozzi's pianoforte over
the Horse Shoe Pass.

The correspondence resulting from this friendship was to be
rather different from that which they were enjoying with Anna
Seward, and perhaps not quite so much to their taste. There was
little of the lush about Mrs Piozzi, although even she could have
her moments; but as she firmly informed Eleanor, 'My Genius
certainly does *not* lead me to Works of Imagination . . .'[15] a statement which must have caused some disappointment at the cottage. It is unsurprising therefore to find her letters less concerned with aesthetics and more with lawsuits, the price of meat,
the effect of the weather, the marriages, advantageous or otherwise, of mutual friends, and the misbehaviour of her daughters.
Nevertheless the two Ladies were to find much to please them in
this stringent association: Mrs Piozzi's impressive learning, her
anecdotes of the great and much admired Doctor, her quick
humour. It says much for the admiration that they entertained
for each other that the Ladies did Mrs Piozzi the honour of
adopting the parody Mr Chappelow had written on her famous
Ode to Society, as a heading for the journal:

> In these blest Shades We two maintain,
> A peaceful unmolested Reign;
> No turbulent Desires intrude,
> In our Repose – and Solitude.

Though not born of 'Desire', turbulence of another kind
would soon interrupt that dignified repose which all through the
first months of 1798 had been supervising, rather oddly, the
making of a 'Potatoe garden'. At times twenty labourers had
been employed on this project, being afterwards rewarded with
copious draughts of ale. The potato garden had been only finished a week when Sarah was expressing doubts to Mrs Tighe
about the way events were shaping in Ireland.

In point of fact only bad weather and worse seamanship had
prevented a French invasion of the country in the previous December. Now, the possibility of a more successful French landing coupled with the fear of the revolutionary body of United

Irishmen, had resulted in the Ascendancy taking exaggerated coercive measures. These had provoked an abortive rising in Dublin, which in May flared up again in Naas, Carlow and Wexford; general opinion interpreting the risings as symptoms of a social revolution on the French pattern.

Both Ladies with the horrors of the September massacres still painfully fresh in their minds were naturally terrified for the safety of their Irish friends, and letters to Mrs Tighe were dashed off daily from Sarah's agitated pen, explaining how her poor head had been turned by 'horrid realities'; her sleep disturbed by terrifying dreams of what might have happened at Woodstock.

Llangollen itself was seething with rumours brought over by the Irish travellers. On 27 May the landlady of the *Hand* had stopped the two friends on their way to church to tell them that she '*suspected* Lady E. Fitzgerald was in her house'. Pamela, who had visited them with Madame de Genlis six years back and who was now married to Lord Edward Fitzgerald, one of the moving spirits in the Irish rebellion, did indeed turn out to be at the inn. 'We could not bear the idea of avoiding her in such a situation' Sarah wrote to Mrs Tighe, 'therefore sent word that if the Lady was as we believed an acquaintance of ours ... we were within call'.[16] There was a brief ten-minute meeting, and both Ladies burst into tears at the plight of the poor fugitive and her children, a small daughter of three and a delicate baby boy of five weeks old. 'She had an idea of passing the day here,' Sarah went on, 'but we persuaded her principally for her own sake and a little for [our] own to proceed as fast and as incognito as possible to London, the mind of the people in this country being so exasperated against the Cause in which she was, I fear deeply engaged, that one dreaded her being insulted. But our Angels, (our neighbours are nearly such at least) suffered her to pass unreproved except in their looks.'[17]

News of the worst kind was now confirmed from Ireland. By the twenty-fifth of the month the rebels had taken the town of Enniscorthy where Mary Carryll's old mother lived, and there were immediate fears for her safety. From all sides the post was bringing sympathetic letters to Plas Newydd, for in spite of past protestations to the contrary, many of the Ladies' affections and interests were still bound up with their home country.

This was well understood by their close friends, and in particular by Harriet Bowdler who had fortunately taken Tower, Mr Whalley's old house in Llangollen, for the summer. She was now only too glad to bestow boundless sympathy.

By the end of June tidings had reached the cottage not only of hairbreadth escapes from the rebels by Harry Tighe and Sarah's own brother, Chum, but news that the rebels had also burned down Borris, Eleanor's brother-in-law's house of unhappy memory, and that her sister-in-law's mansion at Castelcomer had also been attacked and plundered. The last piece of news may have been received with something like equanimity on their part, but not that final news for which they had all been waiting, and which, when it reached them at last, was of the saddest. Mary Carryll's mother had been murdered at Enniscorthy.*

Small wonder that on 16 July Sarah was writing to Mrs Piozzi to decline an invitation to Brynbella for the delicate reason that for the time being they had cancelled all social engagements out of respect for those friends who had suffered in the rebellion.

By September General Lake had in hand what some called the rebellion, and others were now calling the revolution; and Harriet Bowdler, now 'dear, dear H.B.' in the account book, had gone back to Bath. She had left behind the kindest of memories with both Ladies, who now sought to take some sort of retrospective view of the whole terrible Irish episode: 'It is Democratic and French Principles alone – which began with removing their God, and their King – from whence such diabolical Acts can proceed' Sarah wrote to Mrs Tighe. The Irish priests of the old school had all behaved well, she maintained, and had not killed Protestants; the fault had lain with the younger priests, 'They were educated in France.'[18] It was disturbing none the less to hear from Miss Bowdler that Pitt had sympathized with the Irish rebellion, and equally disturbing that Mrs Tighe's eldest son, William, had entertained liberal views on the subject.

* In fact a legacy of five pounds to her mother 'if living at the time of my decease' features in Mary's will made in 1808, which suggests that the report of her death was a rumour.

While they thus pondered the events of this unhappy year, a gift was on its way to them. It arrived in November, a small Alderney cow with an envelope attached to her horns by a ribbon. She had walked all the way from Bath. Inside the envelope was a sheet bearing the following verses:

> From Alderney's far distant shore
> Encircled by the stormy main
> I come that pity to implore
> Which misery asks *not here* in vain.
>
> Oh gentle Ladies of the vale
> Receive a young and friendless guest
> Indulgent hear my artless tale
> And give a weary wanderer rest.

She was a present from Harriet Bowdler. '. . . as gentle as a lamb as tame as a lapdog',[19] Sarah wrote delightedly to Mrs Tighe of this new addition to their farm, which that year had earned them seven guineas from barley and two pounds, seven shillings from potatoes.

Although the end of the world had been so frequently prophesied, life, somewhat surprisingly, had continued. Thirty loads of muck were trundled in to enrich the Plas Newydd policies that January, and the Ladies were by now so completely reconciled with Letitia Barrett that she went down as 'Dear Mrs Barrett' in the account book, when a turkey at three shillings was bespoken in her honour on 14 January. That summer, despite increased taxation on windows and dogs, they were writing and dining serenely beneath the lime trees they had planted. There was the usual stream of visitors, among others the Piozzis and Mr Chappelow, while Anna Seward came to enjoy the autumn tints in the Vale that September.

It was only in October that a note of discord was sounded in the account book: 'Stamp for a Receipt of our Half Years rent to John Edwards which *He says* should be £12:5:9. There fore he is paid £12:5:9.'

This appeared to be a peccadillo over threepence. The rent had stood at twelve pounds, five shillings and sixpence for the two previous years, although it had once been threepence more in 1795 under John Edwards's father. But what at first sight appeared to be no more than petty provocation on John Edwards's part, soon assumed a far more serious aspect. One which rendered the two Ladies almost senseless with terror as a spate of unacknowledged kindness and unanswered letters on their part was to testify.

Inspired, very probably, by the striking improvements made by the two friends to the property, it now became abundantly clear that John Edwards was attempting to terminate their lease.

For a time those lengthening days of early summer, which should have been so lovely, became nightmarish to them; and, as if to point the hateful days, they were pestered and terrified throughout May by a wandering madman. For a time it seemed as though notice to quit Plas Newydd would be not a matter of months now, but of weeks; John Edwards threatening them, as Sarah wrote to Anna Seward, 'with the absolute necessity of removing from a spot so honoured by You – so dear to us – with Our furniture and Books – which a Common Sized Satchell would not speedily convey to seek a new habitation amid these mountains'.[20]

Mrs Piozzi was to be lavish with her sympathy; had she not been litigating herself earlier on in the year over her pert elder daughter's claim to the Crowmarsh estate? 'And how did our Dear Ladies get home?' she wrote that August after a visit from the two Ladies and Mr Chappelow. 'I could not express my concern about the Difficulties with Regard to that dear and Celebrated Cottage which never *never* must slip from the Possession of the Ladies which have made its Very Name Immortal. Miss Ponsonby mention'd *Ten Years* as secure I think: In that Time some Method will surely be lit upon for perpetuating the Quiet and inalienable Tenure . . .'[21]

In fact, as the account book shows, their lawyer, Mr Wynne of Mold, had already been over to comfort them by confirming them in their lease of the cottage. 'Peas and Potatoes' in expectation of his visit had cost two shillings and threepence, his advice three pounds, three shillings. On 7 July they followed this up with a present of five guineas, 'for the Instrument which is to secure us from molestation during the lives of John and Mary

Edwards though he most liberally and earnestly refused any compensation'.[22]

The 'heart worrying business' now happily concluded had quite clearly taxed their nerves beyond endurance. Five days before Mr Wynne's visit Sarah had entered into the account book: '. . . to the mother of the two Boys whom we caught in our part of the Cufflymen. for whipping them 1s.' A day later the two Ladies discovered that overtaut nerves had caused them to commit a terrible injustice: '. . . 6d to the one – 6d to the other' scratched Sarah's repentant quill, 'and 1s to Mr Davies son John in compensation of our unjustly suspecting them of taking our Strawberries.'[23]

Happier times were on the way however. Two days after Mary was to spend nearly a pound at the market for a grand haymaking supper for their fourteen labourers.

The small farm had grown. In addition to Aber Adda field they were now renting a meadow by the Cufflymen from the vicar, another called the Scubba from a Mrs Parry, and a further meadow from Sir Thomas Mostyn, nine acres in all. All the fields had been carefully weeded and enclosed with quickset hedges, and by the end of the year a third cow had arrived from Brynkinalt to swell the tiny herd.

Yet the farm, into which they were now pouring what resources they could spare, was expensive. Taxes on the house, their servants and dogs, were now six pounds, sixteen shillings a year, while Pitt's new income tax was bleeding them to the tune of twenty-one pounds, six shillings and eightpence annually. By the beginning of 1801 their pensions were seven quarters in arrears and they were driven to borrow money once again and to write desperate letters to Sir William Scott the judge, and to their old friend Lord Castlereagh to treat on their behalf with the Irish Secretary of State.

Yet although Sarah would write to Mrs Tighe of 'a combination of circumstances' about which she was not specific, but which had caused her to suffer 'all the apprehensions of what Insolvency might end', she could not help exulting that July over 'the beauty and neatness of our nine acres' continuing, as for their *paying* it is a different affair. We shall make a little by selling Butter as soon as we can purchase a fourth cow, and if potatoes kept their last year's prices (four shillings or five shillings the measure) we should make near twenty pounds by what we shall have to sell of them, but thank Heaven [she went on, her heart with the labouring poor who were suffering so terribly], (for we are not yet sufficient farmers of *monsters* – not to say 'thank Heaven' though we should starve or go to gaol) we shall not make Near a fourth of that sum, for we yesterday heard that 20 measures of good ones had been offered for 18s.[24]

Six months later the fourth cow arrived, 'the loveliest of all lovely cows called Beauty' noted Eleanor in the small orange notebook which now did service as a journal, 'sent by that dearest of Friends Mrs Powys'.[25]

The following February, Sarah, writing to thank Mrs Tighe for an exceedingly welcome addition to her allowance, was describing how they were staying at home, 'wishing to spend all that we can and *cannot* afford in the manuring and Hedging of our four beautiful Fields for our four beautiful cows'.[26]

Bucolic advice now posted back and forth between Miss Ponsonby in Wales and Ireland, where Mrs Tighe, driven by financial necessity, was herself in the process of becoming an 'improving' farmer.

Mrs Tighe dispatches apple potatoes, which are as yet unheard of in North Wales, and Miss Ponsonby causes them to be distributed for poor families to plant; ditto with the Velvet wheat of which Miss Ponsonby has begged a cupful to plant and collect seeds from. What about Mrs Tighe's scheme whereby a family can support itself on two and a quarter acres of land? If the scheme were at all suitable for the poorer soil of their neighbourhood they could get some copies printed in Welsh of how this might be achieved. Does Mrs Tighe plough with horses or oxen, and what are her opinions on the planting of trees? '... we have been assured and our experience confirms, that 20,000 larch would, in twenty years be worth a guinea each ...'[27]

In short, like Mrs Tighe, the two Ladies were gripped by a perfect fever of improvement.

Their financial situation, for the time being, was more secure.

In the summer of 1802 their old friend, Lucy Goddard, had died, worn out with Methodism, the alternating doubt and wild religious enthusiasm, which had attacked her, fatally, in middle life. She generously left Sarah not only the legacy of one hundred pounds, but an annuity of thirty pounds a year, '... totally unexpected by me'[28] Sarah confided to Mrs Tighe in the letter asking if she might be allowed to have the dear G's miniature from the drawing-room at Woodstock.

The annuity, the increased allowance from Mrs Tighe, a good hay harvest, and the fact that, thanks to the intervention both of Sir William Scott and Lord Castlereagh, their pensions were now being paid more regularly, all contributed to their increased comfort and to '... those heavenly Slumbers' as Sarah feelingly expressed it, 'only experienced by those who are not in Debt'.[29]

'Our Gardens over flowing with Green peas and Strawberries, and Our Dairy with Butter and Cream', Sarah was writing as though from some Elysium in the high summer of 1803. In fact life was not without its anxieties, for the lull in the French war brought about by the Peace of Amiens had given way to war once more, so that in the same letter Sarah would write as of old of 'these terrible days of expected invasion and actual taxation'.[30]

As so often public seemed to coincide with private misfortune. Mary Carryll had been ill again, and from Mrs Tighe came the sad news that Harry's wife, Mary Tighe, was ill with consumption. A war too had been developing on the Ladies' own doorstep, one which was 'if possible still more formidable to us'[31] as Sarah explained, than the threat of Napoleon. It was an aesthetic war this time, waged in true Quixotic fashion against the building of two large cotton mills in the Dee valley.

They had long ago campaigned against quarries being opened within view of their windows, they would in the future campaign stoutly against Telford's roads. In the meantime they officered an impressive force of friends against the mill proprietors; attacking the whole notion of mills which were 'destructive' Eleanor wrote to Mr Thomas Jones of Llantysilio Hall, 'of the peace Health and Morals of the Inhabitants' and moreover advanced 'to an insupportable degree Taxes and Rates already sufficiently oppressive'.[32]

By the summer of 1804 they could congratulate themselves that they would be invaded 'neither by Buonaparte nor the Cotton Mills'[33] and they could ignore the pert piece about them which had appeared in the newspapers:

> Lady Eleanor Butler, and her fair friend Miss Ponsonby, who have for so many years been the fair recluses of the Vale of Llangollen in Wales are going to leave their beautiful seat no longer a *retreat* from the 'busy hum of men', by two extensive cotton mills having been erected near their abode.

In fact the army of Myddeltons, Myttons, Mostyns and Williams Wynns, had succeeded in reducing the two extensive cotton mills to one small factory, which Lady Lonsdale saw two years later, and which, for the modest sum of half a crown a year, was permitted to draw two inches of water from the river Dee.

Misgivings about quarries, roads and manufactories were not, it seems, extended to aqueducts. For in the November of the following year, that month in which with mingled 'transport and anguish' Englishmen learned of the victory of Trafalgar and the death of Nelson, the two Ladies attended the triumphal opening of Telford's aqueduct at Pontcysylte. Occupying the second ceremonial barge along with Lady Williams Wynn and Miss Ormsby, Lady Eleanor Butler and Miss Ponsonby with 'a complete sense of security' floated one hundred and twenty-six feet above the river Dee to the accompaniment of cheers from the eight thousand onlookers and heartening salutes from the Seringapatam guns.

They were quasi-Royalty in Llangollen; more sought after by visitors than ever before, their house and garden an object of pilgrimage to every traveller and tourist who passed. It was no small cause for self-congratulation that the Princess Amelia* had sent them Princess Elizabeth's† etchings which, as Sarah wrote to Mrs Tighe, 'are only struck off to be presented to Friends'[34]

---

* Princess Amelia (1783–1810), youngest child of George III.
† Princess Elizabeth (1770–1840), third daughter of George III.

while Countess Woronsov* who had visited them had sent an engraving of the Russian Empress begging them to write something upon it for her in English.

Opinions concerning them varied. 'I found them more unaffected and less clever than I expected' Lady Stanley of Alderly had confessed, while Lady Lonsdale who had visited them at the same time as she had inspected the cotton factory wrote: 'I think Lady Eleanor very clever, very odd . . .'[35]

The cleverness, the oddness, to be seen neither in her inflated correspondence with Anna Seward, nor yet in her archly formal letters to Mrs Piozzi, obviously permeated her conversation. Her conversation comes alive, is exhaled, pungent as the musk they loved to use, from between the pages of the day-book bound in mottled green boards with crimson leather on the spine and corners; that day-book which contains the raw material of her talk. The anecdotes are ticked off, presumably as she uses them:

Miss Seward was one day walking at Lichfield – attended by a little Italian greyhound – She met Dr Johnson – and telling him she had been reading Shenstone with which she was enchanted asked his opinion of him.

Why Madam – said He I think him that dog – who has neither the velocity of the greyhound – the sagacity of the Spaniel the courage of the mastiff or the vigour of the Bull dog – not [but] tis a pretty little thing.

We had a conversation at Brynkinalt with Mr Morhills Sen. who had been for Five years a resident in Russia. He arrived at St Petersburg the day after the assassination of the late Emperor Paul – who had been dreadfull mangled – his Face cut – and one Eye beat out – nevertheless his Body was exposed to the populace the next day – extended on a Bier – Covered with a Black Velvet Pall – his face painted and repaired.

Lady Powys has three rooms at Walcot filled with stuffed Birds in Glass Cases – Amongst them the Argus Pheasant – and the King Bird of Paradise – they require the incessant attention of One Person to preserve them from Damp – or they would melt away – there are not only fires – but stoves in all the rooms.

* Wife of the Russian Ambassador.

Buonaparte has quarrelled with his very virtuous wife – cut off the head of her Favourite Swan in a Passion and picked out of her Garden all her famous English Plants – which she had from Lee and Kennedy.[36]

Occasionally she cannot resist recording her own wit:

'Paris is now a Second Sodom and Gomorrah' declares Dr Glass [she writes Sod. and Gom.].
'No' she ripostes, 'I am sure they were much stricter in those days!'[37]

But her mind, for all its wit, tends to the Gothick, abounds in dark corners though lit with fitful gleams of irony. In the day-book she notes that Mr Weld of Lulworth Castle retires to the tower of the Castle and performs penance, adding, 'perhaps flagellations'; the pregnant Duchess of Montrose is leapt upon by a Newfoundland dog with the result that she gives birth to a monster 'with the face – dewlaps – and tail of a Dog'; the Electress of Bavaria is 'a tall masculine woman – highly rouged – suspected of gallantries – fond of dogs'; a page turns, and here is Frederick of Prussia as she sees and Delacroix might have painted him: 'mounted on a great English charger and surrounded by mutilated men'.[38]

It is this dark, this Gothick quality of her mind which will, increasingly, find expression in her taste. And yet what woman of sixty-seven could have a more active and interested mind? For now, in 1806, as her day-book tells us she is interested in many, many things; in fossils; makers of Aeolian harps; geology; underground passages; the choice of a new lama; witchcraft; ghosts; Egyptology; Russian dancing; a lady who purports to lay eggs; snake charmers; Tipoo Sahib; customs of the Moors; scandalous anecdotes of the French court; feeding poultry by pump at Nancy; Pompeii; making money. No wonder Mrs Piozzi has written to her friend, Mrs Pennington, that 'the unaccountable knowledge these Recluses have of all living books and people and things is like magic'.

At the beginning of 1806 Sarah had written wonderingly to Mrs Tighe of '. . . those years which seem flying so fast after each other'. They were now sixty-seven and fifty-one respectively, and Sarah's hair, once so fair, was white, and, like Eleanor, she had taken to wearing it cropped short and pow-dered. She signed her letters *SPQRST*, the initials standing for Sarah Ponsonby QueRulous with Sarah Tighe who had not been writing frequently enough. The correspondence must have picked up, however, for by the end of the year with her ears full of the clanging of the village bells ringing out to celebrate November 5th she was writing humorously to her friend of the bonfire 'to which Mary always contributes about a soup ladle full of Coals and then expects the Children to shout applauses of her generosity'.[39]

As had now become commonplace, there was a constant pro-cession of visitors to the cottage, among them Lady Bedingfield to stay and long talks with her in her bedroom until three in the morning; Mr and Mrs Peter La Touche; the Bishop of St Asaph's daughter, Miss Shipley; Count Woronsov, the Russian Ambassador; Sir Arthur Wellesley. To him Eleanor gave a small prayer book in Spanish that had once belonged to the Duke of Ormonde, and from this, sailing to Mondego Bay a year later, the future Duke was able, with the aid of a grammar, to learn enough Spanish to stand him in good stead during the Peninsular campaign.

In the journal Plas Newydd had now ceased to be a cottage, and had become a 'mansion', and the precious 'retirement' was in danger of being eroded by a spate of amusements. There were the customary jaunts to what Eleanor was on occasion piqued enough to call the 'filthy booksellers' of Shrewsbury and Oswes-try; and there were frequent expeditions even further afield, to the Shipleys at St Asaph for instance, from where they returned home 'by the light of Jupiter' as Eleanor romantically expressed it. Nearer at hand there were jaunts to Porkington, Brynkinalt, Aston, when they got home often as not, at four or five in the morning. Cards were now mentioned in the journal, having appeared in the account book some time previous, when they lost ten shillings at play at Brynkinalt. There were now cards at the Grove Bow meeting, where they met 'Such a canting, odious, detestable Boasting woman under the trees'; cards at Acton with the Warden of Ruthin, his wife, Miss Gore and Miss

Ormsby Gore; and there were theatricals at Porkington, *The Force of Love* before tea, *The Devil to Pay* after, 'admirably performed', after which they drove home, arriving 'at our peaceful mansion at midnight'.

Yet for all the gaiety Eleanor Butler could still look out on the world with unspoiled eyes: 'Intense frost', she was writing in the last week of the old year, 'air so rarefied that the little cracked Bell of Llantysilio church was as distinctly heard at our door as the village bells. Sun ray less, white, round, and not to be known except from its place in the heavens from the moon.'[40]

This reflective mood was a pointer to the quieter times which lay ahead. By February Mary Carryll was ill once more, and although at first she seemed to recover, weeks passed into months during which they looked in vain for a complete return to health: 'Our lives have ever since been passed in alternate hope and fear' wrote Sarah to Mrs Tighe, 'but all the time an anxiety that knew no abatement.'[41]

By the beginning of the following year what they both now recognized as the inevitable outcome of Mary's illness was to be foreshadowed by the loss of two friends within a day of each another. On 25 March Anna Seward died bequeathing them a mourning ring, and a day after that poor Gabriel Piozzi, who had only been able to bear the agonizing gangrene which was killing him by taking doses of opium and brandy.

By summer Mary had grown so weak that when the King's nephew, the young Duke of Gloucester, expressed a desire to meet the Ladies in August, they had little heart for such an occasion, honour though it was. They made a determined effort not to disappoint the young man however, and entertained him at the cottage, which the newspapers were now pleased to call 'the Fairy Palace of the Vale', that 'rural and sylvan like retreat of those Ornaments of their Sex ...', after which they turned sadly back to doing all they could for their old friend.

Four months later the young man was to add his condolences to many others, for that November the big, raucous, generous woman, who for so long had been their devoted servant and friend, died, in peace, without pain. She died, leaving Aber

Adda field, which she had bought with her life's savings, to Sarah Ponsonby; and leaving, with grim humour, a shilling each to her brother and sister if they cared to come all the way over from Ireland to fetch it. She went, taking with her their last close link with the old Irish past.

Chapter Eight

'. . . Stately and difficult of access'
Sarah Ponsonby to Mrs Tighe

Relationships

They were now famous. 'The most celebrated Virgins', Prince Puckler Muskau was soon to call them, 'in Europe.'

Yet for some time now there had been low but unmistakable rumbles of disapprobation. Although young noblemen like the Duke of Somerset touring North Wales with his tutor in 1795 might dutifully find the Ladies' way of life 'preferable to all the boasted pleasures of fashionable dissipation', there were others who were not so convinced.

There was Madame de Genlis, who, that first day she had met the Ladies, had been quite overcome by them. Next morning, however, she had revised her opinion. Like Anna Seward she had been quick to notice Eleanor's cheerful and robust appearance, '*un charmant visage*' she remembered, '*éclatant de fraicheur et de santé la plus franche*', but contrasting somewhat with Sarah's '*belle figure pâle et melancolique*'. Lady Eleanor, she was convinced, had no second thoughts whatsoever in leaving the world, was perfectly '*à son aise*' in her retirement, but she sensed that Miss Ponsonby might have regrets; though surely, Madame de Genlis reasoned, it was not repentance that had brought her to such a '*désert*'?[1]

Lying awake that first night at Plas Newydd, nay kept awake by the unearthly music of the concealed Aeolian harp, Madame de Genlis had found herself reflecting that the two friends were more properly to be pitied than admired. How terrible to be so devoted to one person to the exclusion of all else; to have no children, though they could, she supposed, but with small conviction, adopt some; to have no family ties! And what if one of them died! How awful for the other. Or even worse, suppose they both became senile at once and could no longer look after one another! What an appalling future lay before them! By morning Madame de Genlis saw the whole *ménuge* with great clarity. Lady Eleanor Butler and Miss Ponsonby were victims *'de la pluse dangereuse exaltation de tete et de sensibilité . . .'* and, supreme horror, were chained to their mountain for ever.[2]

There were others prepared not only to criticize the Ladies' way of life but the Ladies themselves. They were name droppers and name collectors (De Quincey – who had visited them in 1802 and been coldly received); they were flatterers (Lady Lonsdale); they were insincere (Lady Louisa Stuart, who had actually never met them); they were rude, particularly Lady Eleanor (the Reverend Dr Whalley); they kept a gossip shop between England and Ireland (Mr Hamilton), and so far from retiring from the world, had never left it.

'I was yesterday complimented as very tolerant', wrote Lady Louisa Stuart, 'but I cannot be so to the Genus Mountebankum, and they clearly belong to it.'[3]

The sincerity or not of the two friends obviously turned to some extent upon the genuineness of the retirement and of the relationships resulting from it, and about the retirement they were more than a little neurotic. Shenstone, Cowper, Elizabeth Carter among many others had like them celebrated the ideal way of living, but without fuss. Unlike them, however, Eleanor Butler and Sarah Ponsonby had taken violent action in order to lead such a life. The whole reason for their elopement, they maintained, had been to lead the retired life; consequently to depart from its principles in any way would expose them to the censure of those relatives and friends whom they ever felt regarding them with critical and suspicious eyes.

Their early years together had been the most stringent in this respect; had not Sarah written to Mrs Tighe in 1784 confessing how they had infringed their resolution of 'never passing a night from our Cottage' by going to visit the Bridgemans in Staffordshire; had she not declined an invitation from Mrs

Tighe herself, who had taken a house at Harrow, because 'it would totally demolish our system'; and had she not written again in 1787 of how they had resisted an invitation to go and see the theatricals at Wynnstay, and how Lady Bridgeman had had a strong inclination to join their retirement, 'But did not yield to it from an idea that as it might be conveyed from this village to our Irish friends, it might lead them to think our conduct extravagant, and inconsistent with our professed Solitude'?[4]

Years later Sarah, in the face of their busy social life, would feel secure enough to joke, if only tentatively, at the 'retirement', but to begin with, as their friend Anna Seward seemed to understand so well,* the retirement had to be protected not only by personal strength of will but by the adoption of certain strict resolutions. 'My B and I have made our resolution known to the village' Sarah wrote to Mrs Tighe, 'that we would never visit or be visited by any Ponsonby, who became residents in it, as it would subject us to perpetual and sometimes very disagreeable intrusions.'[5] This fiat was unable to prevent the ill behaviour of Lord Meath's nephew, however, who, when the Ladies in accordance with their rule had firmly refused to lend him a book, had broken down their hedge, insulted their gardener, stared impertinently into their shrubbery and scandalized the entire village by guffawing in chapel.

There was also to be considered the awkward question of receiving the friends of friends : 'We have been obliged to adopt the resolution', wrote Sarah, 'of making no acquaintance with occasional neighbours as our village is now almost always crowded with strangers.'[6]

Exceptions had to be made none the less. Two such were Miss Harriet Bowdler and Miss Margaret Davies, close friends of the Barretts, whose intimacy with the Ladies 'entitled their Friends' in their turn 'to every attention in our power to show them'. As a result both Miss Bowdler and Miss Davies had been invited to stay at Plas Newydd in the August of 1785, but amiable as they

---

* 'An influx of company so various and incessant obliges them daily to decline appearing to the parties that request permission to see the place . . .' Anna Seward to Mrs Parry Price, 23 September 1795, H.M.C. Somerset and Buccleugh, I, vol. XV, 7, 8.

had been, close as the friendship that followed with Miss Bowdler was to prove, poor Sarah would write that 'My B cou'd
hardly brook such continual interruptions to her Manuscript
...'[7] and great were the rejoicings when the two guests departed.

It so happened that that very month the retirement had been
further threatened by gentlefolk invading the Vale for the first
time since the two friends had settled there. Mr Whalley a
clergyman from Somerset desiring to paint Welsh views had
taken Tower House, across the Dee, with his wife and children.
For a time both Ladies played it very cool with the newcomers
until they discovered that Mr Whalley was almost as addicted to
Solitude as they were themselves, 'And we can sleep in peace'
wrote Sarah, 'which we before thought we never cou'd do ...
though our rest' she added 'ought to be a little disturbed by the
Consciousness of not having been quite so civil to them as we
ought.'[8]

For their anxiety, and particularly Eleanor's, to protect their
way of life, to prevent it from rendering down into that frivol
of unwanted social intercourse which they had both determined
to escape, made them somewhat over alert to intrusion, and thus
frequently to give offence. Visitors to the garden, which as early
as 1782 was becoming famous, were requested, often imperi-
ously, to present proper credentials or else be denied. Permission
being granted, Eleanor and Sarah, as their journal frequently
tells us, would retire either to the shrubbery or to their bedroom
until the nuisance was past; although not, it must be confessed,
without a certain curiosity of their own: 'Compliments from
Mr White desiring permission for himself, his Son and Daughter to see this place; permitted. They came. An old man with
spectacles, a flaunting daughter in a brown and gold Capotte,
school Boy. He left a Poem (which please God I shall not read)
signed Samuel White.'[9]

When later the tourist flow to North Wales turned into something more like a flood it even became known for people to
broach the 'retirement' by guile. One such was Miss Coates of
Glasgow. This lady had secured a foothold in Plas Newydd by
declaring she had a letter of introduction, '(that has not yet

made its appearance)',[10] from Professor Dugald Stuart.* The Ladies were to find themselves distinctly unimpressed by the manners, conduct and appearance of the bold Miss Coates, who had no sooner satisfied her curiosity about them than she buccaneered off to Mrs Piozzi at Brynbella, gaining admission there, it seems, by bragging that she had been but recently entertained at Plas Newydd. The monstrous deception was completed when, having preyed on Mrs Piozzi's trust in the Vale of Clywd, Miss Coates returned to provoke the Ladies once more by bearing a letter from their friend that had to be delivered 'with her own hands'. The Ladies caught entertaining far more select company than that of Miss Coates, were, as Eleanor Butler indignantly wrote to Mrs Piozzi, 'obliged to employ Methods Very Unpleasant to practice, in preventing her from overstaying'.[11]

In the journal the microclimates of their relationships with other people can be clearly traced. 4 February 1788, is a day of freezing wind, and snow is threatening. A messenger arrives from the *Hand* bringing compliments from a Colonel Mansergh St George, who is on his way to Ireland and is desirous of carrying any commands they might have for that country. His social position is impeccable as he is a member of the Leinster family, and the two friends enjoy receiving visits from the eminent although, as we shall see, not to the point of involvement.

The Colonel is invited to the cottage, he arrives at six and leaves at nine: 'One of the most pleasing men I ever conversed with' records Eleanor in the journal. 'Very pretty, slight figure, pale genteel Face his appearance is rendered even more interesting by the black silk cap he wears upon his head to conceal the terrible wound he has received in the American war.' While the wind howls outside the closed shutters they drink tea before the library fire; they discuss Pompeii and Herculaneum, and the Colonel regales them with anecdotes of the Prince of Wales and amuses them with pencil sketches of their beloved Rousseau in his fur-trimmed coat and large muff. 'We were quite sorry' writes Eleanor later, 'when this agreeable man made his Bow.'[12]

---

*Dugald Stewart (1753–1828), philosopher and mathematician at Edinburgh University and such an effective lecturer that, according to Cockburn, there was 'eloquence in his very spitting'.

Five months later all is changed. News from a mutual friend confirms, horror of horrors, that Colonel and Mrs St George and Mrs St George's sister are all coming to settle in Llangollen. 'We shall care not to be troubled by them' comments the journal grimly. Five days later, Lady Eleanor and Miss Ponsonby are walking the lawn before the library windows when they spy two large straw hats coming up the lane. Beneath them, as they have already guessed, are the St George ladies: '. . . noticed they walked round the clump before the pales' Eleanor noted furiously in the journal, 'stared into the windows and behaved with a degree of vulgarity peculiar to the stile and line of Life those Ladies have wilfully adopted.'[13]

By August the danger was receding. 'A very polite note from Col. St George' announces the journal. Very likely, as with the Whalleys, the two Ladies have found that the St Georges are no such great threat after all.

One says the Ladies, but if Anna Seward, in what appears to be a letter of unusual frankness, is to be believed, it was Eleanor Butler who was chiefly responsible for this somewhat extreme attitude to their social life. Her brilliance had without doubt created the retirement, had stamped it with a novelty and an originality which made it so irresistible to others that it came near to destroying their solitude together. Yet defence of the retirement was not wholly responsible for her suspicious and sometimes *sauvage* attitude to society. There was a flaw in her nature, a violence and an arrogance perhaps due to her masculine nature, perhaps springing from insecurity which had constantly to be redressed by the milder-natured Sarah Ponsonby.

'O, no! no!' Anna Seward was writing in June 1800 to Dr Whalley and to whom the Ladies had been very rude.

It was indeed not the answer which Lady E. Butler and her friend ought to have sent. I am sorry, I am ashamed for them, in a much greater degree than I am surprised. I am sure, however, that neither Miss Ponsonby's will nor heart were in that message; but Lady E., who, when pleased is, one of the most gracious of God's creatures, under a contrary impression is extremely haughty and imperious. Her sweet, amiable friend who, when she has time, can bend and soften that imperious temper, knows she cannot, and therefore does not attempt to assuage its *extempore* sallies. On occasions, in some degree similar I have seen Miss Ponsonby sigh, shrug her shoulders and acquiesce. On those occasions Lady E. always involves her by the words *we* and *us*. Accustomed to incessant homage and compliance, a broken promise, and not even apologized for, would, I know, be a sin in the eyes of both, which scarcely any acknowledged repentence could atone. That sin was your brother's; but I think Miss Ponsonby would not have sought it by unjust rudeness to you. They were, you know, unconscious of the family misfortunes and mental gloom which had produced his breach of promise, and apparent cold neglect of them.[14]

To be fair to the remiss Ladies, Anna Seward was equally unconscious of the mental gloom which was threatening them at the time due to the threatened curtailment of the Plas Newydd lease and the loss of their home. A factor which had resulted in overtaut nerves and rudeness in more quarters than Dr Whalley's.

'Lady Eleanor repents' concluded Miss Seward 'as she often does on other occasions.'[15]

The degree of offence to which the unfortunate prebendary had been subjected may be judged by the fact that eight years later he was still huffily unreconciled.

Anna Seward was not to be the only one who would perceive Eleanor Butler's dominating nature and glimpse the points of disagreement which occasionally rose between the Ladies; others, besides Lady Lonsdale who visited them in 1806, would notice how little Sarah spoke, only seeming to assent to what Eleanor said.

Differences certainly there were. While it was given to Eleanor to fulminate in the journal against 'That little Dirty Village Quack' who had just sent in his bill, 'never paid money with more reluctance'; it was left to Sarah to enter into the account book with gentle irony: 'An Important Bill of the little Doctor £2:2:6.' And while, in the journal, Eleanor railed sumptuously against the treachery of the Barretts in patronizing the *Hand* after their famous quarrel with the proprietor, her Better Half would be sweetly defiant in the accounts. 'Dear Mrs Barrett', she recorded as soon as she could, the rift having been to some degree closed and they entertaining their former favourite

with a three-shilling turkey, 'Dear Mrs Barrett', an appellation
which Eleanor seemed no longer prepared to bestow, although
she was contented enough to borrow money from the tainted
source.

If Eleanor's nature conveyed an impression of feudal temper
touched with extravagance and mingled with a rigid devotion to
the niceties of etiquette, Sarah's partook of the mild rationalism
of the age, and through both journal and account book can be
traced the influence of those milder counsels, those eventual
reconciliations, for which Sarah was doubtless responsible.

Eleanor, given to discharging gardeners like cannon balls, is
frequently persuaded by Sarah to think better of it; a procedure
to be experienced three times in the course of one year by the
unfortunate Moses Jones. Small boys are whipped for stealing
their strawberries and then, proving guiltless after all, hastily
placated with shillings; fallen kitchen maids are turned away
only to be secretly succoured; ill-tempered dogs belonging to the
commonalty are threatened with instant shooting and then, at
the last moment, reprieved; unsatisfactory chimney-sweeps,
thatchers, joiners, tailors, carpet men, doctors, are branded con-
summate villains for a time and then, beneath the healing wings
of Time and Miss Ponsonby, employed again. Everyone it seems
is somehow forgiven in the end, even the *Hand*, even the Barretts.

Of close friendships there were, by nature of their own passionate attachment, rather few, and of these few most had in the
first instance been Sarah's friends. But these friends lived far
from Plas Newydd, and intimacy had to survive the vagaries of
correspondence. Mrs Tighe, whom Sarah dutifully placed
second in her heart to Eleanor, lived either in her 'Hermitage'
at Harrow or in Ireland, seldom visiting them at the cottage.
With Mrs Goddard they were almost entirely out of touch by
1794, her obsession with Methodism and her own acknowledged
irregularity as a correspondent contributing to the breach.
Among the surrounding gentry Lady Dungannon was an old,
rather than a great, friend, invited to stay less for any peculiar
pleasure afforded by her company than for the sake of past

times. Further out on the perimeter were the Kynastons, Ormsbys, Myttons, Myddeltons, Williams Wynns, the Lloydes, the Kenyons and the Parkers; with the Shipleys further off still at St Asaph and Mrs Powys at Berwick, rather especial favourites. The company of these, while being enjoyed, could nevertheless be kept safely and pleasantly regulated by prevailing etiquette, although even here care was necessary. Mrs Mytton, the foolish and doting mother of the famous Squire Jack, had at least once proved unreliable in the matter of repeating confidences. 'Think Twice before We Speak Once' Eleanor had noted tersely in the journal as a consequence.

Further out still were the acquaintances, the Lady Templetons and the Lady Bedingfields, over whom Eleanor might rhapsodize in the journal, but who were not really close in any sense of the word.

The closest friendship had no doubt been with the two Barrett sisters and their especial companion, Margaret Davies; but with the Barretts and with Margaret too, they had quarrelled. The contrast between Eleanor's harsh criticism of them in the journal with Sarah's more liberal treatment in the account book gives added significance to the fact that both ladies lived near by at Oswestry, perhaps representing something of a threat to Eleanor's and Sarah's own relationship. Harriet Bowdler was the only one of this coterie to survive as a close friend. She was clearly more drawn to Sarah than to Eleanor of whom, it appears, she was rather in awe, having in a manner of speaking 'fallen' for the younger woman from the moment she had heard her voice outside Miss Barrett's drawing-room door at Oswestry.* It is difficult not to harbour the suspicion that had she lived nearer to and not at Bath or London, Eleanor would have found some excuse to curtail her visits. As it was she restricted her intimacies to a correspondence which, even when it was addressed to Sarah, was certainly also read by Eleanor.

* '. . . *never* was there a moment since that when I first heard your voice, before you enter'd the room when I was waiting for you at Oswestry – never was there *one* moment in wch I cd possibly write a letter deserving the epithet you employ if my pen did justice to my heart' Harriet Bowdler–Sarah Ponsonby, 9 September 1790. Ormonde MS.

Of the few, the privileged few who had been permitted to enter the Sacred Temple of Friendship, allowed actually to occupy for a few nights the 'State Bedchamber', Anna Seward was not so much a friend as a triumphant literary acquisition on the Ladies' part. So too, to some extent, was Mrs Piozzi, with whom in any case they had to share Mr Piozzi, which meant that the company was 'mixed' and intimacy accordingly restricted. In any case, as with most of the Ladies' friends, the Piozzis never actually stayed at Plas Newydd, but slept at the *Hand* and only took meals at the cottage.

As to their immediate families, with hers Eleanor was more or less in a continuous state of estrangement, although she corresponded with at least one sister, and was always pleased to see her nephews: 'Wandesford said he had wished to come by Llangollen and spend some days with us' she had written of her brother's second son, 'but Lady Anne Butler had insisted on his going from Waterford to Milford, in June however he will be quite his own master and will then please God visit us.'[16]

With her family, such as it was, Sarah had remained in closer touch. Her half-brother, Chambre, not only gave her presents of money from time to time, but frequently called in at the cottage on his way to and from Ireland; she corresponded regularly with Mrs O'Connel her maternal aunt, and occasionally with her mean half-sister, Mrs Lowther. But it was with Mrs Tighe and her family that Sarah felt most engaged. Eleanor seems not to have objected to this, she herself giving up long days to making transcriptions for Mrs Tighe, writing out reading lists and drawing up programmes of instruction for Mrs Tighe's daughters, Bess and Caroline. Later she was greatly to relish her jokes with Harry Tighe; would assure him that his original story was better by far than the one Miss Edgeworth had adapted for *Irish Bulls*; would promise, as a consequence of their mutual impecuniosity, to accompany him to Botany Bay.[17]

But the closest of all friendships outside their own was with Mary Carryll. She threatened nothing, being of a different class from themselves; had been apprised of all or most of their story from the outset; had from the beginning been the mainstay of their small household. Her generous and forceful personality comes vividly off the pages of the journal, for her raucous voice frequently reached Eleanor at work in the library: 'Bought Herrings and Oysters. Loud and violent altercation between Mary and the Fisherman. Mary Triumphant', or: 'Mary in her Glory purchasing Beef for hanging and executing all her powers of Eloquence in bargaining with the Butcher.' 'Ah Madam,' she sighs to Miss Ponsonby, 'you once showed me a fine sight in the heavens, the Belt of O'Bryon; but I suppose we shall see it no more now since the Union.'[18]

In the pages of the account book she is vignetted bowling grandly over to Brynkinalt in a chaise at a cost of five shillings to dine with Lady Dungannon's upper servants or, with a comfortable standby of lemons, ale and rum, returning hospitality in her kitchen at Plas Newydd; or, less happily, rheumatic, emetical, and no doubt crotchety, being attended by the 'little Doctor'.

The Ladies rewarded her staunchness and loyalty with the most tender consideration and affection which extended not only to generous presents to her father and mother over in Ireland, but to the closest personal matters. At a time when she was conducting an acrimonious, and no doubt scurrilous vendetta by post with a sister who had unjustly tried to blacken her good name with the two friends, they begged permission to open her sister's letters for her, so that by tactful summarizing they might soften the harshness of the contents.[19]

Mary Carryll responded not only with love and loyalty but with at least two recorded presents; petticoats and pockets laid out for both at the bottom of their bed on New Year's day of 1790, and, on another occasion, a grand seal for Sarah. A seal upon which, as Sarah dryly wrote Mrs Tighe, was cut '. . . the most Deformed Hope that any mortal ever laid hold upon'.[20]

With their other servants the Ladies were strict but kind; the following memorandum written by Sarah Ponsonby in 1826 gives some idea of the qualities looked for in a Plas Newydd housemaid.

Wages, it was noted, were to be six guineas a year:

Scouring of Rooms – Only required for the Maids and Mangle rooms – and the Hall and porch – which last are of free stone – all

the other rooms being covered with carpets – and only secured thrice
a year – perfect neatness in Appearance and Work – and Simplicity
of attire in which qualities She will have a very excellent pattern
in Gwendolen – A good washer – and a Strong assistant in the
Labourious part of Brewing – a Good Sharpener of Knives is most
particularly requisite to Our peace of Mind – were the present Grinder
– to take her departing Journey upon the edge of one of those which
She sends to assist at Our Dinner – She would have no occasion for
a Side Saddle – Assisting the Dairy Maid in Keeping the Kitchen
and all its utensils and furniture in perfect Neatness – and making
Winter Fires in Our Library – and eating Parlour and at night in
Our Bed Chamber – seems the heaviest parts of her requisite Duty
– A good humoured Willingness – Occasionally to assist in Other
miscellaneous Services – will – We can pledge Our Words – neither
be imposed upon – nor unrewarded. No fine Plain Work nor much
Coarse nor any Ironing of fine or small Linen expected . . .

In addition Lady Eleanor personally asked that the girl 'May
be a Merry Creature Given to talking and Singing – provided
they are neither *Raw* Songs nor Methodist Hymns'.[21]

Most difficulty was experienced with the kitchen maids, who
were tiresomely given to impertinence (one had been caught red-
handed with the Aeolian harp!), uncleanliness, and to losing
their virtue. They were fired, as both journal and account book
show, with moderate regularity; although when they were in
the friends' employment they were always encouraged with shilling bounties for diligent polishing of grates, thorough scrub-
bings, or neat appearance.

Thus with their inside staff at least the two friends were more
than usually thoughtful, for not only did they refuse to take
advantage of a good girl's willingness, but they themselves, as
Sarah had long ago told Mrs Tighe, always retired to the dressing-room at nine each evening, so that their servants could go
early to bed.

With their gardeners the Ladies were rather more exacting;
not only did they demand a high standard of ability in every
aspect of horticultural management and constant rakings and re-
rakings of the gravel paths in all weathers, but they expected
this important member of their staff to be more or less perma-
nently on call. One of their early gardeners had been required to

sleep on the premises every night of the week but Saturday, when he was allowed off to walk the twelve miles to Wrexham to spend the night with his wife and six children. Unsurprisingly their gardeners seemed fatally disposed to drunkenness, and throughout the year were exchanged with frequency. 'Discharged Moses Jones for repeated and outrageous Drunkenness' runs the journal for a June afternoon. 'He had lived fourteen months with us in the capacity of gardener. For the last seven months he has been drunk three days in the Week. This morning he began to mow. He cut three Swards of Grass, laid Down his Scythe, ran to the Ale House. Returned, began to Mow. Then went again.' When he returned his mistresses were waiting for him, 'took the keys of the garden from him, paid him one-and-twenty pence, which was all that was due him for one day's work, as every Saturday from the time we Hired him we paid him Ten shillings'.[22] Moses, to be engaged and discharged a number of times before his final departure, was but one of many, whose failings led to indignant and sometimes apoplectic outbursts in the journal. Yet such entries were often as not accompanied by an air of self-congratulation, of triumph even: 'Richard sent in his keys' runs such an entry. 'We sent out his wages . . . we think we acted with becoming calmness and presence of Mind.'[23] But once again it is the account book which softens an impression which would otherwise be over-harsh. For it is in the account book that the shillings and the sixpences are recorded which were given as bounties and encouragements to the successive gardeners, their wives and their children; and here is the 'drink money' bestowed, not only as a portion of their wages, but often to celebrate the completion of a new garden, a shrubbery or waterworks, while sometimes, as with their favoured Simon, it was given to soften the melancholy parting from a devoted brother.

Nevertheless it must be faced that in the matter of wages the Ladies were exceedingly conservative. Even allowing for the fact that the cost of living in North Wales was low, it is notable that they were paying wages in 1788 that corresponded with the national average as calculated by Arthur Young eighteen years before, and it is more notable still that this rate of wages had not

gone up one penny twelve years later in 1800 and after the
catastrophic rise in the cost of living following on the French
war. To their admirers it is an embarrassing fact that by that
date the Ladies' gardener was actually receiving sixpence a week
less. One can only plead that the Ladies' own income during the
period had risen by but a sixteenth.

Better than most in their relations with their servants, the two
friends were more than usually interesting in their dealings with
the commonalty, for it was here that those sacred principles of
'retirement' which had been imbibed from *La Nouvelle Héloïse*
were most strikingly put into practice. Rarely had such great
ladies been forced to live so simply, and the effect upon them
was complicated.

In their dealings with tradesmen they were, in an age not
overscrupulous in such matters, uncharacteristically impeccable
and courteous; both honour and self-interest demanding that
they paid their creditors as promptly as they could. As Sarah was
to write reprovingly to Mrs Tighe: '. . . my feelings are less
Hurt by the word Pension than the Horror of being asked by a
Tradesman for his Honest earnings without the power of acting
Honestly towards him.'[24] It was a horror that owing to the irregularity of their income they would often be forced to endure, and
one that frequently gave them sleepless nights. Yet for all their
concern and courtesy there existed, and particularly in Eleanor
Butler, a high-handed attitude towards their inferiors which was
a consequence of their breeding. This showed not only in the
rigorous standard of service which they demanded from their
tradesmen – the journal bristles with accounts of unsatisfactory
goods returned and work redone – but in other characteristic
confrontations. 'Saw a family coming to occupy the Weaver's
house' runs the journal, 'Enquired who they were. Blanche
Moses. Not good people. Don't like such neighbours. Sent to our
Landlord. He and his Daughter-in-law, John's wife, came immediately. Said Blanche Moses and her sons should not stay
there.'[25] So with the weaver's dog, which was ordered to be shot
as a nuisance until Eleanor Butler, seeing its mistress's sad face,
ordered it to be reprieved; so with Evans of the *Hand* who was
severely cautioned for having the presumption to open an un-

romantic quarry working on the hillside in sight of their windows.

Yet bound in with this feudal attitude was another, one governed by the prevailing cult of 'sensibility', one in which 'imagination' rather than true feeling predominated. It was a state of mind which at its worst wallowed voluptuously in madnesses and bereavements and thus resulted in some disagreeably mawkish entries in the journal:

> Sitting in our parlour window we beheld a very affecting sight – at least the burial of our old neighbour Mathew the Miller was to us an affecting sight ... This mournful procession came slowly along the undulating path through our field, the passing Bell solemnly tolling all the while, it drew many tears from us and left an impression of tender melancholy which we would rather cherish than seek to dissipate.[26]

It was this attitude of mind which would enable her one moment to see the small child who came to sweep their chimneys as 'the little Prince of Ebony', and the next as 'the odious Brat', who had swept no further than the bend in the flue. It was an attitude which encouraged not only the destitute of Llangollen, but the two friends, to see themselves as far greater benefactors than in fact they were; for so far from spending a tenth of their income on charity, the sum was not always a hundredth.

But another and redeeming thread was intermingled with these feudal and romantic attitudes of Eleanor Butler and Sarah Ponsonby, and this was a true sense of community, of shared experience.

Although neither lady was in the least sympathetic to popular political agitation, the Girondist cry of 'War upon *Châteaux* peace to cottages!' did have a meaning for them where it could have had none for other members of their caste. They had actually experienced the arrogance of those who lived in *châteaux*; they had known what it was like to have too little money for their particular requirements; being women, they had known what it was like to feel legally unprotected and insecure. So it was that when others shared these experiences they were both sympathetic and practical, and it did not matter whether help

consisted in writing to the Lord Chief Justice himself* for the
protection of a villager who was being browbeaten by an attorney; or engaging the help of influential friends to rescue an
elderly gentlewoman from the workhouse ('one murder less for
The Oswestry House of Vice and Oppression' as Eleanor trium-
phantly expressed it); or in sending, with the most sisterly feelings in the world, a hair-raising purge to cure a costive wagoner.

But perhaps their sense of community was at its most attractive when things went well rather than badly; when they re-
joiced with everyone around them over good weather and a fine
harvest; when they were amused and delighted by the village
children; when they took pleasure in the calm happiness of a
married couple, for in this they always saw a mirror of their own
relationship. This found expression time and again in the journal; sometimes it was Evan Williams and his wife '. . . walking
slowly and pensively round their hanging Field, examining the
Thread which lies there for bleaching and counting the Lambs';[27]
once it was a little old woman they had met, aged 'Four-score-
and-eight . . . when she married with thirty grandchildren and
eight great-grandchildren', who, 'from the Night of her Marriage to that of her Husband's Death (she said) they lay side by
side Forty-seven years . . .',[28] a record which they themselves
would actually surpass; and they would revel in the contentment of their old landlord and his wife, drawing her, if only a
little self-consciously, below a spreading ash tree to eat the cherries she had picked for them, and to listen to the tale of her
courtship.

It is at such moments of close self-identification that the journal is at its best, the aesthetics of the retirement most justified, as
on that freezing spring night when Eleanor Butler saw riding
up the field before the cottage, 'A comfortable well clad old
woman . . . with a pipe of Tobacco in her Mouth, the Puffs of
which softened the keeness of the air and must make her journey over the mountains delectable.'[29]

It was perhaps less for their charity than for their sense of
community that they were loved by the people in Llangollen;
those people who liked to bring them small simple presents,

*Lloyd Kenyon, first Baron Kenyon (1732–1802).

wild flowers, trouts, birds' eggs; who mustered in strength to help them when their library chimney went on fire; who celebrated the accouchements of their cows, the mowing of their hay and the lifting of their potatoes as if they had been their own.

Even Lockhart, Sir Walter Scott's son-in-law, who in many respects was to prove their most malicious detractor, would have to admit that 'they have long been the guardian angels of this village, and are worshipped by man woman and child about them'.[30]

Chapter Nine

'Pleasures unknown to Vulgar Minds'
The Journal

Correspondence

Although social intercourse had to be carefully regulated for the sake of preserving the retirement, there was one sphere in which relationships could be safely entered into without threat to the 'system', and this was in the prosecution of a voluminous correspondence.

The account book shows that bills for postage were heavy, the journal reveals that it was not unusual for them to spend six hours out of the twenty-four in continuous writing. Most of their pleasures, as Sarah had told Mrs Tighe, came from using paper. Of this they employed the finest quality, Eleanor's double glazed for preference, Sarah's single, both gilt-edged and sealed, as the whim took them, with wax impresses of Owls, Hopes, Minervas, or quite simply their initials, entwined.

Each was mistress of the contents of the other's letters, frequently they wrote as one. Rules for conducting their correspondence were strict, not to say rigid. They subscribed, in theory at least, to accepted niceties such as not reading other people's letters aloud without their consent, or making transcripts without permission; they were extremely insistent upon prompt replies. 'Letter due from Lady Anne Butler, from Lady Mornington, from Miss Davies, from Page, from Mrs Lowther' notes the journal, adding sternly, 'The same time which these ladies take to answer our Letters shall we take to answer theirs.' But promptness seems to have been more frequently preached than practised judging by anguished lowings from Miss Bowdler for replies from Eleanor Butler.

The correspondence itself ranged through a whole spectrum

comprising routine letters to tradesmen, letters literary, letters politico-religio, letters sentimental, coquetto-patronizing, litigious, formal and insulting.

Five principal correspondents were to emerge from this sea of paper; three single and two married ladies were to elicit from the Plas Newydd friends a variety of moods and opinions.

Sarah Ponsonby's most constant correspondent was, of course, Mrs Tighe. They wrote on average every ten days, the time it took for the post to go and return again.

The correspondence was not one of equals however. There were old feelings of guilt on Sarah's side and a consciousness of dependence, for from Mrs Tighe she received her allowance. This fact, together with Mrs Tighe's own character, high-minded, veering to the Methodistical and a touch mean, called forth a response from Sarah at once cautious and over-anxious to please, one that was only faintly tinctured by her pleasantly dry humour.

Nevertheless there were other safe subjects for discussion besides the perennially delightful one of Mrs Tighe and her five children. There were areas of soothing agreement; upon the excellence of the Boarding School system, or the extreme trust-worthiness of Mr Pitt and the wickedness of the Jacobinical principles with which he was so strenuously contending; there was the wisdom of the Irish Act of Union and the sad unreliability of Mrs Grattan; there was the consuming interest afforded by certain millenary prophecies. There were also areas, notably those concerning the arts and the sciences, in which Sarah was at liberty to express her own, or rather her Better Half's opinions, not only without giving offence, but with some suggestion of actually conferring a benefit upon Mrs Tighe, who was a lady as bent on self-improvement as they were themselves.

These opinions were of no striking originality. Richardson's novels were extolled for their pious examples (did her dear friend know that Nelson's grandfather had served as the model for worthy Sir Charles Grandison?), while the works of Hume, Bolingbroke and Gibbon were condemned for their contrary influence; among works in English, French and Italian now unread and forgotten – works of history, biography, and fiction

– they were especially to recommend those of Ariosto, Tasso, Madame de Sevigné, and Rousseau, along with Charlotte Smith's *Elegiac Sonnets*, Cowper's *Task*, and Ossian, significantly in 'small doses'. As with nearly everyone protesting sensibility the painters Claude and Salvator were lauded, while Angelica was condemned because 'the figures are so gigantic'; Bunbury was praised as a cartoonist, Cosway as a miniaturist, Payne Knight as a gardener.

There were even areas where, greatly daring, Sarah could sometimes venture emendatory if not quite contrary opinions. Thus she could prevail on Mrs Tighe to study Mr Clarkson's pamphlet upon the slave trade, which had caused both her and her Better Half radically to alter their previous line of thinking on the subject; or, disapproving in any case of all manufactories, she could provide a list of work, neither unhealthy nor too hard, for the young orphan girls in whom Mrs Tighe had become interested; plain work and service were much to be preferred, but netting for fishing nets and making wig curls were both healthier she opined than ribbon or lace making. And when Mrs Tighe, contemplating, in addition to all her other good works, the gift of a cow and Bible to all her married Protestant tenants at Woodstock, she could be gently worked upon by Sarah to 'extend a little comfort to those of Roman Catholicks also – such as a little Pig or Cock and Hen – a few trees to plant round the Cottage – or some other mark of your favour – As they will feel the being totally excluded from it'.[1]

Yet all this came perilously close to those zones of discussion in which the very greatest tact had to be exercised, namely those of money and religion.

About money Mrs Tighe was sensitive. At the time of the elopement all those years ago her father, Sir William, had offered to double Sarah's allowance of thirty pounds a year. Mrs Tighe had nearer trebled the sum despite the claims of a large family and an estate that was only beginning to pay its way. In view of this generosity Sarah's success in securing a pension from the Civil List had seemed a personal affront, a reproach, and only a sequence of humble and conciliatory letters was able to correct the impression. Therefter great delicacy had to be employed on both sides of a correspondence which was apt to be punctuated with small wounded silences, implied accusations followed by temporary reconciliations. It was only when Mrs Tighe herself came near financial disaster and it was borne in upon her what Sarah had already suffered, that some sort of sympathy was re-established and Sarah's allowance augmented; although throughout Sarah had never been backward in acknowledging '. . . the income I Gratefully owe to Your Friendship – an income which is my sole dependence, for if I could have existed without it – I would have resigned it on the first suspicion that it would be useful to you'.[2]

The religious question was a nearly equal hazard, for throughout their long correspondence Mrs Tighe was steadily developing into a full-blown Methodist. Here indeed was a cause for some embarrassment, for the Beloved, repelled doubtless by certain egalitarian features of the sect, detested it. Sarah herself, as her letters to Harriet Bowdler make clear, was disturbed by the histrionic character of the religion and by the depressing effect it had had on the spirits of her friend the once gay and extrovert Goddard. Yet, conciliatory as ever, she sought to bridge the theological crevasse that appeared to be widening between her and her friend.

Mrs Tighe, hiding behind the person of her erstwhile governess, 'thinks' that she, Masquerier, is a Methodist. Sarah, aware that sly Mrs Tighe is testing her responses to this strange piece of news, responds nobly, 'I *wish* she was one for though not perfectly acquainted with the meaning of that term It is a Gratification to me to associate it with what I conceive from the word Christian',[3] a piece of gentle insincerity in view of the Beloved's violent experiences with Methodist gardeners. Mrs Tighe, encouraged, now emerges into the daylight with her opinions and expresses great admiration of Mr Wesley. Sarah in her turn inquires anxiously whether Mr Wesley would disapprove of her opinion that Astronomy and Botany, 'Rather tend to the Cultivation and increase of our Religious Principles than otherwise',[4] waits, breathlessly it would appear, for Mrs T's answer, is thankfully confirmed in her opinion, and is awarded a volume of Mr Wesley's works. She reads them, and discovers, quite genuinely it would seem, that in fact they 'breathe in my Humble opinion a still purer Spirit of True Religion'.[5]

For a time it almost looks as though Mrs Tighe might be making a convert. Sarah asks whether it would not be possible for Mr Wesley to visit Plas Newydd since he has chapels in both Bath and Chester, a risky suggestion one would have thought in view of the Beloved's declared prejudice. How sincerely intended the invitation was is hard to say. Sarah's nature was one to which Methodism might have appealed. She was highly sensitive, prone to guilt, repressed; her mind was of a melancholy cast, and this was accentuated in her middle thirties by anxieties about her health. Death had perforce to be contemplated: 'Is it possible' she was to inquire of Mrs Tighe with something near horror, 'that the Great Deceiver can have power to ensnare us to the very latest moment of our lives?'[6]

It is not recorded whether Mr Wesley did ever call at Plas Newydd, in any case Eleanor Butler would have had no truck with her Sally's Methodistical flirtings. By 1790 the times had changed dramatically and the correspondence became full of financial distresses, the fear of revolution and of war, and by the time these dangers had abated farming had ousted religion as the subject of greatest mutual interest.

Limitations notwithstanding Mrs Tighe was unquestionably one of Sarah's most intimate correspondents, for although Sarah might hope that 'I shall *always* prefer the Bottling of my stock of little vexations for my *private* drinking to uncorking them for the entertainment of those whose tranquility is dear to me',[7] she could and did confide in Mrs Tighe the sharp vexation that rumours about her marriage had occasioned, as well as her anxieties about money, and the pain caused by the Ormondes' ill-treatment of her Beloved. On this subject she felt obliged to warn Mrs Tighe not to repeat what she had told her, 'I have never to any other person even hinted . . .'[8]

In fact she had already confided in someone about the ill-behaviour of the Ormondes and about other close matters too. Someone who, had it not been for the Beloved, might have been an even closer friend, closer even than Mrs Tighe. This was Harriet Bowdler.

Evidence for this view is contained in a letter from Harriet Bowdler to Sarah Ponsonby; a letter since lost, but mentioned by Sarah's niece, Caroline Hamilton, in her memoirs. It was a letter which appears to have hinted at the unmentionable, the unthinkable, which was that there were times when Sarah regretted leaving Ireland; a letter in which Miss Bowdler had conjured Sarah Ponsonby 'not to give way to useless lamentations and to forget her Irish friends, as they were not worthy of her'.

This suggests a degree of intimacy never accorded Mrs Tighe, and the impression is reinforced by a fragment of another of Harriet Bowdler's letters written in 1809, a letter apparently concerned with Sarah's ill-treatment by one of the Bessborough family: 'My dearest angel . . . my dearest dear love' it begins, ending 'O that I cd. shelter you in my arms and guard you from every danger',[9] which, extravagant and sumptuous as sympathy then was, is none the less unusually warm.

Apart from these brief flashes, which suggest a friendship closer than was ever apparent, the surviving correspondence (all on Harriet Bowdler's side) between her and Sarah Ponsonby, is of an earlier date, and at this time her position with regard to the Plas Newydd friends had by no means become so equivocal.

Her role, it seems, was to supply the friends with political intelligence, and in the better parts of her letters she favoured them with long and clear accounts of current matters like the King's madness, the first stirrings of the French Revolution, Pitt's resignation and the controversy over the Act of Union with Ireland. That Eleanor herself valued these accounts is made clear by the fact that she frequently transcribed long sequences from Miss Bowdler's letters straight into the journal. But Harriet Bowdler, born of a clever family and gifted, as Sarah had written to Mrs Tighe, in practically everything but music, had other talents to offer. One of her anonymous works of theology had been so well received that a bishop had offered her a living on the strength of it; she was the acknowledged authoress of a number of poems and essays and a work of fiction pleading the cause of old maids; she was an authority on the education of the young. Miss Bowdler in short had much to say upon questions

relating to morals, manners and taste. In her correspondence
appreciations were written on favourite works ranging from
Hannah More's *The Progress of the Pilgrim Good Intent in
Jacobinical Times* to the less demanding *Mysteries of Udolpho.*
Favourite Italian sonnets were transcribed; also verse, which one
fears was, but hopes was not, written by herself.

From such a collection, transcribed in Sarah Ponsonby's elegant hand, illustrated with pen and wash drawings as meticulous as Baxter prints and withal dedicated to H.M.B., the
following poem *To Miss Harrap* will give some notion of what
was admired by Miss Bowdler at Bath and the two friends at
Plas Newydd:

> What numbers are these on my senses that steal
> Through night and thro' silence so sweetly convey'd
> No Mortal I cry'd ever warbled so well,
> Tis Philomel tunes her sad note in the glade
> Tis the wood's lovely Chantress with sorrow oppress'd
> That tunes her sad note with a thorn in her breast!
> But when Harrap her numbers melodiously rais'd
> So sweet was the music that fell from her tongue
> That enraptured I swore as I listen'd and gaz'd
> Twas an Angel I look'd on, an Angel that sung!
> Long ... long may she sing each rough passion to rest,
> But never, ye Gods! with a thorn in her Breast.[10]

Harriet Bowdler was also able to relay Bath gossip for which
the Ladies may secretly have pined; and although her accounts
of Bath society can scarcely be called scintillating, they at least
enabled the friends to enjoy tittle-tattle without actually endan-
gering the purity of the 'retirement'. In addition to all these
benefits which her correspondence conferred was that of sympathy, for she was close enough to be apprised of their most
pressing troubles, their financial anxieties, the possible consequences of the appalling article in the *General Evening Post,*
and, as we have seen, the cruel behaviour of the Ormondes.

From the Ladies themselves poor Miss Bowdler principally
desired affection; affection and constant remembrance of her
perfect visits to them: '... let me believe that I am as dear to
you as I was at that blessed period'; 'indulge me with a line to

say that you are well and have not forgotten me'; '. . . it is only from your own dear hand that I can learn what I most wish to know – that you still love me'.[11]

Her passionate need for affection tended to make this gifted and intelligent woman both foolish and slavish. While greatly preferring Sarah she sought, as we have seen, to placate the jealousy of the Beloved by making believe that she was a man, 'the *Viellard*', with whom she was in love. She carried out the fantasy in a manner which, had she paused to take stock of herself, she would have recognized as being both ridiculous and dangerous since her pretended '*affaire*' was broadcast to her circle of women friends at Bath. Thus, writing of their mutual friend, Miss Shipley, the sister of the Dean of St Asaph, she informed Sarah, apropos her '*affaire*' with Eleanor, 'I am still more gratified by her approbation of *my marriage*, for her judgement has more weight with me than a whole Theatre of others. Indeed as far as I have had an opportunity of knowing the opinion of the world, I find that everybody thinks as she does on the subject, and I receive the kindest and most flattering congratulations from all quarters.'[12]

Yet this subservient flattery did not always achieve that consistent affection and favour for which she yearned. From time to time her letters provoked wounded even querulous responses from Plas Newydd. Yet, written by Sarah as they were, the nature of the complaints suggests that they emanated in the first instance from the demanding *Viellard*: Why, for example, has not Miss Bowdler told them before of their mutual friend Mrs Morgan's marriage? And why has she announced it in the manner she has?

All that poor Miss Bowdler had had to say on the subject had been this: 'The only real objection is that the Lady is some few years older than he is; but young as he is, his steadiness has been tried by very uncommon circumstances, and nobly has he behaved in every instance',[13] with which there seems little enough to find fault. Yet in her friends' opinion, by her mild criticism of the match, she had committed an offence, one that had weakened the bonds of 'Affection, Friendship, Sympathy' which bound them all together.

On such an occasion the imagined wrappings of love, of intimacy, of gay flirtations with the *Viellard* vanished into thin air, and poor Miss Bowdler, left naked and frightened, cringed: 'If there was anything wrong in my *manner* of announcing Mrs M's marriage I can only intreat your pardon for an Offence of wch I am unconscious. God forbid that I should keep copies of my own letters and I do not recollect what I sd on the subject wch cd displease you. I am sure nothing ever came from my heart wch ought to offend you.'[14] After which eminently satisfactory apology Miss Bowdler was readmitted to a Temple of Friendship that had been newly scoured and whitened, and the sad and lonely game of make-believe began again.

By contrast the exchanges with Anna Seward were decidedly more equal. But unlike poor Miss Bowdler, Miss Seward was emotionally independent of the Ladies; was moreover, as one who had sung the great events of the era in verse, 'improved' *Beowulf*, and been roundly acclaimed as a critic, a celebrity in her own right. 'Queen Muse of Britain', as Sarah Ponsonby expressed it.

There was, however, as they must soon have found out, need for caution even in this correspondence. For while, like them, Miss Seward was a devotee of Richardson's *Clarissa* and Dr Darwin's *The Loves of the Plants*, doted on Salvator, Claude and Romney, she nevertheless detested the Ladies' much admired Tasso and Ariosto. More seriously she even had reservations about Dr Johnson, whom they wholeheartedly revered, and she hated their favourite, Pitt, for leading England into the devastating French war. More painful to tolerate perhaps than anything was the unhappy fact that she much preferred Mary Wolstonecraft's *Rights of Women* to what she considered the specious theories on women's education propounded in the works of Dr Gregory and the Ladies' adored Rousseau.

Lamed, unquestionably, by such grave differences, the correspondence managed to survive upon a certain compatibility of sentiment.

Politics penetrated this correspondence to but a limited extent, and only then at the raging heights of the Napoleonic war, but social tittle-tattle never found a place in letters which were almost entirely given over to literary criticism. However, place in the correspondence was reserved for experiences of an aesthetic nature, and these were presumably of mutual interest, or how else can one account for Miss Seward's strange outpourings, of which the following from the resort of Buxton is typical: 'I now sit writing by a good fire in very commodious lodgings' she writes Miss Ponsonby. 'My neat light parlour looks backward, is on the first flight of stairs, and, from its aspect, is quiet and silent. When I close one of the sash windows that looks on the superb stables, which are built on the rise of the hill, above this splendid, this golden half moon, the other window shows me only a sloping range of bare fields, without hedge or tree, and intersected by stone walls. They present a perfect picture of a barren country' she concludes with triumph, 'of rudeness, silence and solitude.'[15]

The correspondence was to be published in the Ladies' own lifetime, but unfortunately only that part of it which had been penned by Miss Seward, so that there are only second-hand glimpses of what the Ladies had to say to the poetess. One such reveals that Eleanor Butler was given to expressing herself in the grand manner to her friend, 'Fatally spreads the pestilential taint of insubordinate principles' she had written by way of comment on the events in Europe, a phrase so well liked by Miss Seward both in terms of expression and sentiment that she had quoted it back to her friend in a subsequent letter.

Flattering this must have been, yet what in her 'Edenic' solitude could E.B., the satirical, have thought of Miss Seward's account of a recent visit to yet another spa, Harrogate this time, an account which exhibits a fatuity of which she must surely have been aware? '... during one whole week, I lived unknowing and unknown, in a seclusion never in my whole preceding life experienced ... I rose at seven, and swallowed at intervals of twenty minutes between each draught three half pints of that superlatively nauseous fluid, impregnated with salt and sulphur, that makes it taste like putrid eggs'.[16]

Did these accounts really find echo in the Ladies' aesthetic hearts, or was it because Miss Seward was 'Queen Muse of Britain' that such letters were kept and not thrown, as tiresome

Lady Dungannon's, upon the dressing-room fire? And would Eleanor Butler have minded their cherished Mrs Piozzi, who anyway thought Miss Seward had a good deal less sense than she ought, knowing that they exchanged such stuff? Mrs Piozzi who was intellectually disinclined to works of the imagination, and had been trained by the great Doctor to hate 'feelers'.

For this reason their letters to Mrs Piozzi were a good deal more temperate than those to Miss Seward; the correspondence being conducted for the greater part by Eleanor, possibly deemed more fit than Sarah to engage with a lady as gifted as the mistress of Brynbella.

There were few dangerous zones of difference between them however. Mrs Piozzi, like them, greatly admired Pitt; she was as disturbed at the spread of Jacobinical principles as they were themselves; she was quite as given as they and Miss Bowdler to being impressed by doomful prophesies, *'Apollyon'* she had been pondering gloomily in the July of 1803, *'Apollyon'* while in the next valley her friend, Lady Eleanor, had been feverishly consulting almanacks.

But Mrs Piozzi was without question the more relaxed correspondent. Even allowing for the inflated mode of expression current at the time, it must be admitted that Eleanor Butler's letters were not only expressive of the highest gratification at being able to correspond with Mrs Piozzi at all, they were even a thought wheedling:

... permit us to remind you of the Friends whom you seem to have forgotten.

Dearest Mrs Piozzi We trust you will hold yourself bound to make us Ample recompense for the Many and Cruel disappointments We have experienced in hearing that you had so frequently Journeyd to and from Brynbella without bestowing a Single glance Upon us.[17]

When Mr Piozzi crowned their highest expectations by having his pianoforte lugged over the Horse Shoe Pass, which intervened between Plas Newydd and Brynbella, for a musical evening, their response was elegantly ecstatic: 'We should say a little of the trouble to yourselves and danger to the precious little Instrument' wrote Sarah, 'and the infinite indulgence to us – of sending it on Horseback down Bwlah y Rhw Odin – a feat never attempted much less Performed before as We Believe, since either Mountains or Pianofortes came in existence.'[18]

Perhaps slightly less impressed by the Ladies than they were with her, or she with herself, Mrs Piozzi committed herself confidently and amply to paper; would recommend them to read Beddowes on *Oxygen Air and Gas*, to which Eleanor would counter with 'Mr Cobbett's most entertaining and most impertinent paper';* would go blow for blow through the semantic errors perpetrated by the critics who had torn her *Retrospection* to pieces; would candidly reveal the anguish caused her by the lawsuit with which her elder daughter was threatening her: 'I brought their Papa more than £20,000, first and last – as the Phrase is; and I now see that if he had not remembered me in his Will, These Ladies would have driven me completely on the Pavé.'[19] To which the Plas Newydd friends responded with indignant twitters, for it was unthinkable that such a horror could happen at Brynbella, where reigned Harmony almost Celestial, where Taste, Genius and Talents and Benevolence presided in the most Sublime of all Regions. 'Miss Thrale will not enjoy an Estate so unscrupulously gained'[20] they promised sternly. But for all their sympathy, they do not seem to have been prepared to confide with equal frankness in Mrs Piozzi. Those tender subjects like shortage of cash and the disappointments caused by friends, seem not to have been discussed at all.

But there was one person with whom Eleanor Butler seemed able to conduct a correspondence of an altogether more relaxed kind, one very much younger than herself, who could evoke from her that ironic humour in which she showed at her best.

Miss Harriet Pigott, the niece of their nearby neighbours, the Myttons of Halston, was of impeccable family, she was also high-spirited, but poor. Nearly half a century separated her in age from Eleanor Butler, and yet they shared an affinity. Had not Miss Pigott been the youngest in a family of two girls and one boy, and had she not received unmerited ill-treatment from

* *Cobbett's Political Register*, a radical weekly paper that first came out in 1802.

them all? 'Was I *carresante*' she had told the two Ladies, 'I was artful; if grave and tearful ill-tempered, if animated, bold and rude; and to crown it all, there was no occasion to bring me out.'[21]

Her story bore a strong resemblance to Eleanor's own, so that when Miss Pigott, at the age of thirty, finding her family intolerable, decamped in a rage from her brother's rectory at Chetwynd and took up residence at an inn called the *Butcher's Arms*, Eleanor was both sympathetic and amused. 'Tho' not eligibly – we trust you are at least comfortably situated in your Butcher's Arms'[22] she wrote teasingly.

The intrepid Miss Pigott now withdrew for an interim period to live with a friend at a cottage in Lancing. Meanwhile in letters to and from Eleanor Butler a plan for her future began to mature. It was simple enough, but, for the times, daring. It was that she should accompany a French lady to France and help look after her two children. 'Let your residence in France be for so short a length of time you will be quite the fashion in Shropshire when you return' wrote Eleanor approvingly, 'and it will be "Who shall invite Miss H. Pigott. She is just home from Paris and is so agreeable so entertaining. She has seen everything – lived in the first society – and all that sort of Thing." '[23]

Early in the year of Waterloo Miss Pigott set forth for Paris armed with a letter of introduction from the Ladies to their acquaintance, Mrs Popkin. The letter of introduction remained unused, but her experiences, which included a round of balls and a visit to the famous battlefield, she gathered into a bulky scrapbook bearing the warning 'Do not touch these drawings, the eyes are not in the fingers'; she also relayed her experiences in letters to Plas Newydd.

These letters gave Eleanor the most genuine delight: 'Your Account of Paris and all you have Seen is particularly interesting to me and gave me a Sort of Maladie du Pays' she wrote. 'Write to me Dearest Miss Harriet – such Letters as yours are not to be met with for Love or Money – I devour I live upon them – in the Circle of your delicious french friends.'[24]

Her own letters to Harriet Pigott were not only relaxed but pleasingly malicious. Miss Pigott must have smiled to read that

'You would be terrified to behold the Multitude of persons who are conjured up to prevent My Writing ... Sir John Cotterill and his three Most hideous Daughters ... Mr and Mrs Becker he a German of immense Opulence. She built on a Very large Scale – with a Magnificent face in the Rubens Stile a Massish Beauty – then we have had the Algernon Grevilles – we like them very Much – if he could be Convinced of how much More becoming it is to stand erect than to Lounge – and Sweep the Carpet with his head he would be very handsome Graceful and pleasing.'[25]

The style was as sharp and vigorous in the woman of seventy-five writing in 1815 as it had been writing to the Goddard of a 'Batch of Irish' that had passed through Llangollen thirty-three years before:

The Father a good humoured good natured Honest Looking Man in Continued Wonder and admiration at Every Thing he Sees. which Though a Childish is I believe a very pleasant State. The Mother. a plain Scorbutic good woman a pretty Sloppy daughter. a gawky Son. and a cousin. who I fancy means to exhibit his person this season. to the Highest Old bidder ...'[26]

So she emerged when writing to someone of sympathetic temper; E.B. given in most of her letters to hiding herself, laughing or furious, behind bland formality, Johnsonian verbosity or fatuous rapture. Eleanor Butler, tart, arrogant, sardonic and a shade cruel, a vivid contrast to Sarah Ponsonby.

For even in her most intimate correspondence Sarah Ponsonby never let herself go beyond gentle teasing or certain dryly humorous comments.

Surely Miss Bulley is rather a dolorous name for a governess? she demands of Mrs Tighe; or might not Muff, the Woodstock dog, benefit from a dose of the Bark? Perhaps if she opened to anyone it was in her lost letters to Harriet Bowdler. Harriet Bowdler as sensitive as she was herself, the sympathetic recipient of sorrows that we do not know about, though sorrows unspecified we know there were.

What, if anything, resulted from this life lived out so painstakingly in the quires of gold-edged paper that they covered with their small neat handwriting? Not only the power to bid wine and books and beaver hats and marble and Gothick patterns and the Reeves paints, with which Sarah Ponsonby adorned her MSS., to come jogging by mail and carrier and horseback to their remote cottage. Together they constituted a kind of diplomatic chancery through which, by means of a complex of introductions, recommendations and minute inquests, they could exert very real power and influence. So that they could make or break reputations : 'She begs you will not be Civil to those Butlers' writes Sarah Ponsonby to Mrs Tighe. 'She thinks they are the Children of a Cheese Woman.'[27] Or, 'We are very materially interested in the appointment of a Master to Harrow School. Having been told that if Our Acquaintance Mr Foster shou'd be the Successful Candidate it will be more advantageous to Him – than it is likely to prove to His Pupils.'[28] Or, 'She is descended from, and connected with some of the first families in Shropshire who have long been in the number of Our particular friends – has many agreable and valuable qualities . . .'[29] So that they could, knowing Bishops, make recommendations for curacies. So that, knowing many rich people, they could boost suitable charities. So that, knowing many influential people, they could champion their just causes.

They expected their services to be reciprocated none the less, though this was not strange in the age in which they lived. Insomuch as they had written a letter of introduction for Miss Pigott to Mrs Popkin at Paris, it behoved Miss Pigott not only to respond with letters but to present them, perhaps, with a new receipt. '. . . something *Very Good* out of *Nothing*' Eleanor Butler would demand of her, 'the cheaper the more convenient. the french understand these things better than any people upon earth – therefore I appeal to you to assist us in performing that Miracle – of making a great Show for nothing.'[30]

But reciprocation was not confined to their correspondence. Their world was built upon it, and it permeated every aspect of their daily life. For out of Plas Newydd was daily, monthly, yearly, spun a great web of obligation and counter-obligation, which entrapped willingly, and sometimes not, man, woman and child to a radius of several miles. Their Iris, the old Irishwoman, daily trudged hither and thither with hand notes and nostrums and rare plants, and back came hares and trees and eggs and kittens, while the *Hand* in exchange for their continued patronage regularly sent up those 'culinary presents' which Eleanor Butler so detested.

For in that age of patronage they were great patrons; had, over the years by the skilful employment of social influence, honesty, service and charm, built up from small insecure beginnings, a kingdom. It was a kingdom in which they were absolute, with power over such diverse matters as unruly children, curacies, ill-behaved dogs, beggars, dirty streets, the preservation of rural beauty, the ordering of celebratory bell peals and bonfires.

Those who criticized them tended to disregard the fact that a way of life tends to evolve in spite of those who live it, and they would contrast the Ladies' small splendour in 1809 with the protested retirement of their early days.

'Faugh!' their erstwhile acquaintance, Mrs Preston, used to cry whenever their names were mentioned, or so Lady Louisa Stuart tells us. But then Eleanor Butler had always known that Mrs Preston was an hysteric, and had been prescribed green nettle whippings by Dr Darwin,* and she herself had always considered the unfortunate lady 'twaddling'.

* Dr Robert Waring Darwin, father of the naturalist.

Chapter Ten

'Nine till Twelve. In the Dressing Room.' 1809–29

By the end of 1810, a whole year after Mary Carryll's death, Sarah was still lamenting '. . . the dreadful vacancy made in Our family and our comfort by the fatal event of November 22nd. 1809'.[1]

Many evenings had been whiled away recalling 'the angelic countenance' of the dead woman, and in consoling themselves with the remembrance of the visions that had been vouchsafed to her before she died. She had seen a beautiful young child sitting by her bed, had heard the music of sweetly playing flutes, at which, smiling, she had cried out, 'Beat on! Beat on!' while Sarah, steeling herself to read the commendatory prayer, had been rewarded by the attendant apothecary telling her that Mary had drawn her last breath 'just as the most Important Sentence in it had passed my lips'.[2]

The Llangollen people had shown their love and respect for the dead woman by turning out in great numbers to sweep the road clean along which the coffin was to be drawn to the church; their own friends had also testified to their affection for Mary, Mr Parker of Sweeney Hall helping them to design the Gothick memorial over the vault, and Dr Dealtry composing the epitaph:

> 'Patient, industrious, faithful, generous, kind,
> Her conduct left the proudest far behind;
> Her virtues dignified her humble birth,
> And raised her mind above this sordid earth.'

There had been letters of condolence from the greatest: from the Princess Amelia, from the Duke of Gloucester, as well as from their personal friends, friends who now did all in their power to take their minds off their sad loss. Indeed it was at one of Miss Ormsby's theatrical parties, where Harriet Pigott so amused them in her part of Busy the maid, that a new and pleasing friendship sprang up between the Ladies and the young woman. Notes were soon flying back and forth that spring of 1810, notes which showed that life at Plas Newydd was at last returning to normal: 'I dare say we could have discovered Aches and pains in Abundance had we professed leisure sufficient to attend to them' wrote Eleanor Butler to Harriet Pigott, 'but Tuesday — we had an M.P. — and a Young Divine to entertain — Wednesday we had that most interesting of Beings Lady Erne to admire — Thursday we had Lady Erne Again — and this day our beloved Ancient Cow Beauty — for so Many — Many years the Grace and Pride and Ornament of our Pastures — Well — this day — No matter — I am convinced She is now grazing in the Elysian Fields'.[3]

Outside affairs were engrossing their attention once more, and in particular Telford's scheme for his new Holyhead road to which, as already in the case of unsightly quarries and the even worse manufactories, both Ladies had taken instant exception. By the July of 1811 Sarah was referring angrily to 'the number of counties the great Land Anatomist has occasion to digest at the same time',[4] while Eleanor had already expressed her disapproval with characteristic vigour to the engineer himself. On receiving a polite and well-reasoned reply however, she had immediately shed her prejudices: 'As my voice has been loudest in expressing resentment of your supposed contumely' she wrote with engaging frankness, 'I feel it incumbent on my pen to make you Amende honorable and request you will show my recantation wherever you have heard, or may hear, of my complaints, as your obliging explanation has perfectly convinced me of their injustice.'[5]

They were not only occupied with roads, however. They were using influence to persuade their friends to grant custom to Mrs Parker of the *Hand*, were themselves trying to secure the appointment of her son to a curacy; they were persuading yet other acquaintances to patronize poor Mr Jones 'the Oswestry China man', whose business was not thriving; were petitioning Mr

Parker to save unfortunate Elizabeth Longford from being sent to the Oswestry House of Industry.

Agriculture was still claiming their attention; they had been to the Wynnstay agricultural meeting that autumn; had been seeking advice about new types of manure; were levelling one of their fields and experimenting with the culture of potatoes.

Meanwhile in the realm of the arts Robert Southey, whose Joan of Arc they had so greatly admired, had honoured them with a visit and had written 'a manuscript poem' beneath their roof. They themselves were currently laughing at a jingle of Mr Sheridan's, which seemed perfectly to reflect the morality of the times:

> To ready Scotland Boys and Girls are carried
> Across the Tweed, impatient to be married,
> More prudent grown, the self same road they run
> With equal haste to get the knot undone
> Th'indulgent Scots, when English law too nice is
> Our Follies Sanction first, and then our vices.[6]

Sarah commenting dryly in her letter to Mrs Parker of Sweeney Hall that 'Marriages in future may terminate with the Honeymoons – and unbridled Licentiousness become the Disorder of the day.'[7] Meanwhile in their own words they were entertaining 'Company from Ten am to Ten pm' and were themselves visiting, arriving home often as not in the early hours of the morning.

In contrast to such enviable vigour some of their older friends were failing. Mrs Tighe was ill, and would soon make the painful journey over from Ireland to consult Dr Darwin; Letitia Barrett had died, and when Harriet Bowdler wrote for a description of her tomb in Oswestry church, which was in all conscience near enough for them to visit they rather oddly wrote to Mrs Parker to supply them with the necessary details.

Other friends had already gone, Elizabeth Barrett, Anna Seward, poor Gabriel Piozzi. In the June of 1813 his widow drove over to Plas Newydd after hearing that Eleanor Butler had had a severe fall, fractured her arm and painfully dislocated her shoulder. She found her well and merry, however, and as she wrote to Dr Whalley, the seventy-four-year-old patient 'was not confined to her bed an hour it seems so strong is her constitution'.[8] And soon Sarah was informing Mrs Tighe that Eleanor, like Lazarus, had 'dismissed all her bandages'. By October they were entertaining as vigorously as ever, and Sarah was sending Mrs Parker, with whom she was becoming increasingly intimate, an enormous list of visitors, to 'show You the sort of life we *sometimes* lead in our *strict* retirement'.[9]

Strong constitutions were needed. The year 1814 made its debut with sleet and snowfalls so heavy that towards the end of January the coach returning over the Horse Shoe Pass from depositing Mrs Piozzi at Ruthin after a visit to Plas Newydd was caught in a drift, Patrick, the Ladies' driver, being 'providentially discovered when quite exhausted after crawling on his hands and knees within twenty yards of the only habitation on that dreary road,' and one of the horses, apparently blind, having, as Sarah described it, 'the extraordinary sagacity to remain stationary until she was sought and found in the morning'.[10] During this exceptionally hard time Sarah was proud to record how 'Our Parish have really done wonders for the relief of Our Unfortunate Neighbours – in the late dreadful Weather – both in supplying them with Coals and Food.'[11]

By May such horrors were forgotten. Lord Byron had sent them a complimentary copy of *The Corsair*, 'May we not be proud' commented Sarah to Mrs Parker, and they were turning their attention to beautifying the cottage.

Taste had changed. Gothick had evolved towards Tudor, oak was becoming the rage. 'Seized' as Sarah admitted with 'the Oak carving mania' they now, indefatigably and inexorably, set about transforming Plas Newydd.

While in Europe their friend Castlereagh was engaged in negotiating a peace treaty with France, the Ladies at Plas Newydd, unblushingly owning that for them the choosing of a new pair of wafer tongs was 'as important as the restoration of the Bourbons',[12] were filling the cottage with workmen.

The upheaval was immense, and Harriet Pigott was to hear from Lady Eleanor how they had been obliged '. . . to remove every article of furniture from the lower to the Upper regions –

which we now inhabit. The difficulty was where to stow Books. Pictures. Treasures. Tables. Chairs etc etc. – it is now Accomplished and the Spare bedchamber and Dressing room, are Converted into a State Apartment fit for the acceptance of that Gadding Dss of Oldenburgh* should her S.H. – (which heaven Avert ramble into this Principality.)'[13]

Meanwhile below stairs, the hall, staircase and one room were panelled in the dark richly carved oak which twenty years later would put a lady tourist in mind of an enormous cupboard. By October the great work was finished, and the visitor would gaze upon a transmogrified Plas Newydd; its lower windows strangely lidded by oaken canopies, its porch a rich and appalling riot of carving. Since this last item was the *pièce de resistance* its completion called for a celebration, a 'Porch warming', to which a number of their friends were invited. Nine days later Eleanor was writing feelingly that if she had only known that Harriet Pigott had been seeing Lord Ormonde's agent, Mr Williams, 'I should have besought you to speak to him on My Behalf and Gently hint of what essential – what incalculable service a little Money would do me – The trifle Lord Ormonde Could So *well* Spare would be Absolute Wealth to *poor* me'.[14]

Their pensions were most likely in arrears again. Three years later hectic appeals to Castlereagh would result in all too familiar disappointment, 'I owe it ... to you both to impress upon your mind the extreme difficulty of procuring, in the indigent state of the Pension Fund in both countries, Provision from that source',[15] he would write sternly.

But even as Castlereagh was thus cautioning them life at the cottage was continuing, and departing, moreover, not one tittle from previous high standards: 'two or three dozen ... of what you recommend as the best and most fashionable white wine ...' had been ordered in September, while only a fortnight before they received Castlereagh's sober warning an order had been dispatched for 'Two dozen very finest Old Red Port'.[16] Orders to their tallow chandler were equally particular, whether for the 'best purified and perfumed Windsor Soap' or for those candles which must not only burn brightly and clearly and be

* The Czar's sister.

free from 'Tallowish smell', but must also be 'very handsome to look at'.[17]

They were old hands at coping with financial embarrassment after all, adept, after nearly forty years practice, at living as though no such nuisance existed. But they were getting old, seventy-nine and sixty-three respectively, and, as they increasingly bewailed, many of their old friends and acquaintainces had already gone, while they themselves were beginning to be regarded as eccentric, laughable even by a younger generation.

When Harriet Pigott had accompanied them to Oswestry to watch the ceremony by which the French prisoners of war had had their passports returned to them, she had noticed how the prisoners had stared transfixed at Lady Eleanor, viewing with amazement the order of the *Croix St Louis* that she wore about her neck. Their interest was pardonable, the *Croix* being a pre-revolutionary award made only to officers and gentlemen for outstandingly meritorious conduct on the field of battle. The order had been discontinued during the Revolution, however, and it is possible that the exiled King had considered it no unsuitable souvenir to send to so ardent and distinguished a supporter of the Bourbons; one so ardent indeed that some time later she was, as a matter of principle, to refuse the tempting offer of a lock of Napoleon's hair.

Eleanor wore the *Croix* on every important occasion; round her neck, as a cordon round her waist, and in triplicate in her button hole, together with a large harp brooch signifying allegiance to loyalist Ireland. In addition she sported a life-size silver *fleur-de-lis* pinned to her breast.

But this was not all. During the 90s both Ladies had begun having their hair cropped in the fashionable 'Titus' style, and this, together with the adoption of a mode more fashionable in France than in England, namely the wearing of beaver hats with their habits, gave them, to unpractised eyes, an oddly masculine appearance.

To some degree the Ladies themselves seem to have been aware of the eccentric impression they were creating, for, as a jingle of Eleanor's shows, even she had a modicum of self-knowledge:

Hymn to Diana

Since thou and the stars my dear Goddess decree
That old maid as I am, an old maid I must be,
Oh hear the petition I offer to thee
For to bear it must be my endeavour!

From the griefs of my friendships all drooping around
Till not one that I loved in my youth can be found
From the legacy-hunters that near us abound
Diana! thy servant deliver.

From the scorn of the young, and the flouts of the gay,
From all the trite ridicule rattled away
By the pert ones who know nothing better to say,
Oh a spirit to laugh at them give her!

From repining at fancied neglected desert,
Or vain of a civil speech bridling alert,
From finical rudeness or flattering dirt,
Diana! thy servant deliver.

From over-solicitous guarding of pelf
From humour unchecked, that most obstinate elf,
From every unsocial attention to self
Or ridiculous whim whatsoever,

From vapourish freaks or methodical airs
Apt to sprout in a mind thats exempted from cares,
From impertinent meddling others affairs,
Diana! thy servant deliver.

From spleen at beholding the young more carest,
From the pettish asperity tartly expressed,
From scandal, detraction and every such pest,
From all, thy true servant deliver.

Nor let satisfaction depart from her lot,
Let her sing if at ease, and be patient if not,
Be pleased if remembered, content if forgot,
Till the Fates her slight thread shall dissever.[16]

It was left to Sarah in her letters to Mrs Parker to be ironically humorous about their failings in prose. There was the Better Half's response to a box of eye ointment from kind Mrs Parker, how she 'contented herself with Opening the Box – giving it one look – and having it laid by very Carefully – being her customary mode of treating almost all prescriptions'.[19] In addition they both knew themselves to be more than ordinarily fussy about the return of borrowed books, and Sarah would describe them 'smarting – and fretting – and grumbling – and almost Despairing'[20] when Mrs Mytton of Garth was slow to return their treasured copy of *The Antiquary*.

But for all their age and reputed eccentricity they could still charm, especially the young. For although Dean Stanley confessed to being terrified out of his wits when he visited the Ladies as a child, he seems to have been an exception, for a succession of children were to find themselves delighted by the Plas Newydd dogs and kittens and Eleanor's two tame crows 'with three legs between them'. And in May 1818 Sarah recorded the no mean achievement of keeping six small grand-nephews and grand-nieces entertained for an entire afternoon with one of the newly invented kaleidoscopes.

The great war which had lasted twenty-two years was over at last. It was some time now since they had nervously speculated upon the effect of the 'Demon's' escape from Elba; some time too since they had read their answer in the Mail galloping into Llangollen festooned with laurel to celebrate the great victory; some time since they had sat up late at night to watch the new and amazing gaslights illuminating the Llangollen cotton factory over the river. And they had seen that very factory go bankrupt, so that, in Sarah's words, 'Scores of poor little Creatures would be 'dismissed from that odious employ ... unfit for any other whatsoever', and they two would have only 'the miserable *Vain* Consolation – of having prophesied five and twenty Years ... that such things would eventually be'.[21]

Time had passed, but in the eighteen months which separated Castlereagh's dispiriting letter on the subject of their pensions from Eleanor Butler's first entry in the 1819 journal, there had occurred some unrecorded stroke of good fortune. For, 'thursday the fifth of January – 1819' ran the clear hand of the eighty-year-old woman, 'We this day completed the Purchase of our House.'[22]

Where had the money come from? In 1800 at the time of the quarrel with their new landlord, Sarah had written to Anna Seward that they had thankfully been confirmed in their rights 'for the remaining term of our Lease – viz. about 85 years', yet at the time of their deaths Plas Newydd was undoubtedly free-hold.

Their anxious applications to Castlereagh hardly suggest that they had sufficient money to make gradual payments for the house, and Mrs Goddard's legacy of a hundred pounds and Mary Carryll's savings could scarcely have been sufficient, and in any case both had been left them quite ten years previously.

It is possible that they anticipated a legacy briefly mentioned in July 1822 in a letter from Sarah Ponsonby to a Mrs Reynolds. The donor appears to have been a woman, but was not Mrs Piozzi, who died in 1821 leaving everything to her adopted son. It is more likely that Eleanor's Ormonde nephew, now richer by some half a million pounds after selling the family rights to the prisage of Irish wines, had not forgotten his aunt before his own early death in 1820.

By whatever means, Plas Newydd, in which they had lived for so long, was legally theirs at last, and a year later Eleanor made a new will leaving all she possessed to Sarah, and appointing her sole executrix.

With the possession of the cottage the financial anxieties which had dogged them for so long seemed to be receding at last. Three years later Lord Kenyon's* patronage would secure them not only regular but increased pensions, while correspondence with Miss Pigott shows that by 1822 Eleanor was in receipt of an additional allowance of sixty pounds a year from her nephew James, the new Lord Ormonde.

For the time being, however, the mere ability to pay a bill at all still evoked a fervent *Laus Deo!* in the journal. The entries

* George, 2nd Baron Kenyon. Bencher of the Middle Temple.

were sometimes only a couple of lines long now and, because of worsening sight due to a spreading cataract, in a difficult scrawled hand.

Their routine had changed in some particulars; breakfast was now at a more indulgent time, dinner had progressed to the more fashionable hour of four or even five o'clock; yet their daily activities remained much as before, seeming almost to suggest lives that would continue for ever. 'Perfect Spring day – Soft – Smiling – Verdant – employed in planting hollies'[23] records the eighty-year-old hand, and drops an early violet between the pages. Their fields were prospering, thirty people sitting down under the trees to celebrate at their haymaking dinner in a July so burning that all she could write was 'heat intense' and afterwards note down Lady Glynn's receipt for ginger beer.

Indoors improvements still had not ceased. The glazier had been to put up new painted glass in the bedchamber, and the builder had taken down the old chimney-piece and replaced it with one of Shropshire marble. They were still collecting books, having them handsomely bound by Price of Oswestry; they were also collecting rarities specially employing Mr Davies as their 'Antiquarian Researcher', and they were still obsessively hoarding oak; the Warden of Ruthin having recently sent them a 'beautiful lion couchant'* and another admirer 'Two Noble Bed posts'.

The journal reveals a mind as far ranging in its interests, as amused as ever. In October of the following year the actor, Charles Mathews, meeting them at a dinner party at Porkington would see, as he thought, 'a couple of dear antedeluvian old darlings'[24] and would long to pop Lady Eleanor, mannified dress, decorations, vast brooches and all, beneath a bell jar to take back to Highgate to show Mrs Mathews.

He would little guess at the snug laughs that the antediluvian old darling was enjoying between the pages of the little red journal. Lady Strangford's 'ludicrous letter about the blue pill'; Lady Donegal's joke that 'the PR in consequence of the advice of his physicians had left off wearing stays – and his stomach

* Still keeping guard in the porch today.

had fallen down to his knees', Mrs Scott commenting dryly 'that it was a moveable feast'.[25] Would Mr Mathews have any idea of the many interests that flock through the old darling's head? How, for instance, you could tell a true from a composite stone by licking it, or how for a cancer, 'a poultice of Bruised and pounded Water Cresses fresh from the Spring – changed twice in the day each time quite fresh prevents the offensive smell so dreadful in this disease'.[26] Doubtless her conversation would already have given the lie to her keen interest in births, marriages and, most particularly, deaths. There was the old Duke of Hamilton who had left 'Eighty thousand pounds to an *improper*'; there was the poor Queen of Spain who had undergone a Caesarian operation while alive and fully conscious, 'Murdered' the old darling notes passionately, 'by the Inquisition'. Could Mr Mathews believe that at eighty-one she still enjoys lying awake in the early hours listening to distant thunder; still notes with pleasure that there has been 'delicious rain all night'; that Christmas still revels in the 'Beautiful French perfumes from Nightingale Shrewsbury – the gift of My Beloved'?[27]

The press of people coming to visit them is now phenomenal, especially in the summertime; 'Mr Loyd of Rhagatt' records the journal for 5 August 1821, 'Mr, Mrs, Miss and Mr Augustus Morgan in the morning, then Lord Ormonde and Lord Thurles, then Lord Mayborough and Lord Burguish to Luncheon, then Lord, Lady Ormonde and Lord Thurles to dinner. Then Lady Harriet, Lady Anne, Lady Louisa, Mr Walter, Mr James, Mr Richard, Mr Charles Butler to Supper. Prince Paul Esterhazy for a short time in the evening, and Lord and Lady Ormonde slept in our State Apartment.'[28]

No wonder that not a few people, Lady Louisa Stuart among them, sneer at the 'retirement' the Ladies profess. But not only are they receiving a stream of visitors but, as the flat orange notebook tells us, a stream of presents: Herculaneum Grapes, Pears, Partridges, Woodcocks, Pheasants, Cherry Brandy, Geraniums, Porcelain, Eggs, and, of course, Oak.

They acknowledge these gifts with interest, however, and when the plump Regent ascends the throne that July they celebrate his coronation by gorgeously illuminating Plas Newydd with transparencies to the huge delight of 'all the Mob-ility of Llangollen', and the Shrewsbury paper reports the event in full the following week.

They are enjoying life greatly, almost too greatly were that possible, for there are approaching shadows. In France their old acquaintance Madame de Genlis has recently been visited by their friends, Clorinda and Georgina Byrne, and they tell her that the Ladies are threatened with tragedy; poor Miss Ponsonby has dropsy: '*Ainsi*' comments Madame de Genlis with something like a touch of triumph at her somewhat obvious prophecy being realized, '*l'une des deux survivra à l'autre*.'[29]

There seems to have been truth in the rumour, for a water-colour sketch taken by Lady Delamere some time later, whether from life or memory it is not certain, does portray with great tenderness the elder friend childlike and smiling being led round the library by the younger, whose cheeks are gaunt, and below whose waist can be seen a great swelling like some monstrous pregnancy. Contemporaries tell us that it was now Sarah's main concern to survive her friend, since she knew all too well that Eleanor would be intolerably wretched without her.

By now Eleanor's writing in the 1821 journal was growing ever more illegible, the thicker quill and blacker ink unable to compensate for the rapidly failing sight.

By February of the following year they decided to resort to surgery and Eleanor underwent an operation to cut the cataract. It was popularly reported that as soon as the surgeon had done his work his patient, scorning a blue eye-shade, put on her decorations and, covering her head with a large-brimmed hat, went and sat in the library. True or not the story is expressive of the fortitude which could endure such an operation and the weeks of pain that followed it.

By June inflammation was spreading from the weaker eye to the eye that they had hoped to save, and Sarah was writing to Mrs Parker of 'unconquerable pain', of 'Sleepless nights and miserable days'.[30] On the afternoon of 23 June two more leeches were applied to Eleanor's temple 'In addition to the number it had already enclosed',[31] and the inflammation appeared to be subsiding so that Sarah, writing during a thunderstorm, 'the finest We have long enjoyed', could tell Mrs Parker not only of the 'most Sublime thunder – but long unexperienced Content of Heart'.[32] A second operation soon followed while the going was good, and by Tuesday night on the sixteenth of July Sarah wrote Mrs Parker that the doctors had high hopes of Eleanor making a good recovery and that, most cheerful of all for one devoted to such comforts, 'She has been Allowed for the first time since the 13th April – to eat one Mutton Chop for her Dinner.'[33]

In fact she was never, in any useful sense, to recover her sight again. For when, a year later, loyalty to the Bourbon cause forbade her to accept the lock of Napoleon's hair, her letter politely declining this memento was written by Sarah, and her own signature at the bottom of the page was illegible.

Two years later, however, William Wordsworth, writing to Sir George Beaumont of an evening spent drinking tea with the two friends, informed him that 'Lady E. has not been well, and has suffered much in her eyes, but she is surprisingly lively for her years. Miss P.' he added, 'is apparently in unimpaired health.'[34]

The following day the poet sent a sonnet from Ruthin, which he had composed in the grounds of Plas Newydd, and which he had dedicated to the two friends, the pertinent lines of which ran as follows:

> Glyn Cafaillgaroch, in the Cambrian tongue,
> In ours the Vale of Friendship, let this spot
> Be nam'd where faithful to a low roof'd Cot
> On Deva's banks, ye have abode so long,
> Sisters in love, a love allowed to climb
> Ev'n on this earth, above the reach of time.[35]

It was hardly one of his best compositions, and what Eleanor Butler and Sarah Ponsonby thought of Plas Newydd, which for some time they had been referring to as a 'mansion', being called 'a low roof'd Cot' is not recorded. They must have been only too sadly aware, however, that their love would not for long be beyond the reach of time.

John Lockhart, visiting them with Sir Walter Scott the following year, saw only two odd old women, 'the one almost blind, and every way much decayed', the other, 'the *ci-devant* groom' as he expressed it, 'in good presentation'.[36] But Prince Puckler Muskau calling on them three years later in 1828 was to be less struck by their oddity than by Sarah's indefatigable tenderness to Eleanor Butler, her sympathetic anticipation of her beloved friend's every small need.

The older woman had been extremely ill in 1827, recalled from death's door ironically enough, among other nostrums, by the fervent prayers of the Llangollen Methodists, whom for so long she had despised. But she was failing, was no longer the small vital figure she had once been. People noticed that the front of her habit was now spotted with dropped food and that the treasured *Croix* was coated with spilled butter and sprinkled with falling hair powder. It was hardly surprising since she was by now almost blind. Now when she wanted to move out of the library where they habitually sat among piled-up newspapers, albums, autograph books, exuding, as Lockhart had heartlessly commented, 'the incarnation of bluestockingism', Sarah had to lead her. It was in the library in the year of her serious illness that there was taken what was reputedly the first and last sketch of them together. Mrs Parker's daughter Mary, who was a gifted amateur artist, made secret drawings from the shadow of the library curtains, while Miss Ponsonby and her mother engaged Lady Eleanor in conversation, that decided lady having always detested the mere idea of having her portrait taken, or so we are told.

Late in their day as it was they still made plans for the future, still shared their own quiet fun. Another cow was needed for the farm, and Sarah wrote on behalf of them both asking Mrs Parker to find them 'A Whole Alderney or Guernsey or Half Alderney or Guernsey – and Half Devon – None of Your pale-face Herefordshires ... Holdernesses – or Gigantic Denhams' which, in their combined opinion, were merely 'Gorgeous machines of Skim Milk'.[37]

Although she could write no longer Eleanor's voice sounded strongly in the letters to Mrs Parker. Mrs Silk, the cat, is expecting kittens, 'but has not yet produced her promised offspring –

for which Lady Eleanor calls her Johanne Southcote'.* There
was the perennial concern about the return of those borrowed
books which she could now no longer read. What has become of
their *Vathek* that they leant Mrs Parker? 'Lady Eleanor Vows
par Diana that the Second Volume of *Segan Histoire de
Napoleon* – left here as a Substitute for the Caliph Shall not be
restored till you come to replace the Potentate on his too long
Usurped throne.'[38]

It was Sarah who was now reading Eleanor the books which
interested them as much as ever, and in particular Sir Walter
Scott's novels of which they were ardent admirers. Sometimes
they amused themselves trying to solve *Enigmes* like the following, which a friend had sent them:

> A word I am of plural number
> Foe to Peace and tranquil slumber
> Add to it the Letter S
> How Great the Metamorphosis,
> Plural is Plural now no more
> And Sweet what bitter was before.[39]

The solution, gracefully supplied in verse by the vicar of
Oswestry, was no less than a statement of their life together,
Cares transformed into *Caress*.

Summer 1828 ended, and the days began to shorten, days
which in the past they had welcomed for the long evenings
which followed and the subsequent peace in which to enjoy their
'retirement': those mornings spent reading *La Nouvelle
Héloïse*, while Sarah drew her maps; autumn afternoons walking up the Bache to collect holly berries for hedges; evenings
spent before the library fire learning Italian, learning Spanish,
for sadly there had, after all, not been enough time to learn
Latin; and those quietest, most intimate times of all, chatting
in their curl papers before the kitchen fire or reading in the
dressing-room late at night before bed.

As then, so they were in spirit this last winter together, snow
and cold contracting their world; yet small as it was it was only

* Joanna Southcott (1750–1814), religious fanatic. In October 1802 she
described herself as 'bringing forth to the world . . . the second Christ'.
The pregnancy was hysterical and came to nothing.

through Sarah that Eleanor could make contact with it at all. As they moved about the library tenderly hand in hand people noticed that their roles had reversed at last, Eleanor grown quiet and submissive while Sarah gently directed her.

Did she lead her through the shrubbery that spring to smell the white lilacs again, that shrubbery where nearly fifty years ago they had walked away their 'little troubles' in the moonlight? And did she, as the days lengthened out once more and summer approached, describe their favourite plants as they reappeared in the border once again; the huge white violets, the great bed of gentian aucaulis that they had planted together? There may even have been time for her to pick her one of the first roses, but she was sinking fast.

On the second of June, that month which she so loved describing in the journal; when the streams were full, and the dark green shadows were flying over the woods and meadows, on just such a day when she and her Beloved would have gone walking along the Cufflymen to the Pengwern woods in the cool of the evening; the tired eyes, which for nearly a century had looked out on the world, now bitter, now amused, but at Sarah Ponsonby always with love, closed at last.

Chapter Eleven

'Midnight.' 1829–31

She had seemed indestructible, immortal, and Llangollen was stunned. 'It is impossible almost to describe the feelings of the inhabitants', wrote the reporter in the Shrewsbury paper, 'all the shops were closed, business at a stand and scarcely a dry eye to be seen. All who could afford it were attired in deep mourning, and the poorer classes to whom she was a most liberal benefactress bewailed the loss of her . . .'

The funeral was almost royal. The bier, supported by twelve bearers, was followed by a procession which included four clergymen, two physicians and two surgeons. These were in turn followed by the chief mourners; Eleanor Butler's nephew, now the Marquess, and his wife and the Marquess's brother, all of whom had been with Sarah Ponsonby from before the death. The newspapers, as she ruefully pointed out, had unfortunately failed to mention the mourners from her side, among whom were her brother Chambre's son and one of the young Mrs Tighes. Sarah herself, as she confessed to Lady Richmond, had been too overcome to attend.[1]

Strange tales would gather round this event, and Miss Pigott's day-book would disclose that at least two emanated from Sarah herself. 'The year Lady Elinor died' scribbled Miss Pigott, 'Miss P related that her Cows all produced black calves. Doctor Wolfe the missionary believes there may be evidence in the spirits of the departed appearing to their friends but only for some particular purpose.'[2]

The doctor's theory was to be strikingly, not to say characteristically, borne out by yet another supernatural experience vouchsafed to Miss Ponsonby. On the day of the funeral a stray dog attached itself to the Plas Newydd household, and appearing to be without a master, was kept and christened Chance. Some weeks after, Miss Pigott tells us, two ladies paid a visit to Miss Ponsonby, and while all three were sitting in that summerhouse which overhung the brook and which contained a small library, Miss Ponsonby took down a volume with the idea of giving it to her visitors as a keepsake. She had no sooner placed the book in her friend's hands when Chance, who was with them, 'began to howl in the most fearful manner looking up in Miss P's face as if reproaching her for giving away the book ... Miss P. (confessed) went on her knees to it to appease its howling but in vain – its anger after the book was given cd not be appeased and Miss P wrote the following day to beg the friend wd exchange that book for another.'³

But these supernatural happenings would take place some time after the sad event which inspired them. For the moment Sarah was concentrating all her will in trying to live at all, in trying to assimilate 'the Sad Sad Event, which has annihilated as far as concerns this world the happiness, that for nearly Fifty One Years – the Almighty Giver of All Good, has Generously permitted me to enjoy –'⁴ For no amount of foresight on her part, it seems, had been able to prepare her for the appalling actuality of her loss.

The Ormondes, she wrote a friend, had been kindness itself, and now that they had gone back to London, her young nephew was with her and proving a wonderful consolation, and more especially as it was within her power to offer him comfort, for, young as he was, he had also experienced sorrow, was tragically separated from his beautiful but mad wife.

Her wishes were now of the simplest: 'I hope it will be in my power to pass the remainder of My Days under this little Roof – without lessening the number of my present and faithful establishment'⁵ she wrote.

Elizabeth and Jane Hughes had been twenty years in her service now, and were almost as great a comfort as dear Mary Carryll had once been, but whether or not she would be able to afford to keep them would depend upon her friends, for Eleanor's pensions and allowances had died with her.

She was not to be kept long in suspense. News both hearten-

ing and to the point reached her a month later from their old
admirer, the Duke of Wellington:

My dear Miss Ponsonby, I have this morning received your note
of the – [*sic*] July acknowledging the receipt of the second Half of
the Bank Notes transmitted to you.

I have now the pleasure to inform you that the King was yesterday
most graciously pleased to grant you a Pension on the Civil List of
200 a year net, of which I sincerely congratulate you.

I hope this will secure your comfort as far as it can be at present.

Believe me ever yours most affectionately,

Wellington[6]

Meanwhile she occupied herself in answering the letters of
sympathy which were pouring into Plas Newydd from all quarters and with them occasional threnodies:

Hush'd is that voice whose gay and courtly greeting,
Welcom'd the Noblest in the Sister Isles,
To her Elysian Bower!
Closed is that Hand, whose ever open Bounty,
Obey'd the dictates of her Generous Heart!
That Heart oe'r which the lapse of Ninety Years
Shed not *one* chilling drop!
Silent that wit, which quick and brilliant
Like the summer lightening, illuminated all,
But scathed not,
A mind of rare endowment, whose high powers
Are now in full fruition!
How blest was she to find a Kindred Soul!
Bound in the Sacred ties of holy Friendship
With her she passed the pleasant days of Youth,
Shared every pain, and doubled every joy,
She like a Guardian Angel watched her steps,
With all the intensity of deep Affection!
Long may *She* live; Honored, Admired Beloved.
Then sinking gently in the arms of Death,
Join her twin spirit, in the realms of Bliss.[7]

She kept this, which, for all its naïveté, yet conveyed something
of her lost friend and love. But the obituary which appeared
in the *Gentleman's Magazine* could only have aroused her

contempt and caused her grief. Not only was her friend not accorded her correct title, but there were all the old and hurtful lies of how she had refused five offers of marriage in order to elope with Sarah Ponsonby; and there was, which was worse, that sketch of her life and character lifted verbatim from the 1790 copy of the *General Evening Post*, which had caused them such anguish all those years back.

Perhaps she no longer cared. Perhaps since Eleanor, the furiously indignant, was no longer at her side, she even smiled to read, if read it she did, the fatuous account of their life together which appeared in the pages of the *British Magazine* a year later. She was, after all, but waiting.

Feeling now that it might not be for long she made her final will that February, leaving an annuity of twenty-four pounds a year to each of the Hughes sisters, 'who have lived with my late most loved and most lamented friend the Lady Eleanor Butler and myself upwards of twenty years', and bequeathing the remainder of her estate and all her private papers to Mrs Tighe's grandsons, the children of Caroline Hamilton.

She was waiting, but true to their 'system', that precious way of life, she did not wait in idleness. As 1830 drew to its close, while giving Mrs Parker leave to keep a borrowed book 'till after Christmas — should I then be alive, and if not — for ever,'[8] she was also writing to Mr Jerome the Chester bookseller for drawing paper and 'Indian Rubber', so that those candlelit winter nights spent on her own beside the library fire should not go unfilled.

Did she in her solitary days and nights reread the journals of the life they had shared together, did she ever unfold and scan again those anxious misspelt letters from poor Lady Betty to Mrs Goddard that had been written over half a century ago? For Mrs Goddard, Harriet Bowdler tells us, had for some reason not found it in her heart to burn those letters, and some time before her death had returned them to Sarah Ponsonby along with her own journals:

My dear Mrs Goddard I cant Paint our distress. My Dr Sally lept out of a Window last Night and is gon off . . .

I talked to Miss Pons, not to dissuade her from her purpose but to discharge my conscience of the duty I owed her as a friend by letting her know my opinion of Miss Butler and the certainty I had they never would agree living together.

... Said if the whole world was kneeling at her feet it should not make her foresake her purpose she would live and die with Miss Butler.

This, in all truth, she had done.

That she never burned these intimate papers could indicate that some part of her intended that a select few should know the truth of their story, on the other hand the immediate present may have been too full for her even to consider the matter.

As 1831 opened, their garden came to life again claiming her attention, and as usual the summer visitors came flocking and, as in the past, were taken round the Home Circuit or dined beneath the great limes. Whereas in the past it had naturally been Eleanor who had most commanded their attention, not a few now found, like Mr John Murray the publisher, that Miss Ponsonby was 'a most inexhaustible fund of entertaining instructive and lively conversation'. And when George Borrow visited Llangollen in the summer of 1854 his guide remembered both Ladies, but particularly 'the last, who lived by herself after her companion died. She was a good lady and very kind to the poor, when they came to her gate they were never sent away without something to cheer them.'[9]

But now and again, for all her courage, she was unable single-handed to combat the feelings of intense loneliness which swept over her. This was to happen one evening late that June, an evening of such beauty, yet with no one to share it, that she sat down then and there to write to Mrs Parker to come over from Sweeney and keep her company. For the most part, however, she was tranquil, lulled no doubt by the continuing regularity of the life they had made together.

That July she was writing jokingly to Mrs Parker that 'The three *Great* Meadows on this *great* farm were Cut Yesterday – by *Only* Eighteen Mowers' and she was begging her friend to come over and see a bed full of pinks 'which I think you would like to see and *inhale*'.[10]

Summer went. Her correspondence was full of flowers and politics; the dahlias in full bloom in the middle of October, her new greenhouse, 'which its inhabitants seem to find very constituent'; the Reform Bill pending, to which she scarcely knew 'whether to wish good or ill'.[11] She was writing, she told Mrs Tighe's daughter, Caroline Hamilton, on a morning that had been delightfully interrupted by 'a friend who Brought me 16 geraniums, 14 of which are perfectly new to me, though already possessed of, I think, fourscore varieties. . .' She promised Caroline Hamilton a list of them 'for though Infants at present they may be parents in Spring and, some at least, be acceptable additions to yours in their Descendants at that Season'.[12]

But Providence was to spare her another solitary winter. Early in December, before the spring brought the passing of the Reform Bill and the still more important potting of the geraniums, Sarah Ponsonby was lying once again beside her 'beloved companion'.

Did she ever regret that impulsive elopement of fifty years ago? Caroline Hamilton wrote, 'I have no cause to think that Lady Eleanor Butler ever repented the steps she had taken, but from a letter I found of Miss Harriet Bowdler I suspect Miss Ponsonby sometimes expressed regret at having left Ireland. The two ladies continued to the last devoted to each other' she continued, 'and if they had a difference of opinion, they discussed it in a particular walk where they could not be overheard, for as they felt themselves bound to give to the world, an example of perfect friendship, the slightest appearance of discord would have tarnished their reputation – but' concluded Caroline Hamilton, 'they could not quarrel often as Miss Ponsonby's sweet, affectionate disposition always inclined her to yield to her companion'.[13]

'. . . at the time truth told you might have intitled yourself to a dowager's Income from the Estates' Sarah Ponsonby's aunt, Mrs O'Connel, had long ago written of what might have come from Sir William's penchant for her niece, 'but surely you chose the wiser part'.[14]

'. . . a well furnished library, a charming neighbourhood, an even-tempered life without material cares, a most intimate friendship and community amongst themselves – these are their treasures,' Prince Puckler Muskau had written of them, 'they must have chosen not quite badly'.[15]

As though by some tacit understanding Sarah Ponsonby's obituary in the *Gentleman's Magazine* was, by contrast with her friend's two years before, a model of tact and decorum.

Six months later Plas Newydd was put up for sale. Mr George Robins, the famous auctioneer, produced a fulsome description of it in his sale catalogue, one which was for the most part but a re-hash of poor long-dead Miss Seward's original encomiums. The cottage and its grounds he was pleased to call 'a Little Paradise'. So, for two women, it had been.

The sale of their possessions followed that August. 'I read the catalogue of the poor Ladies of LL. with a melancholy interest' wrote Mrs Hughes.* 'All their personal ornaments, presents of friends etc offered to public sale, to be pulled about by the curious and vulgar and then dispersed in every direction ... The place' she went on 'is bought for £1400 by two ladies long resident in the village, come from Manchester; one of them is a Miss Lolly and poor Lady Eleanor Butler used to call them the Lollies and the Trollies.'[16]

On the auction day Plas Newydd was crowded. Their books attracted special interest. A friend of Mrs Hughes managed to buy an album of views by Miss Bowdler and other of the Ladies' friends for thirty-five shillings. A very rare edition of Froissart went for thirty-two shillings and sixpence. 'From a memorandum in the title page it belonged to the Sorbonne library in Paris' Mrs Hughes wrote, 'and was probably one of the spoils of the Revolution.'[17]

The cottage was stripped. There remained only a cupboard full of letters, 'several of Mrs Piozzi' wrote Mrs Hughes, 'Miss Seward and Mrs Harriet Bowdler, the latter Dr D[ealtry] thinks Mrs H[amilton] would let me have. I know my valued friend dreaded the idea of her letters being made public.'[18]

The sale was said to have made two thousand and thirteen

* Grandmother of the author of *Tom Brown's Schooldays*.

pounds, six shillings and sixpence, 'enough money', as Mrs Hughes observed 'to pay all the debts and purchase comfortable annuities for their old servants'.[19]

Characteristically, they had left nothing undone.

Chapter Twelve

'... those abnormally self advertised old frumps.'
A. M. Broadley

The Myth

They were dead yet they lived. The seven-day auction at Plas Newydd had been attended by scores of their friends and acquaintances, besides a horde of the curious and the prying, all seeking relics.

Of these there were a great number, ranging from silver bells engraved with their initials to that large Aeolian harp which had kept Madame de Genlis awake all night; from Sarah Ponsonby's box of Reeves' paints sent her by the Princess Amelia, to the *Memoires of the Duke de Montpensier* presented to them by the French King, as well as a profusion of oddities: telescopes, kaleidoscopes, tigers' feet, walrus, whale and seal teeth, elephants' hair, pistols, a monkey made out of a sponge, a basket of flowers and fruit very finely modelled in chocolate ... Lady Eleanor's *Croix* it seems had never come up for auction, had last been seen in the hand of a tall and handsome man with a foreign accent.

These objects were soon dispersed countrywide, and along with them memories and anecdotes of the two women which, over the years, were to coalesce into a strange and self-perpetuating myth.

The process had already begun in their own lifetime, popular interest fastening with peculiar tenacity upon the kind of clothes they wore, the reputedly eccentric pattern of their daily lives and the mysterious circumstances of their elopement.

As early as 1790 the reporter in the *General Evening Post* had remarked on Miss Butler's constant wearing of a 'riding habit'. It must be admitted that Addison, still exercising an influence, had found the habit immodest, even 'amphibious', thinking it 'absolutely necessary to keep the partition between the two sexes, and to take notice of the smallest encroachments which one makes upon the other'.[1] But to the country eye, as that most correct of women Mrs Delany tells us, the wearing of the habit was not all that extraordinary; people in Ireland did not consider it necessary to change whilst in the country, the habit being far better suited to the exigencies of rustic life. It would thus seem likely that it was not only for reasons of economy, but in pursuance of Irish custom that the two Ladies continued to wear this form of dress after they had settled in Wales.

By 1809, however, a note from the Duke of Gloucester does suggest that the Ladies themselves felt doubtful that their habits, however suitable for Plas Newydd and even for visiting the surrounding gentry, were quite the garb in which to receive Royalty. For, in a letter of charm and tact, the young man was to write expressing mortification 'in consequence of their not chusing to dine with me in the Dress they usually wear, as I hoped they considered me *as a Friend* and therefore would not have thought it necessary to make any Alteration in their Dress on my Account'.[2]

Eleven years after this the actor, Charles Mathews, would find himself convulsed with laughter at their odd appearance glimpsed in the theatre box in the September of 1820 when he was performing at Oswestry: 'As they are seated, there is not one point to distinguish them from men' he wrote to his wife, 'the dressing and powdering of the hair, their well-starched neckcloths, the upper part of their habits which they always wear, even at a dinner party, made precisely like men's coats, and regular black beaver men's hats.'[3]

Needless to say John Lockhart, not for nothing nicknamed 'the Scorpion', hammered home the point five years later, '... heavy blue riding habits' he wrote recording his visit to Plas Newydd with Sir Walter Scott, 'enormous shoes, and men's hats, with their petticoats so tucked up, that at first glance of them fussing and tottering about their porch in the agony of expectation, we took them for a couple of hazy or crazy old sailors ...'[4]

Mathews mistook them for clergymen and Lockhart, if only to make a better story, for sailors. But in 1885 the Reverend Thomas Mozley, who had never known either of them, declared that until 1835, 'it was a very ordinary thing to meet with ladies, who, to save the trouble and cost of following the fashion never wore anything but a close-fitting habit'. While General Yorke, who was to live in Plas Newydd himself, stoutly declared that such habits, such hats, had been worn by many Welsh ladies of the time. Had not Mrs Dawkins Pennant worn similar dress in 1832 when introduced to the Princess Victoria on board a boat in the Menai straits, and was not this sufficient confirmation of its propriety?

As always the answer seems to lie somewhere between the two extremes. If not eccentric the two friends were certainly old-fashioned in using hair powder after the turn of the century; they had, moreover, never left off having their hair cropped in the 'Titus' style which, like the hair powder, had gone out of fashion after the seventeen-nineties. Similarly with their habits and their beaver hats which, though fairly common in France during the Directoire, had never been so fashionable in England, where they were deemed oddly masculine particularly to urban eyes and more especially because the Ladies, as Charles Mathews remarked, made a regular practice of wearing them on both formal as well as informal occasions.

Taking this all into consideration it is unsurprising to discover that by 1898 visitors to Plas Newydd on asking 'Why were the Ladies so famous?' generally received the simple answer, 'Oh they went about dressed like men.' While by the beginning of the next century the intriguing question as to whether they had or had not actually worn trousers, was to give rise to a prolonged and vivacious correspondence in the *Field*.

The popular misapprehension that they wore men's clothes was to be matched by another concerning their way of life; that conviction, still current in North Wales and in Llangollen itself, that they never spent a single night away from home.

This belief, for some reason the most earnestly adhered to of any, had a simple enough origin. As we have already seen, the Ladies had been neurotically anxious to prove the sincerity of the 'retirement' to their critical Irish friends. At the beginning of their life together they had hardened themselves to resist temptation in the guise of agreeable invitations, though on occasion, they had succumbed. Apart from their holiday spent at Barmouth in 1797, we know that they spent a night with the Barrett sisters at the beginning of 1784, and two nights with the Bridgemans in Staffordshire at the end of that year. There were possibly, and probably, other occasions, for Mrs Piozzi tells us that it was common practice among the Welsh gentry to sleep at one another's houses after an evening's entertainment. The Ladies' dogged determination to keep to their system, however, caused them so frequently to flout this custom, to insist, to everyone's amusement and amazement, upon driving home, no matter at what hour, 'by the light of Jupiter' if need be, that it was not long before such unusual behaviour gave rise to the myth that they had never spent a night away from their cottage.

The development of the myth is clear to trace. Ten years after they had left Ireland their friend, Robert Stuart, later Lord Castlereagh, had, for Madame de Genlis's benefit, wound up a highly-coloured biography of the two women, by declaring that they had never been absent from their cottage for a single night. Seven years after this Miss Anna Seward was informing the Reverend Henry White of the remarkable fact that they had only been away thirty hours in seventeen years. Mr Chappelow to Mrs Piozzi a year later conceded two nights in eighteen years. By 1820 the old story had re-established itself, and Charles Mathews was writing to his wife that the two Ladies had 'not slept one night from home for above forty years',[5] the version which survives to the present.

But it was to be the elopement and its attendant circumstances which was to give rise to the most prolific mythologizing.

The development was gradual. The true story had been told by the Ladies themselves to close friends, and by these friends to the friends of friends, and, drawing nourishment from human inaccuracy, malice, and misapprehension, it spread on and out to people who had never known them. Meanwhile, as Mrs Piozzi testifies, not only manners but attitudes were changing radically, with the expected result that the two women were exposed to ever-growing misinterpretation.

By 1790 the story of the elopement had reached its widest audience yet by way of the distressing piece in the *General Evening Post*. This piece, though ripe with innuendo, was not all that inaccurate as far as the actual elopement was concerned, but it did introduce one innovation, which was that Eleanor Butler had refused several offers of marriage expressly in order to live with Sarah Ponsonby. Meanwhile the myth was waxing strong in more private quarters; Thomas Creevey staying at Woodstock had written to his stepdaughter of 'those *chiennes* Lady Eleanor Butler and Miss Ponsonby', and described how Eleanor Butler in making her escape had climbed over the wall of Kilkenny Castle, fallen and broken her arm. This was an acknowledgement, one can only suppose, of her proven proneness to accident. For although a similar plight had once been ascribed to Sarah in yet another version, this feature of the story was to remain Eleanor's ever after.

Later still Miss Harriet Pigott noted down in her untidy daybook the reasons, as she understood them, for the elopement: 'Lady Elinor forced into a convent' she wrote in her spidery lopsided handwriting, 'her mother a horrid woman. She ran to Miss Ponsonby who lived with an unkind Aunt. They ran off with Mary Miss P's nurse.'[6] A version which did less than justice to the memory of poor Lady Betty Fownes.

By 1825 with the publication of Madame de Genlis's *Souvenirs de Felicie*, the myth had been considerably enlarged. Eleanor Butler born in Dublin, orphaned from the cradle, while yet preserving all the female virtues of modesty, sweetness of temper etc. etc. is nevertheless determined not to marry. She and Sarah Ponsonby meet and realize in a flash that they are made for each other to 'glide down the stream of life, in the bosom of peace, the most intimate friendship, and delicious independence'. They run away, Sarah aged seventeen, Eleanor thirty-four. They are brought back by their families, but on Sarah attaining her majority they run away to Llangollen, build a cottage and settle down for ever.

By the time Lockhart's life of Sir Walter Scott appeared in that same year there had been further developments. Sarah now promoted to the rank of a peer's daughter had emerged as 'the Honourable Miss Ponsonby'. The reason given for their elopement was that they had both been crossed in love. We are told that 'in the heyday of youth beauty and fashion' they selected Llangollen for the repose of their now time-honoured Virginity'. For the first time, however, there was a piquante addition, Lady Eleanor arrived here in the natural aspect of a pretty girl' writes Lockhart, 'while Miss Ponsonby had condescended to accompany her in the garb of a smart footman in buckskin breeches . . .'[7]

This malicious transposition of the disguise they had both necessarily assumed in the first elopement, to the period of their unhindered arrival in North Wales, was no doubt a concession to sophisticated contemporaries, for in *The Romantic Agony* Mario Praz tells us that owing to the influence of George Sand at this time 'the vice of Lesbianism became extremely popular'.

Prince Puckler Muskau was to be similarly influenced, for in his otherwise fair account of them which appeared in 1830 he asserts, quite untruly, that the two women unitedly hated the male sex, ceasing to be 'noble, handsome and fashionable young ladies' in order to live with each other. More than this he had little to add, and it was left to the *British Magazine* for the same year to carry the story a stage further.

In this version both Ladies are, with incredible coincidence, born in Dublin on the same day and the same year, lose both sets of parents at the same time, and are brought up together. They elope, are found in disguise on board a merchant vessel at Waterford, are brought back, separated, and 'every means taken to wean them from this extraordinary, and as it appeared to their friends, most injurious attachment for each other'. The rest of the story continues as its predecessors.

In 1847 with an idea, no doubt, of cashing in on the developing tourist trade in North Wales, a gentleman called Mr Hicklin brought out a collection of memoirs of the Ladies. This was little more than a rearrangement of all previous accounts, the only innovations being that the Ladies had eloped, 'impelled by a desire to lead a secluded life of celibacy', after which they build a cottage in what Victorian Mr Hicklin considers to be 'a remarkably unique and somewhat grotesque style of architecture'.

In 1856 the *Visitors Handbook to Llangollen* contained another re-hash of the previous stories but included, by way of garnishing, the Lockhart tale of Sarah Ponsonby attired as a footman, thus spreading the scandalous innuendo to yet wider audiences.

Clergymen's stipends being small, it is unsurprising to find the Reverend J. Pritchard, D.D., putting in his oar at about the same time. In his *Account of the Ladies of Llangollen*, printed at the 'Atmospheric Gas Printing Works' in Llangollen, he not only gave his own rather charming pot-pourri of memoirs, but daringly added top boots to Sarah Ponsonby's buckskin breeches, after which he blossomed out into a M'Gonegal-like poem in praise of his heroines. The lines, in their own coy fashion, sum up the general state of the myth thus far :

> Once two young girls of rank and beauty rare,
> Of features more than ordinary fair,
> Who in the heyday of their youthful charms
> Refused the proffer of all suitors' arms,
> Lived in a cottage here rich carved in oak,
> Though now long passed from life by death's grim stroke.
> Plas Newydd's gardens then displayed much taste,
> And nought about them e'er allowed to waste.
> The umbrageous foliage of surrounding trees
> Gave them a shelter from the stormy breeze,
> Whilst in a snug retreat about south-west,
> Was bird-cote placed as shelter for redbreast,
> For sparrow, chaffinch, blackbird or for thrush,
> These ladies did not wish the cold to touch.
> Then did all species of ferns abound
> In every nook and corner of the ground,
> Then none were known to come unto their door
> That was not welcomed with kind words or more.
> These ladies to each other kind and true,
> Around Llangollen's vale, like them were few.
> E'en now I see them seated in yon chair,
> In well-starched neckcloths, and with powdered hair,

Their upper habits just like men's they wore,
With tall black beaver hats outside their door;
To crown it all my muse would whisper low,
With hair cropped short, rough, bushy, white as snow.
They at death's summons, God's commands obeyed,
And were in fair Llangollen's churchyard laid,
As they through life together did abide,
E'en now in death they both lie side by side,
Of them remains nought save dark mould and sod,
Who lived their neighbours second to their God.
Sweet peace be theirs – by death to dust allied,
Through him who near a century was their Guide;
Beloved, respected by the world were they,
By all regretted when they passed away.

The boom in the Ladies continued, and was extended to the plastic arts. Already during their lifetime two Swansea potteries had been producing services of a pattern which was called 'Ladies of Llangollen', and which depicted a rural scene with two ladies on horseback talking to a man with a scythe over his shoulder. Some time after 1831 an engraving made from Mary Parker's clandestine sketch of the Ladies in the library was published, the proceeds going to charity. It was not long, however, before the engraving was pirated and the Ladies' faces lifted and placed in a new context, in which they were to be found standing before the Valle Crucis font with an unfamiliar whippet cavorting at their heels. It was the pirated version of their portraits which was to appear upon a succession of not uncharming fairings; numerous strange Bristol-blue vessels of odd shape and indeterminate usefulness; also a *biscuit* of the Ladies in black habits and beavers, with sweet bland faces like Christmas cake babies.

In 1888 General Yorke, who had known the Ladies as a boy, and who admired and loved them, brought out his own book of recollections. In these, Eleanor Butler, living under the strict guardianship of her aunt, Lady Kavanagh of Borris, flees to Dublin to meet Sarah Ponsonby leaving her clothes on the banks of the river Barrow to mislead the family. In other words Eleanor's sister at Borris had by now turned into an aunt, and that tell-tale ruffle dropped near the barn at Waterford, had become a suit of clothes. In other respects General Yorke's version did not differ greatly from those that had preceded it, although it was refreshingly free from scandalous innuendo.

But it was in 1897 with Mr Charles Penruddock's version, or rather four intertwined versions, that the myth was to reach its fullest blooming.

Here is all that has gone before and more. In the course of escaping Eleanor Butler falls again, only this time it is in negotiating the park gate at Woodstock. She is found. The plot is discovered. Six months later there is a second attempt, and, with the same object of misleading her family, Eleanor leaves her clothes, not by the river this time, but at the edge of the garden pond. The two girls get as far as Park Gate Chester, Miss P. still in breeches, but are captured again. This time Miss B. is sent to London to repent, where, as soon as she reaches her majority, Miss P. joins her, and they spend two rattling years in society, leading the life of the gayest of the gay before retiring to North Wales for ever.

In Mr Penruddock's final Ouida-esque version, the successful elopement occurs on the night of a grand ball given at Kilkenny Castle to celebrate John Butler's accession to the family titles. Next morning Mary Carryll is found to be missing, at five that evening it is discovered that the two girls are also missing. They have all three travelled to Waterford, boarded a fishing smack, and set sail for Milford Haven.

It was this final version which, forty years later in 1937, would be adopted with minor adjustments in the first full-scale biography of the two friends.

Yet their lives had been reintroduced to public notice seven years before in 1930 with the publication of *The Hamwood Papers of the Ladies of Llangollen*. This charming book, drawing upon Sarah Ponsonby's private papers that she had left to Mrs Tighe's daughter, Caroline Hamilton, contained not only excerpts from Eleanor Butler's journal, but a number of Lady Betty Fownes's letters to Mrs Goddard concerning the elopement. It thus presented the Ladies' lives in more accurate detail than ever before. Yet the publication of *The Hamwood Papers* did little to halt the evolving myth. Two years after its appearance Colette, certainly influenced by Proust's *À la Recherche du Temps Perdu*, probably by Radclyffe Hall's *The Well of Loneliness*, incorporated into *Ces Plaisirs* only those extracts from *The Hamwood Papers* which suited her theme.

Her interpretation of the two women, though sympathetic, was very much in terms of her own times as her conclusions show :

'Can we possibly imagine the Ladies of Llangollen in this year of 1930 ?' she asks. 'They would own a car, wear dungarees, smoke cigarettes, have short hair, and there would be a bar in their apartment. Would Sarah Ponsonby still know how to remain silent? Perhaps with the aid of crossword puzzles. Eleanor Butler would curse as she jacked up the car and would have her breasts amputated.'

By the time Simone de Beauvoir had published *The Second Sex* in 1949 it was taken for granted that Eleanor Butler and Sarah Ponsonby had been lesbians, although, oddly enough, Eleanor was no longer seen as having been the dominant partner. 'The union of Sarah Ponsonby with her woman companion lasted for almost fifty years without a cloud,' writes Mlle de Beauvoir of them, 'apparently they were able to create a peaceful Eden apart from the ordinary world.'

Yet there was something incongruous in a vague phrase like 'life without a cloud' escaping into a treatise that pretended to be so scientifically specific. We know quite well, and Mlle de Beauvoir could have guessed, that for Eleanor Butler and Sarah Ponsonby, as for anyone else, life was not without a cloud. Could it be that for all her typing and categorizing Mlle de Beauvoir recognized that in both her own and in the popular consciousness the Ladies represented something more than just a lesbian couple ?

For throughout the evolution of the myth it is clear that the two women had inspired not only personal but universal interest. It is as though, in the course of one hundred and thirty-seven years, popular fantasy, born of some craving for perfection, had created an archetypal pair.

In the case of their own period they seem perfectly to have embodied the contemporary yearning for retirement; for rural innocence and simplicity without any loss of the comforts and cultural benefits of civilization; for freedom from the shackles of unbridled passion without any loss of pleasure. For them, as for succeeding admirers, the Ladies seemed successfully to reconcile those absurd and tiresome polarities of existence, which are the bane of all mortals.

For nearly a hundred and fifty years these quasi-goddesses have, thanks to popular fantasy, led a becomingly protean existence. Have, while remaining perpetually young and beautiful, painlessly and continuously changed sex; have, while remaining romantically poor, never wanted; while living in a cottage, yet mixed with princes; have, while remaining eternally celibate, yet been touched by that dark wing of perverse passion so as to render them for ever interesting.

Thus by the mysterious operation of time upon the popular imagination have two spinsters of no great beauty, of uncertain age, little money, living in a remote cottage, become a paradigm of the heart's desire. Small wonder that at least three pairs of women fell beneath their spell.

As early as 1788 the journal tells us that two ladies in Sussex were impersonating Eleanor Butler and Sarah Ponsonby. 'Odd circumstance', commented Eleanor of these impostors, and pondered with some amusement the discomfort of the people they had deceived.

It was not until Sarah Ponsonby's death in 1831, however, and the consequent sale of Plas Newydd, that two other spinster ladies, Miss Charlotte Andrew and Miss Amelia Lolly, were able, by buying the cottage, to assume the faery mantle.

By the time Catherine Sinclair had visited the famous cottage two years later, the 'Lollies and Trollies' as Eleanor Butler so disrespectfully called them, had made their own additions to the Shrine of Friendship.

Continuing what they must have supposed to be the Ladies' eccentric taste, Miss Lolly and Miss Andrew had caused a large stuffed bear to be set up at the corner of the cottage, and the white front palings, as a contemporary engravings shows, had sprouted a number of grotesque devices. Miss Sinclair herself glimpsed a 'gim-crack model of a wooden house stuck on a wooden pillar'.[8] It is not to be wondered that Miss Costello, visiting the cottage eleven years later, found the 'whole place had a vulgar and commonplace appearance'.[9] On his Welsh tour in 1854 George Borrow saw only a small gloomy mansion that was empty and deserted. Miss Lolly had died, and the property had gone to a relative living far off in Devon. Miss Lolly herself was resting beneath a Gothick obelisk in Llantysilio churchyard where, in 1861, Miss Andrew joined her. Thus ended a not very successful attempt to emulate the lives of the first Plas Newydd friends.

But the most remarkable instance of the continuing influence of the Ladies was to occur in the next century.

Mary Gordon had been one of the first woman doctors to be trained in England, she had been medical officer at Holloway during the height of the Suffragette agitations, and she was the author of a treatise on prison discipline. Sometime during the nineteen-thirties she happened to be staying with the psychologist Carl Jung at Bollingen. Moved perhaps by Jung's curious tower-like house that he had had built by the lakeside, 'a place of psychic wholeness', 'a place of maturation – a maternal womb in which I could become what I was, what I am and will be',[10] Doctor Mary Gordon dreamed a dream that profoundly impressed her. She dreamed that she had revisited the ruins of Valle Crucis Abbey near Llangollen, where she had not been since she was a girl of seventeen.

Immensely interested, Jung insisted that she must return to Valle Crucis where he believed an explanation, or at least an amplification, of the dream awaited her.

Obedient to the master's advice the Doctor soon found herself back in Llangollen after an absence of fifty-six years. She was not to find her answer in Valle Crucis however. While staying in the town she determined to revisit Plas Newydd of which she retained no girlhood memories. Accordingly one autumn day the custodian of the cottage saw, as he imagined, the incarnation of Lady Eleanor Butler walking down the path; a short, stocky woman with grey hair neatly cropped.

The Doctor had no sooner entered Plas Newydd than she became immediately and intensely aware of two presences, whom she at once took to be the Ladies. This she found strange, for hitherto their personalities had in no way interested her. After two hours she left the cottage, determined, in the course of the winter, to read up all she could about them. Eight months later, well primed with information, she returned to Plas Newydd, but this time the presences had coyly withdrawn.

Deeply disappointed the Doctor left the cottage and began slowly walking up the hill towards the Bache, where, in the past, the Ladies themselves had so often gone gathering holly berries for their hedges. She had only gone a little way when she suddenly and very clearly heard a dog bark, and then, rounding an outcrop, she saw sitting by the hill path and outlined against the strong sunlight, two figures whom she recognized instantly. They were wearing light blue linen habits and fine muslin shirts, and they were sitting so still that it seemed to the Doctor that they must have been asleep for some considerable time.

'They were strong, healthy experienced refined' wrote the Doctor rather quaintly in *The Flight of the Wild Goose*, 'ladies to their fingertips.'

The Doctor in her tweeds and homespun stockings shyly made her presence known and, after delicate introductions, it was agreed that she and the two spectres should rendezvous at the cottage at nine that evening. This was possible to achieve without anyone knowing since Plas Newydd was uninhabited, as it had been in the Llangollen Town Council's possession for the last three years.

That night the Doctor, herself well over seventy, affected a clandestine entrance by a back window, entered the library, and sat waiting on a sofa until her hostesses should appear. Time passed and she grew drowsy. All at once she saw a figure cross the room and replace a book in the shelves which in daytime she had particularly noted to be empty. A moment later a form that she recognized as Lady Eleanor's came and sat softly on the sofa beside her, while another, which proved to be Miss Ponsonby, took a near-by chair.

There now followed in the weird half-light, and until cock-crow brought it to an end, a wide-ranging conversation between the Doctor and the two friends. The conversation, by the

Doctor's account, struck a highly emancipated note, touching not only upon feminine education, but the problems of birth control and twentieth-century marriage, which, considering the Ladies' proven formality, seems a thought daring. Dawn arrived without incident, however, the interview came safely to an end, and the spry old Doctor swung a leg over the window-sill and, much moved, returned home to write up her experience.

The result, *The Flight of the Wild Goose*, a fictional biography based mainly on *The Hamwood Papers* and the anthology of Mr Penruddock, is a strangely moving piece of work though abounding in wild embellishments.

'... She has a debauched mind' Mrs Goddard warns the Doctor's Miss Ponsonby on the eve of the elopement to Wales. This, lifted from Mrs Goddard's own journal, is in order, but what follows is highly questionable:

'Why my dear Miss Ponsonby' continues the Doctor's version of Mrs Goddard, 'when she, gets you away ... why ... she might make love to you.'

'I hope she will love me Mrs Goddard' ripostes Miss Ponsonby cheekily, 'she does it so beautifully.' 'Mrs Goddard for once in her life looked genuinely shocked, and Miss Ponsonby laughed merrily.'

In Doctor Mary Gordon's version it is not long before Lady Betty Fownes begins to share Mrs Goddard's doubts about the propriety of the friendship, or, as the Doctor curiously expresses it: 'The frothing scum of sordid experience which made Mrs Goddard's mind had blown in Lady Betty's direction ...'

It appears that the Doctor herself either could not or would not make up her own mind about the propriety or otherwise of the friendship. In effect, however, Eleanor Butler's character emerges in the Doctor's narrative as the epitome of a gallant Great War officer, while Sarah Ponsonby, unrecognizably more self-opinionated than in real life, and all too given to honey-like Irish phrases like 'Heart o' mine', is a fairly representative emancipated woman. Thus, as so often with history, were the features of the past redrawn to answer the fashions of Doctor Mary's own time.

The Flight of the Wild Goose sold moderately well, and with the proceeds Doctor Mary commissioned a plaque of the two friends for the interior of Llangollen church. The artist was Miss Violet Mathews, and it appears that while Miss Mathews executed a self-portrait to represent Miss Ponsonby, the Doctor, seemingly now in thrall to some form of self-identification, posed as Lady Eleanor.

The plaque itself did and does arouse mixed feelings. To some it was not only unaesthetic but papistical. Though when a Llangollen councillor argued that he wanted a 'Protestant church' he was routed by the Doctor who informed him cuttingly that there was no such word in either Bible or Prayer Book. She was to be entirely mollified by the dedication service, however, at which Lord Howard de Walden unveiled her controversial gift, and an Archdeacon crossed and dedicated it. Afterwards the congregation stood in a large circle in the yard of the *Hand* inn, and the sculptress was presented with a large bunch of pink roses.

'We have been wondering whatever we can do to show our gratitude to you for what you have done' said a woman in a Llangollen shop next day.

'Keep' replied the Doctor briskly, 'the Ladies' memory clean and fresh.'

To ensure this she deposited a brief history of the two friends in the church archives, and, being already old and delicate, the first great modern champion of the Ladies of Llangollen died soon after.

There remained only the cottage. 'I long to get someone to buy it or preserve it properly', the Doctor had written wistfully in 1936. 'No one lives there now, sir', George Borrow's guide had told him in the summer of 1854; 'all dark and dreary; very different from the state of things when the ladies lived there – all gay and cheerful . . . the house is cold and empty; no fire in it sir; no furniture.'[11]

At Miss Lolly's death the property had gone to her relative Mrs Couran. She, having owned it fifteen years, sold it in 1876 to Mr Richard Lloyd Williams, who after only two months' possession resold it to General Yorke.

The General, himself something of an eccentric, had known the Ladies as a boy. He had kind memories of them brushing down his coat and filling his pocket with oranges when his pony had thrown him during a hack up Dinas Bran. It was he who remembered the oddity of Lady Eleanor's appearance, and how, as her sight grew worse, she had dropped melted butter from her crumpets and showered hair powder over her decorations. He recalled how in order to ward off deafness both Ladies had placed wads of brown paper 'lightly in the orifice of their ears'; and he remembered how once, when the cottage had been invaded by cockroaches, the friends had been convinced that the unwelcome creatures had issued from a baker's shop on the other side of the Dee, and had marched over the river to take possession of Plas Newydd by way of the thirteenth-century bridge.

The General himself, who had commanded the Royal Dragoons at Balaclava and had been severely wounded, now set himself to devote the remainder of his life to restoring Plas Newydd to its former beauty.

This was in part achieved by covering the entire front of the cottage with oak battens in imitation of the Elizabethan style, adding an extensive wing at the back, and building a neo-Gothick lodge, the Hermitage, to the north-west of the property.

As popular belief insisted that the Ladies had never spent a single night away from Plas Newydd, so now it declared that the new owner had never spent one night in it. True or not the General nevertheless found time to convert the interior of the cottage into a museum that even the Tradescants might have envied. Here genuine relics of the Ladies, the collar of Miss Ponsonby's dog, Chance, Lady Eleanor's cairngorm brooch and her ormulu bell, jostled with objects as various as a china model of Madame Vestris's leg, a scourge of human hair and the head of a Llangollen ram born with four horns.

Outside, however, the garden was slowly decaying; the Gothick bird-cote was rotting, and Lady Eleanor's bower overlooking the Cufflymen became so dangerous that it had to be dismantled, its oriel window being attached to one of the gable ends of the cottage along with the numerous carvings of lions and Irish harps that had been executed by the General himself.

When in 1890 the General died at last, the property with all its accretions was bought by Mr G. H. Robertson, a well-known Liverpool cotton broker. As ardent an admirer of the Ladies as the General himself, Mr Robertson now made his own contribution to the Shrine of Friendship. Beneath his wand Plas Newydd burgeoned into a mansion of two halls, seven reception rooms, eleven principal bedrooms and four bathrooms.

It had reached its apotheosis, would never be so grand again.

Photographs testify to the splendour of the interiors, the meticulous care taken of walks and gardens; to the crowning splendour of Mr Robertson's term of occupation, which was a magnificent pageant, doubtless as entertaining to the 'mob-ility of Llangollen' as the Ladies' own transparencies had been so long ago on the accession of George IV. Now, however, it was the Ladies' own lives that were portrayed, Mrs Roberston in full hunting rig playing Lady Eleanor, and looking so dashing as to give everyone the most idealistic conception of the original.

In 1910, and to everyone's regret, Mr Robertson retired, and sold Plas Newydd to a Lincolnshire lady who only lived there eight years. It was the last time that Plas Newydd was a permanent home. It was bought in 1919 and resold three months later to the 7th Earl of Tankerville, who used it as a summer residence until his death in 1932, when it was acquired by the Llangollen Town Council in whose hands it has been ever since.

There are still traces of the Ladies to be found in Llangollen. There is a public house named the *Ponsonby Arms*; there is a small lane leading to Plas Newydd (that selfsame lane up which Lady Eleanor and Miss Ponsonby glimpsed the menacing straw hats of the St George ladies that summer long ago) which is called, for obvious reasons, Butler Hill. The *Royal* hotel, the old *King's Head* in their day, has the engraving taken from Mary Parker's sketch of them hanging on an upper landing; and the Ladies and Plas Newydd figure in blue on the white tiles of the hall fireplace.

There are even tenuous connections with them. People still remember an old man who boasted of being dandled by Miss Ponsonby, while his mother talked to Lady Eleanor; the late Mrs Rowlands used to knit an Irish stocking stitch taught her by her grandmother, who in turn learned it from Miss Ponsonby;

the Misses Lloyd Jones possess locks of the Ladies' hair set in brooches, which were given by the two friends to their great-great-grand-aunts, those self same Misses Hughes who served the Ladies so faithfully for the twenty years after the death of Mary Carryll.

In Llangollen itself the cult of the Ladies is dying. Variously christened 'the Miss Ponsonbys', 'Miss Butler and Lady Ponsonby', 'the Misses Ormonde'; they are vaguely famous for being suffragettes, spies, nymphomaniacs, men dressed as women, women dressed as men. Yet for those few who are close in imagination to them their memory is still loved: 'I would not' one man told me gravely 'even like to go up to Plas Newydd without putting on my best suit.'

The cottage is as cold and empty as when George Borrow saw it one hundred and fourteen years ago; reduced to something like its original size by the ravages of dry rot and the consequent demolition of General Yorke's and Mr Robertson's additions. But the Warden of Ruthin's oak lion still lies beneath that elaborate porch over which there was such rejoicing in the year before Waterloo, and when the heavy door swings open, the visitor still treads upon those elegant black and white marble squares which Eleanor Butler was so delighted to see replace the vulgar tiles.

Inside the cottage it becomes hard to distinguish between those additions made by the Ladies and those enthusiastic but mistaken alterations of the General's.

Nevertheless, on the left at the top of the stairs, now wrongly labelled Miss Ponsonby's bedroom, can still be seen that room which, half grave, half gay, they were pleased to call the State Bedchamber, and where, among others, Margaret Davies, Harriet Bowdler, Anna Seward and Madame de Genlis all laid their serious and sentimental heads. But only the small Georgian grate, the coloured glass of the oriel window, and the powder closet serve to remind one of what it was once like.

Across the landing is their Bedchamber and, leading off that, all that remains of the Dressing-room from whose window the London coaches could be heard, and glimpsed, drawing in at the

Hand, and where, most nights for nearly fifty years, they retired punctually at nine o'clock to read and write, play backgammon or simply to chat. The Bedchamber with its grey carpet, moreen hangings, Gothick stools and large bookcase has vanished, and a poor stripped apology for their 'capital four poster' stands forlornly in the corner.

It is only downstairs in the Library that one feels on surer ground, for here, beneath the Gothick arch of the doorway, is that lamp-like contrivance in coloured glass which sent Miss Seward into such raptures; and here, as one can recognize from Lady Delamere's sketch, are the Gothick bookcases that once housed their small but sumptuous library; and here is that triple Gothick window overlooking the shrubbery, which Eleanor Butler opened one early spring night long ago, so that the birds came flocking and singing to the lighted candle which she had placed upon the sill.

Their garden, with its shrubbery, its flower borders, its winding gravel paths so painstakingly raked by the Richards, the Simons, the Moses Jones, has gone. Only the small round dairy house, so much admired by Miss Seward, the cow house, and the foundations of Lady Eleanor's bower, where the dog Chance so vividly rebuked Miss Ponsonby for parting with the wrong book, remain to bear witness that it existed at all.

Down by the river Cufflymen, where their wild garden once was, their avenue of birch trees has long been cut down, though the two mills once glimpsed along it remain; one now a farm, and the other ruinous with water cascading from its broken conduit.

The rustic bridges so carefully copied from *L'Art des Jardins* have rotted long ago and been replaced by bridges of stone; but the font that they purloined from Valle Crucis is still there, though the spring which once fed it has burst its pipe, and, like the spring far away at that other home at Woodstock in Ireland, has become a meandering rivulet once more.

Tout passe, tout lasse, tout casse. Only the Cufflyment is unchanged. Foaming and clear as ever, his rushing noise can be heard in the empty cottage, in the still library, where the wind blows coldly through the broken window glass, and where Sarah Ponsonby's account book lies yellowing in its glass case.

'But they shall no more return to their house,' she had caused to have carved on their tombstone from the Book of Job, 'neither shall their place know them any more.'

Abbreviations and Collections

Bod. MS	Bodleian Library.
EB	Eleanor Butler.
Hamwood MS	Hamwood House, Dunboyne, Co. Meath; owned by Major C. R. Hamilton.
Hamwood Papers	*The Hamwood Papers of the Ladies of Llangollen and Caroline Hamilton*, ed. Bell (London 1930).
HB	Harriet Bowdler.
HLP	Hester Lynch Piozzi.
HP	Harriet Pigott.
NLI	National Library of Ireland.
NLW	National Library of Wales.
Ormonde MS	Cantley, Wokingham, Berks.; owned by the Marquis of Ormonde.
Parker MS	Loton Park, nr. Shrewsbury; owned by Sir Michael Leighton, Bt.
Rylands MS	John Rylands Library, Manchester.
SP	Sarah Ponsonby.
ST	Sarah Tighe.
Tighe MS	Weybread, Ightham Common, Sevenoaks, Kent; owned by Evelyn Webber, Esq.

Reference Notes

Chapter One
'. . . your being Totally Ignorant who we are.'

1 *The Orrery Papers*, ed. Countess of Cork and Orrery (1903), v. II, p. 56.
2 Arthur Young, *A Tour in Ireland* (1780), p. 142.
3 ibid., p. 128.
4 ibid., p. 81.
5 Memoirs of Mrs Caroline Hamilton, NLI MS 4811.
6 ibid.
7 SP–ST, 17 January 1788, Tighe MS.
8 Memoirs of Mrs Caroline Hamilton, NLI MS 4811.
9 ibid.
10 ibid.
11 SP–ST, 28 August 1786, Tighe MS.
12 J. N. Brewer, *Beauties of Ireland* (1825), p. 416.
13 William Tighe, *Statistical Survey of the County of Kilkenny* (1802), p. 636n.
14 *Romantic Slievenamon*, ed. Maher (1954), p. 38.
15 *The Ireland of Sir Jonah Barrington. Selections from his Personal Sketches*, ed. Staples (1968), pp. 3–5.
16 *The Kenmare Manuscripts*, ed. MacLysaght (1942), p. 73.
17 *The Prose Writings of Jonathan Swift*, ed. Davis (Blackwell) v. V, p. 219.
18 NLI Ormonde MS, v. 179, p. 109.
19 ibid.
20 ibid.
21 Memoirs of Mrs Caroline Hamilton, NLI MS 4811.
22 James Butler–John Butler, 9 November 1753, NLI Ormonde MS, v. 179, p. 179.
23 Memoirs of Mrs Caroline Hamilton, NLI MS 4811.
24 J. N. Brewer, *Beauties of Ireland* (1825), p. 416.
25 Robert Harrison–Madam Butler, undated, NLI Ormonde MS, v. 180, p. 49.
26 Dominick Farrell–Madam Butler, undated, ibid., p. 129.

27 Nicholas Highly–Madam Butler, undated, ibid., p. 143.
28 Will of Helen Butler, 10 April 1746, NLI Ormonde MS v. 178, 1725–47.
29 Francis Butler–Walter Butler, 17 June 1752, NLI Ormonde MS, v. 179, p. 109.
30 Francis Butler–Walter Butler, July 1762, NLI Ormonde MS, v. 179, p. 423.
31 Margaret Stanley–John Butler, 15 August 1753, NLI Ormonde MS, v. 179, p. 155.
32 EB–HP, 22 January 1815, Bod. MS Pigott, d.9.g. (fol. 130).
33 *Misc X* (Catholic Record Society 1915), p. 157.
34 *The Diary of the Blue Nuns*, ed. Gillow and Lomax (Catholic Record Society 1910), p. 296.
35 *The French Journals of Mrs Thrale and Dr Johnson*, ed. Tyson and Guppy (1932), p. 122.
36 ibid., p. 120.
37 Memoirs of Mrs Caroline Hamilton, NLI MS 4811.
38 *Mémoires*, ed. Garnier, v. IV, p. 517.
39 John Prim, *Notes on Kilkenny Inns and Taverns* (Transactions of the Kilkenny Archaeological Society, New Series 1862–63), v. IV.
40 Memoirs of Mrs Caroline Hamilton, NLI MS 4811.

Chapter Two
'How charmingly might you and I live together and despise them all!'

1 *Hamwood Papers*, p. 19.
2 SP–Lucy Goddard, undated, NLI Wicklow MS 4239.
3 *Hamwood Papers*, p. 20.
4 Memoirs of Mrs Caroline Hamilton, NLI MS 4811.
5 *Hamwood Papers*, p. 20.
6 Memoirs of Mrs Caroline Hamilton, NLI MS 4811.
7 *Autobiography and Correspondence of Mary Granville* (1861), v. I, p. 31.
8 John Ponsonby–Lady Betty Fownes, undated, Tighe MS.
9 Lady Betty Fownes–Lucy Goddard, 'Tuesday Nigh', NLI Wicklow MS.
10 *Hamwood Papers*, p. 27.
11 ibid., p. 28.
12 ibid., p. 28.
13 ibid., p. 29.

14 ibid., p. 30.
15 ibid., p. 27.
16 ibid., p. 30.
17 ibid., p. 31.
18 ibid., p. 35.
19 ibid., p. 31.
20 ibid., p. 32.
21 ibid., p. 33-4.
22 Memoirs of Mrs Caroline Hamilton, NLI MS 4811.
23 ibid.
24 Lady Betty Fownes–Lucy Goddard, 'Monday', NLI Wicklow MS 4239.
25 ibid.
26 ibid.
27 Lady Betty Fownes–Lucy Goddard, 13 April 1788, MS in possession of Miss Katharine Kenyon.
28 ibid.
29 *Hamwood Papers*, p. 34.
30 ibid., p. 36.
31 ibid., p. 36.
32 ibid., p. 37.
33 ibid., p. 37.
34 ibid., p. 38.
35 ibid., p. 38.
36 ibid., p. 39.
37 ibid., p. 39.
38 ibid., p. 39.
39 ibid., p. 39.
40 Lady Betty Fownes–Sir William Fownes, undated, MS in possession of Miss Katharine Kenyon.
41 Lucy Goddard, Journal, 2 June 1778, Hamwood MS.
42 *Hamwood Papers*, p. 40.
43 Lucy Goddard, Journal, 2 June 1778, Hamwood MS.

Chapter Three
'This awfull scenery makes me feel as if I were only a worm or a grain of dust on the face of the earth.'

1 William Gilpin, *Observations on Several Parts of the Counties Cambridge, Norfolk, Suffolk, and Essex also on Several Parts of North Wales* (1809), p. 180.
2 Thomas Pennant, *A Tour in Wales 1773* (1778), pp. 278-9.

3 Account of Journey in Wales Perform'd in May 1778 by Two Fugitive Ladies. Hamwood MS.

4 Thomas Pennant, *A Tour in Wales 1773* (1778), pp. 278–9.

5 Account of a Journey in Wales Perform'd in May 1778 by Two Fugitive Ladies. Hamwood MS.

6 ibid.

7 ibid.

8 Bod. MS Pigott f. 1, p. 197.

9 SP–ST, 14 June 1787, Tighe MS.

10 SP–Mrs Parker, 1 March 1818, Parker MS.

11 Bod. MS Pigott f. 1, p. 197.

12 SP–ST, 14 June 1787, Tighe MS.

13 ibid.

14 *Collected Letters of Anna Seward* (1811), v. III, p. 56.

15 Bod. MS Piggott f. 1, p. 197.

'Rose at Eight.' 1780–83

1 EB, Ladies Pocket Book, 8 November 1784, Hamwood MS.

2 *Millenium Hall*, by a Gentleman (1762), p. 139.

3 SP–ST, 11 April 1785, Tighe MS.

4 SP–ST, 13 February 1789, Tighe MS.

5 *Hamwood Papers*, p. 52.

6 ibid., p. 53.

7 ibid., p. 47.

8 EB–Lucy Goddard, [c. May 1783], NLI Wicklow MS 4239.

9 *Lady Louisa Stuart's Letters*, ed. Home (1901), pp. 187–8.

Chapter Four
'Nine-thirty till Three.' 1783–8

1 EB–Mrs Paulet, 1 August 1783, Tighe MS.

2 SP–ST, 28 August 1786, Tighe MS. 'I am Grateful to Dr Dealtry, since my Friends must amuse themselves with Creating reports on my subject, his was by far the kindest of many that I have been surprised at. was it not better than my wearing out my dear B's patience by cruel usage, and making it impossible for her to endure me any longer – nay absolutely putting her in fear of her life by my Barbarity – etc etc? Which I was said to do two years ago.'

3 *Hamwood Papers*, p. 51.

4 EB, Journal, 20 November 1785, Ormonde MS.

5 EB, Ladies Pocket Book, 2 January 1784, Hamwood MS.
6 SP–ST, 5 October 1784, Tighe MS.
7 EB, Ladies Pocket Book, 2 January 1784, Hamwood MS.
8 SP–ST, 8 January 1785, Tighe MS.
9 EB, Journal, 12 October 1785, Ormonde MS.
10 EB, Journal, 1 October 1785.
11 SP–ST, 11 April 1785, Tighe MS.
12 SP–ST, 15 November 1785, Tighe MS.
13 EB, Journal, 1 October 1785, Ormonde MS.
14 SP–ST, 11 April 1785, Tighe MS.
15 *Hamwood Papers*, p. 57.
16 Jean-Jaques Rousseau, *Julie ou La Nouvelle Héloïse* (Éditions Garnier), p. 90.
17 ibid., p. 31.
18 EB, Journal, 12 November 1785, Ormonde MS.
19 SP–ST, 25 August 1786, Tighe MS.
20 SP–ST, 7 February 1785, Tighe MS.
21 SP–ST, 16 December 1787, Tighe MS.

1788–90

1 EB, Journal, 9 January 1788, Hamwood MS.
2 ibid., 21 January.
3 ibid., 22 January.
4 ibid., 29 April.
5 *Hamwood Papers*, p. 85.
6 ibid., p. 143.
7 EB, Journal, 24 June 1788, Hamwood MS.
8 *Hamwood Papers*, p. 72.
9 ibid., p. 149.
10 ibid., p. 150.
11 EB, Journal, 25 April 1789, Hamwood MS.
12 ibid., 17 May.
13 ibid., 10 May.
14 ibid., 30 June.
15 *Hamwood Papers*, p. 216.
16 ibid., p. 219.
17 ibid., p. 233.
18 EB, Journal, 22 March 1790, Hamwood MS.
19 *Hamwood Papers*, p. 252.
20 ibid., p. 265.
21 ibid., p. 257.

22 ibid., p. 259.

23 HB–SP, 25 August 1791, Ormonde MS.

Chapter Five
'Impossibilities . . . whenever two Ladies live too much together.'

 1 *Thraliana. The Diary of Mrs Hester Lynch Thrale 1776–1809*, ed. Balderston (1951), p. 740.

 2 ibid., p. 770.

 3 ibid., p. 868n.

 4 ibid., p. 949.

 5 Arthur Johnston, *Enchanted Ground. The Study of Medieval Romance in the Eighteenth Century* (1964), p. 210.

 6 *Mrs Carter's Letters to Miss C. Talbot* (1809), v. I, p. 2.

 7 ibid., p. 57.

 8 ibid., p. 61.

 9 ibid., p. 42.

10 *Letters from Mrs E. Carter to Mrs Montagu* (1817), v. I, p. 27.

11 ibid., v. IV, p. 33.

12 ibid., p. 51.

13 *Millenium Hall*, by a Gentleman (1762), p. 77.

14 ibid., p. 76.

15 ibid., p. 144.

16 ibid., p. 145.

17 *The Life of George Crabbe by His Son* (1947), p. 127.

18 *Boswell's Life of Johnson* (Everyman), v. II, p. 513.

19 *The Works of Miss Catharine Talbot* (1809), p. 96.

20 H. M. Bowdler, *Essay on the Proper Employment of Time, Talents, Fortune* (1836), p. 36.

21 HB–SP, 29 April 1794, Ormonde MS.

22 HB–SP, 6 September 1794, Ormonde MS.

23 *Journals and Correspondence of Dr Whalley*, ed. Wickham (1836), p. 392.

24 HB–SP, 1 February 1794, Ormonde MS.

25 *Collected Letters of Anna Seward* (1811), v. III, pp. 29–30.

26 *The Swan of Lichfield*, ed. Pearson (1936), p. 260.

27 *Journals and Correspondence of Dr Whalley*, ed. Wickham (1863), p. 247.

28 *The Swan of Lichfield*, ed. Pearson (1936), p. 275.

29 *Journals and Correspondence of Dr Whalley*, ed. Wickham (1863), p. 251.

30 *Collected Letters of Anna Seward* (1811), v. III, p. 55.

31 HB–SP, 3 December 1793, Ormonde MS.
32 H. M. Bowdler, *Essay on the Proper Employment of Time, Talents, Fortune* (1836), p. 37.

'When shall we be quite alone ?'

1 Verses by Mrs Grant inscribed to Lady Eleanor Butler and Miss Ponsonby, Bod. MS Eng. Letters, *c.* 144 (fol. 224).
2 HB–SP, 6 April 1793, Ormonde MS.
3 *The Intimate letters of Hester Piozzi and Penelope Pennington*, ed. Broadley (1910), p. 149.
4 *Mémoires inédits de Madame de Genlis* (1825), v. III, p. 282.
5 *Thraliana. The Diary of Mrs Hester Lynch Thrale 1776–1809*, ed. Balderston (1951), pp. 957–8.
6 SP, Day Book, 1789, Hamwood MS.
7 ibid.
8 EB, Ladies Pocket Book, 29 August 1784. 'After dinner went to Church laugh'd shamefully.' Hamwood MS.
9 EB–Lucy Goddard, undated (*c.* May 1783), NLI Wicklow MS 4239.
10 *Particulars and etc. of Lady Eleanor Butler and Miss Ponsonby's Little Paradise ... which will be sold by Auction by Mr Geo. Robinson ... on Thursday, the 28th of June 1832*. Hamwood MS.
11 ibid.
12 EB, Journal, 2 December 1785, Ormonde MS.
13 ibid., 6 December.
14 EB, Journal, 13 January 1788, Hamwood MS.
15 ibid., 9 August 1788.
16 ibid., 13 August 1788.

Chapter Six
Three o'clock. Dinner. 1791–4

1 *Hamwood Papers*, p. 268.
2 ibid.
3 SP–ST, 30 April 1791, Tighe MS.
4 Mrs O'Connell–SP, 27 April 1791, Hamwood MS.
5 Countess of Ormonde–EB, 18 May [1791], Hamwood MS.
6 Henry Phillips, *Sylva Florifera the Shrubbery Historically and Botanically Treated* (1823), v. I, p. 32.
7 *Collected Letters of Anna Seward* (1811), v. IV, p. 101.
8 *The Works of Samuel Johnson, LLD* (1796), v. II, p. 278.

9 *The Works in Verse and Prose of William Shenstone Esq.* (1777), v. 2, pp. 111–31.

10 Thomas Love Peacock, *Headlong Hall* (Everyman), p. 72.

11 *Gleanings from an Old Portfolio*, ed. Clark (1898), v. III, p. 158.

12 EB, Journal, 8 June 1799, Hamwood MS.

13 *Collected Letters of Anna Seward* (1811), v. IV, p. 99.

14 *A New Guide to Fonthill Abbey* (1822), p. 23.

15 *Collected Letters of Anna Seward* (1811), v. IV, p. 99.

16 EB–'Sir', 30 December 1792, NLW 18428 E.

17 SP–ST, 25 March 1793, Tighe MS.

18 SP–ST, 29 July 1791, Tighe MS

19 HB–SP, 27 December 1791, Ormonde MS.

20 *Thraliana. The Diary of Mrs Hester Lynch Thrale 1776–1809*, ed. Balderston (1951), p. 851.

21 E. P. Thompson, *The Making of the English Working Class* (1968), p. 118.

22 HB–SP, 3 August, 1793, Ormonde MS.

23 HB–SP, 6 April 1793, Ormonde MS.

24 SP–ST, 4 April 1793, Tighe MS.

25 SP–ST, 25 October 1793, Tighe MS.

26 HB–SP, 31 December 1793, Ormonde MS.

27 SP–ST, 25 October 1793, Tighe MS.

28 SP–ST, 3 February 1794, Tighe MS.

29 ibid.

30 HB–SP, 16 January 1794, Ormonde MS.

31 EB–Anne Ormonde, 24 February 1794, Tighe MS.

32 Anne Ormonde–EB, 4 March 1794, Tighe MS.

Chapter Seven
'Three-thirty till Nine.' 1794–1809

1 HB–SP, 16 January 1794, Ormonde MS.

2 HB–SP, 2 January 1794, Ormonde MS.

3 SP–ST, 25 June 1796, Tighe MS.

4 ibid.

5 SP–ST, 26 September 1796, Tighe MS.

6 *Thraliana. The Diary of Mrs Hester Lynch Thrale 1776–1809*, ed. Balderston (1951), p. 909.

7 *Collected Letters of Anna Seward* (1811), v. IV, p. 103.

8 SP–ST, 26 September 1796, Tighe MS.

9 SP–ST, 11 December 1796, Tighe MS.

10 The Rev. W. Brigley, *North Wales* (1804), p. 24.

11 *Collected Letters of Anna Seward* (1811), v. IV, p. 98.

12 ibid., p. 209.

13 ibid., p. 211.

14 *Thraliana. The Diary of Mrs Hester Lynch Thrale 1776–1809,* ed. Balderston (1951), p. 957 n. 2.

15 HLP–EB, 23 September 1801, NLI Wicklow Papers MS 4239.

16 SP–ST, 25 June 1798, Tighe MS.

17 ibid.

18 SP–ST, 31 October 1798, Tighe MS.

19 SP–ST, 7 December 1798, Tighe MS.

20 SP–Anna Seward, undated [June or July 1800], Bod. MS Eng. Letters *c.* 144 (fol. 224).

21 HLP–EB, 27 August 1800, NLI Wicklow MS 4239.

22 Account Book, 7 July 1800, Llangollen Town Council MS.

23 ibid., 2 July 1800.

24 SP–ST, 30 July 1800, Tighe MS.

25 *Hamwood Papers,* p. 322.

26 SP–ST, 11 February 1802, Tighe MS.

27 SP–ST, 17 May 1802, Tighe MS.

28 SP–ST, 3 July 1802, Tighe MS.

29 SP–ST, 20 April 1802, Tighe MS.

30 SP–ST, 20 June 1803, Tighe MS.

31 SP–ST, 'April' 1804, Tighe MS.

32 *Denbighshire Historical Society Transactions* (1966), v. 15, p. 124.

33 SP–ST, 'April' 1804, Tighe MS.

34 SP–ST, 5 November 1806, Tighe MS.

35 *Gleanings from an Old Portfolio* ed. Clark (1898), p. 159.

36 EB, Day Book, 1806, NLI Wicklow MS 4806.

37 ibid.

38 ibid.

39 SP–ST, 5 November 1806, Tighe MS.

40 *Hamwood Papers,* p. 343.

41 SP–ST, 27 December 1809, Tighe MS.

Chapter Eight

'. . . Stately and difficult of access.' Relationships

1 *Mémoires inédits de Madame de Genlis* (1825), v. III, p. 282.

2 ibid., p. 287.

3 *Lady Louisa Stuart's Letters,* ed. Home (1901), pp. 187–8.

4 SP–ST, 12 January 1787, Tighe MS.

5 SP–ST, 13 April 1787, Tighe MS.

6 ibid.

7 SP–ST, 21 August 1785, Tighe MS.

8 SP–ST, 27 September 1785, Tighe MS.

9 *Hamwood Papers*, p. 127.

10 EB–HLP, undated, Rylands Eng. MS 892.

11 ibid.

12 *Hamwood Papers*, pp. 74–5.

13 ibid., p. 118.

14 *Journals and Correspondence of Dr Whalley* (1863), p. 138.

15 ibid.

16 *Hamwood Papers*, p. 140.

17 SP–ST, 30 July 1801, Tighe MS.

18 *Intimate Letters of Hester Piozzi and Penelope Pennington*, ed. Broadley (1910), p. 213.

19 SP–ST, 11 April 1788, Tighe MS.

20 SP–ST, 12 January 1787, Tighe MS.

21 SP–Mrs Parker, 1 July 1826, Parker MS.

22 *Hamwood Papers*, p. 212.

23 ibid., p. 85.

24 SP–ST, 14 June 1787, Tighe MS.

25 *Hamwood Papers*, p. 251.

26 ibid., p. 128.

27 ibid., p. 195.

28 ibid., p. 133.

29 ibid., p. 195.

30 J. G. Lockhart, *Memoirs of Sir Walter Scott* (1882), v. VIII, p. 50

Chapter Nine
'Pleasures unknown to Vulgar Minds.' Correspondence

1 SP–ST, 19 December 1788, Tighe MS.

2 SP–ST, 26 September 1796, Tighe MS.

3 SP–ST, 7 December 1786, Tighe MS.

4 SP–ST, 31 January 1787, Tighe MS.

5 SP–ST, 11 March 1787, Tighe MS.

6 SP–ST, 26 February 1787, Tighe MS.

7 SP–ST, 11 December 1796, Tighe MS.

8 SP–ST, 25 October 1793, Tighe MS.

9 HB–SP, 18 January 1809, Hamwood MS.

10 Hamwood MS.

11 HB–SP, Ormonde MS.

12 HB–SP, 18 October 1794, Ormonde MS.

13 HB–SP, 10 August 1794, Ormonde MS.

14 HB–SP, 23 August 1794, Ormonde MS.

15 *Collected Letters of Anna Seward* (1811), v. IV, p. 237.

16 ibid., p. 247.

17 Rylands Eng. MS 892.

18 SP–HLP, undated, Rylands Eng. MS 892.

19 HLP–EB, SP, 2 May 1800, Hamwood MS.

20 EB–HLP, 16 April [1800], Rylands Eng. MS 892.

21 Bod. MS Pigott d.9.g (fol. 116).

22 EB–HP, 10 June [1814], MS Pigott d.9.g (fol. 116).

23 EB–HP, 13 August [1814], MS Pigott d.9.g (fol. 116).

24 EB–HP, 14 January [1815], MS Pigott d.9.g (fol. 116).

25 EB–HP, undated [Oct. 1814], MS Pigott d.9.g (fol. 116).

26 EB–Lucy Goddard, undated [May 1783], NLI Wicklow MS 4329.

27 SP–ST, undated, Tighe MS.

28 SP–ST, 7 February 1785, Tighe MS.

29 SP–Mrs Popkin, 14 January 1815, Bod. MS Pigott d.9.g (fol 116).

30 EB–HP, 14 January 1815.

Chapter Ten
'Nine till Twelve. In the Dressing-room.'

1 SP–ST, 30 December 1810, Tighe MS.

2 SP–ST, 27 December 1809, Tighe MS.

3 EB–HP, 16 March [1810], Bod. MS Pigott d.9.g (fol 116).

4 SP–Mrs Parker, 29 July 1811, Parker MS.

5 EB–Mr Telford, a copy undated, Parker MS.

6 SP–Mrs Parker, 29 July 1811, Parker MS.

7 ibid.

8 *Journals and Correspondence of Dr Whalley* (1863), p. 364.

9 SP–Mrs Parker, 7 October 1813, Parker MS.

10 SP–Mrs Parker, 2 February 1814, Parker MS.

11 SP–Mrs Parker, 27 January 1814, Parker MS.

12 SP–Mrs Parker, 5 April 1814, Parker MS.

13 EB–HP, 5 May [1814], Bod. MS Pigott d.9.g (fol. 116).

14 EB–HP, 29 October 1814, Bod. MS Pigott d.9.g (fol. 116).

15 *Hamwood Papers*, p. 352.

16 EB–Mr Hesketh, 2 December 1817, in possession of Mrs Florence MacClellan.

17 EB–Mr Bouchier, 11 November 1818, NLW 18428 E.

18 Parker MS.

19 SP–Mrs Parker, 18 December 1818, Parker MS.

20 SP–Mrs Parker, 26 January 1819, Parker MS.
21 SP–Mrs Parker, 4 March 1819, Parker MS.
22 EB, Journal, 5 January 1819, NLI Wicklow MS 4789.
23 ibid.
24 *Memoirs of Charles Mathews the Elder*, ed. Yates (1860), p. 232.
25 EB, Journal, 1819, NLI Wicklow MS 4789.
26 ibid.
27 ibid.
28 EB, Journal, 5 August 1821, Hamwood MS.
29 *Mémoires inédits de Madame de Genlis* (1825), v. VI, p. 175.
30 SP–Mrs Parker, 22 June 1822, Parker MS.
31 ibid.
32 ibid.
33 SP–Mrs Parker, 16 July 1822, Parker MS.
34 *The Letters of William and Dorothy Wordsworth, 1821–1850*, ed. Selincourt, v. I, p. 152.
35 *Hamwood Papers*, p. 354.
36 J. G. Lockhart, *Memoirs of Sir Walter Scott* (1882), v. VIII, p. 49.
37 SP–Mrs Parker, undated [1825], Parker MS.
38 SP–Parker, 18 April 1826, Parker MS.
39 Parker MS.

Chapter Eleven
'Midnight.' 1829–31

1 SP–Lady Richmond, 13 June 1829, Bod. MS Autogr. C.23 (fol. 291).
2 Bod. MS Pigott, v. VIII, 'Ladies of Llangollen' 23439–40 (fol. 1, p. 48).
3 ibid.
4 SP–Lady Richmond, 13 June 1829, Bod. MS Autogr. C.23 (fol. 291).
5 ibid.
6 *Hamwood Papers*, p. 381.
7 SP–Lady Cunliffe, 16 September 1829, NLW MS 18428 E.
8 SP–Mrs Parker, 14 September 1830, Parker MS.
9 George Borrow, *Wild Wales* (World's Classics), p. 81.
10 SP–Mrs Parker, 5 July 1831, Parker MS.
11 SP–Mrs Parker, 16 October 1831, Parker MS.
12 *Hamwood Papers*, p. 382.
13 Memoirs of Mrs Caroline Hamilton, NLI MS 4811.
14 Mrs O'Connell–SP, 27 April 1791, Hamwood MS.

15 *Notes and Queries*, 4th Series (1869), pp. 220–1.
16 MS Private Collection.
17 ibid.
18 ibid.
19 ibid.

Chapter Twelve
'. . . those abnormally self advertised old frumps. The Myth.'

1 *The Spectator* (1819), v. VI, p. 230.
2 Duke of Gloucester–EB and SP, undated [1809], NLI Wicklow MS 4239.
3 *Memoirs of Charles Mathews the Elder*, ed. Yates (1860), p. 231.
4 J. G. Lockhart, *Memoirs of Sir Walter Scott* (1882), v. VII, p. 48.
5 *Memoirs of Charles Mathews the Elder*, ed. Yates (1860), p. 232.
6 HP, Day Book, undated, Bod. MS Pigott (f. 1, p. 197).
4 J. G. Lockhart, *Memoirs of Sir Walter Scott* (1882), v. VIII, p. 48.
8 *The Ladies of Llangollen as Sketched by Many Hands* (1847).
9 ibid.
10 C. G. Jung, *Memories, Dreams, Reflections* (1963), p. 214.
11 George Borrow, *Wild Wales* (World's Classics), p. 81.

Index

More about Penguins
and Pelicans

Penguinews, which appears every month, contains
details of all new books issued by Penguins as they are
published. From time to time it is supplemented by
Penguins in Print, which is a complete list of all available
books published by Penguins. (There are well over four
thousand of these.)

A specimen copy of *Penguinews* will be sent to you free
on request. For a year's issues (including the complete
lists) please send 30p if you live in the United Kingdom,
or 60p if you live elsewhere. Just write to Dept EP, Penguin
Books Ltd, Harmondsworth, Middlesex, enclosing a
cheque or postal order, and your name will be added to the
mailing list.

Note: *Penguinews* and *Penguins in Print* are not
available in the U.S.A. or Canada